RAMPARTS OF

Ramparts of Resistance

Why Workers Lost Their Power
and How to Get it Back

SHEILA COHEN

Pluto  Press

LONDON • ANN ARBOR, MI

First published 2006 by Pluto Press
345 Archway Road, London N6 5AA
and 839 Greene Street, Ann Arbor, MI 48106

www.plutobooks.com

British Library Cataloguing in Publication Data
A catalogue record for this book is available from the British Library

ISBN-13: 978–0–7453–1534–8 hardback
ISBN-10: 0–7453–1534–8 hardback
ISBN-13: 978–0–7453–1529–4 paperback
ISBN-10: 0–7453–1529–1 paperback

Library of Congress Cataloging in Publication Data applied for

10 9 8 7 6 5 4 3 2 1

Designed and produced for Pluto Press by
Chase Publishing Services Ltd, Fortescue, Sidmouth, EX10 9QG, England
Typeset from disk by Newgen Imaging System (P) Ltd, Chennai, India
Printed and bound in the European Union by
Antony Rowe Ltd, Chippenham and Eastbourne.

Only a social order which can solve the problem of employment and unemployment can solve the problem of war and peace.
Max Cohen, *I Was One of the Unemployed*, Gollancz 1945, p. 244

To Lauren & Berry
& Kim
of course

Contents

Acknowledgements

The first and foremost acknowledgement must be to my husband and comrade, friend and helpmate, Kim Moody. Few authors have the advantage of an infinite source of wisdom in their own field sitting (often literally) feet away from them. Countless are the occasions when I have asked, 'Was that strike in 1986 or 1988?' and the answer has come instantly from that Mastermind of all things labour-oriented (particularly in his native America). This in addition to being one of the foremost, most consistent, committed activists in the rank-and-file labour galaxy.

Few can match that. But among others who have contributed immeasurably both to the material in this book and to my morale while writing it, I would like to include the many union activists clustered around both *Labor Notes*, the rank-and-file union project Kim co-founded in 1979, and my own shorter-lived British effort *Trade Union News*. They include, on the British side of the equation, Davey Ayre, Graham Griffin, Jon Johnson, John Kelly, Pat Longman, Kenny Murphy, Tony Richardson, Roy Wenbourne and above all Glenroy Watson. My many comrades in *Labor Notes* and related networks, including Martha Gruelle, William Johnson, Chris Kutalik, Marsha Niemeijer, Ken Paff, Charlie Post, Teofilo Reyes, Simone Sagovac, Tim Schermerhorn and Jane Slaughter, helped to make my long stay in the US easier as well as contributing in countless ways to the ideas and information contained in *Ramparts*.

Labour activists who kindly provided interviews – not all of which, unfortunately, I had space to use – include, in Britain, Micky Britton of the GPMU, John Johnson of USDAW, Jack Owen of the TGWU at Lucas, Dave Ward of the CWU and once again Glenroy Watson of the RMT. In the US, a hero of rank-and-file struggle, Jim Guyette of the 'P-9ers', allowed me to record his memories of that strike and its bitter legacy of bureaucratic betrayal. And a posse of West Coast activists, including Bill Balderstone, Kay Eisenhower, Caroline Lund and Barry Sheppard, gave much-valued help and information, enabled by the hospitality of beloved friends and life-long rank-and-file activists Erwin and Estar Baur.

More personal friends and stalwarts, as well as union activists, include lifelong TDU supporter Steve Kindred, UAW militant and assembly-line poet Gregg Shotwell, to whom I owe a huge debt, Mick Sullivan of the CWU, who always makes me laugh, and AFSCME's Lynn Taylor, who gave both me and Kim enormous help and friendship in New York.

This book would not exist without the patience, encouragement and support of the person preferably known as 'Beech' – my wonderful editor at Pluto Press. Thanks also to Robert Webb on that score.

And finally, again I would like to 'acknowledge' my beloved daughters Lauren and Berry, who helped with useful editing and publishing advice, listening, encouraging, and, really, just existing.

Abbreviations and Acronyms

ACTSS	Association of Clerical, Technical and Supervisory Staffs (section of TGWU)
AEEU	Amalgamated Engineering and Electrical Union
AEU	Amalgamated Engineering Union
AFGE	American Federation of Government Employees
AFL-CIO	American Federation of Labor-Congress of Industrial Organizations
AFSCME	American Federation of State, County, and Municipal Employees
Amicus	Merger of AEEU and MSF
ASE	Amalgamated Society of Engineers
ASLEF	Associated Society of Locomotive Engineers and Firemen
ASTMS	Association of Scientific, Technical and Managerial Staffs
AUD	Association for Union Democracy
AUEW	Amalgamated Union of Engineering Workers
BALPA	British Air Line Pilots Association
BL	British Leyland
BSC	British Steel Corporation
BT	British Telecom
CCI	Corporate Campaigning, Inc.
COHSE	Confederation of Health Service Employees
COLA	Cost of Living Allowance
CSEU	Confederation of Shipbuilding and Engineering Unions
CWA	Communications Workers of America
CWU	Communication Workers' Union (merger of UPW and POEU/NCU)
DRUM	Dodge Revolutionary Union Movement
EETPU	Electrical, Electronic, Telecommunications and Plumbing Union
EI	Employee Involvement
EPEA	Electrical and Power Engineers' Association
FASH	Fraternal Association of Steel Haulers
FBU	Fire Brigades Union
FLOC	Farm Labor Organising Committee

GM	General Motors
GMB	General, Municipal and Boilermakers' Union
HERE	Hotel Employees Restaurant Employees
HRM	Human Resources Management
IAM	International* Association of Machinists
IBEW	International Brotherhood of Electrical Workers
IBT	International Brotherhood of Teamsters
ILA	International Longshoremen's Association (East Coast)
ILWU	International Longshore and Warehouse Union (West Coast)
ISTC	Iron and Steel Trades Confederation
JSSC	Joint Shop Stewards' Committee
LIUNA	Laborers' International Union of North America
MFD	Miners For Democracy
MSF	Manufacturing, Science, Finance
NACODS	National Association of Colliery Overmen and Deputies
NALC	National Association of Letter Carriers
NALGO	National And Local Government Officers' Association
NCB	National Coal Board
NCU	National Communications Union
NGA	National Graphical Association
NJNC	National Joint Negotiating Committee
NLRA/B	National Labor Relations Act/Board
NUM	National Union of Mineworkers
NUMMI	New United Motors Manufacturing Inc.
NUPE	National Union of Public Employees
NUR	National Union of Railwaymen
NUS	National Union of Seamen
NUT	National Union of Teachers
PATCO	Professional Air Traffic Controllers' Organisation
PCS	Public and Civil Services
POEU	Post Office Engineering Union
QWL	Quality of Working Life
RMT	Rail, Maritime and Transport (merger of NUR and NUS)
RSC	Rotherham Strike Committee
SEIU	Service Employees' International Union
SOGAT	Society of Graphical and Allied Trades
TDC	Teamsters for a Decent Contract
TDU	Teamsters for a Democratic Union
TGWU	Transport and General Workers' Union
TQM	Total Quality Management

TSSA	Transport Salaried Staffs' Association
TUC	Trades Union Congress
TURF	Teamster Union Rank and File
TWU	Transport Workers Union (of America)
UAW	United Auto Workers
UCS	Upper Clyde Shipbuilders
UFCW	United Food and Commercial Workers
UMWA	United Mine Workers of America
UNC	United National Caucus (in UAW)
UNISON	Merger of NALGO, NUPE and COHSE
UNITE	Union of Needletrades, Industrial and Textile Employees
UPIU	United Paperworkers' International Union
UPW	Union of Postal Workers
URW	United Rubber Workers
USDAW	Union of Shop, Distributive and Allied Workers
USWA	United Steel Workers of America

* 'International' indicates that the union has members in both the US and Canada.

Introduction: Focusing on the Rank and File

... But when it is a question of making a precise study of strikes, combinations and other forms in which the proletarians carry out before our eyes their organisation as a class, some are seized with real fear and others display a *transcendental* disdain.

Karl Marx, *The Poverty of Philosophy*, Progress Publishers 1973, p.151

This is a book with an ambitious aim: to reverse the focus of debate on rebuilding the labour movement. While many recent contributions to that debate emphasise a grass roots orientation, most continue to centre on a set of programmatic injunctions as to what 'the unions' ought to do, rather than focusing on what they – or rather their members – are actually doing. By contrast, this book suggests putting workplace-based rank-and-file organisation and resistance at the head of strategic discussion, rather than leaving it as a largely neglected footnote.

FOCUSING ON THE RANK AND FILE

The trade union history covered here, from the 1968–74 upsurge to the present, tells its own story of the class power of rank-and-file struggle – whether in defiance of anti-union legislation, in defence of jobs, or simply in the day-to-day trench warfare of workplace resistance. It illustrates the uncomfortable truth that the main threat to ruling-class demands and strategies has come, time after time, not from lofty political protest but from 'raw', workplace-based, rank-and-file resistance.

A consistent criticism of such resistance is that it is 'economistic' – it lacks the broader political awareness and commitment to social ideals that would be necessary to transform the system, or at least to turn the trade union movement around. The answer to that criticism within this book is not that politics, ideals, ideas and ideology

1

don't matter. It is that the shortest road to political awareness, for workers without the luxury of a formal political education, is via the experience of struggle. Experience itself is not sufficient for a fully informed, sophisticated critique of the system and a strategic commitment to its transformation. But immersion in the raw politics of class conflict – rarely sought by those involved, but a life-changing experience for many – is surely a powerful starting point.

That conflict is itself most likely to be rooted in the concrete issues and concerns which most directly affect rank-and-file workers; and these are experienced, resisted and organised around most often within the workplace. A central focus of this book is recognition of the workplace as a central source of trade union renewal and class struggle. As the site of the central contradictions of capitalist relations of production, the workplace generates the need for organisation and resistance irrespective of the preexisting consciousness of those involved. And it is rank-and-file workers and union members who form the troops and the cadre of that resistance.

The activist layer

This signals the importance of the workplace union structures within which workgroup leaders both represent their members and, in most cases, share their work experience, pay and conditions. Rank-and-file activists – whether bank clerks, car workers, healthcare aides or building labourers – are workers themselves. Occupying as they do a territory between the exploitation-driven concerns of the workplace membership and the institutional concerns of the bureaucracy, these activists are uniquely placed to maintain independence from the demands of capital, and to develop an overview of the shared impact of production relations on different sections of the workforce. Their close, everyday links with the membership enforce an attention to the workplace issues most likely to mobilise workers and maintain the dynamic of direct, member-led democracy.

A central argument of this book is that this layer of activists holds the key to the objective most of us seek: trade union renewal. But this is an argument based on the understanding that the recurrence of mobilisation and struggle within the movement is not the main problem. Episodes of rank-and-file resurgence will take place without needing to be conjured up by visions of social movement unionism; impelled by economic necessity rather than idealistic aspiration, grass-roots resistance is almost always forthcoming at different times, in different sections, even in the most discouraging circumstances. What this resurgence requires is not external calls to action – the contradictions of capitalism will do the job for us – but a conscious strategy of developing and sustaining such forms of resistance as they arise and where they are. The class-conscious, committed layer of rank-and-file activists already existing in the movement is the force with the best potential for doing that.

THE CRUCIAL CONSIDERATION OF CONSCIOUSNESS

This reversal of perspective requires, if anything, an even sharper focus on issues of ideology and consciousness. Working-class struggle and organisation are weakened, in this analysis, not by the absence of 'broader' political principles per se, but by a different kind of absence: the absence of explicit awareness on the part of many of the most militant activists of the need for independence from the objectives of capital, and attention to member-led democracy. It is these two central principles which lie at the heart of the rank-and-file perspective advocated in this book.

Contrary to much of the thinking in this area, ruling-class ideology does not maintain an impenetrable lid on the consciousness of 'ordinary' workers; whatever the subjective awareness of those involved, the stability of the system is continually undermined by ragged, unpredictable, contradictory eruptions of struggle. Strike after strike described in this book explodes from some previously unconsidered 'last straw' of exploitation and repression; striker after striker describes the massive transformation in consciousness, the reversal of perspective and awareness generated by such materially based conflicts.

Yet the development of this exciting potential into long-term, consistent movement building requires conscious awareness, on the part of the activists at its heart, of the crucial need for class independence and workplace union democracy. The dominance of reformist ideology in even the most militant sections of the movement acts as a block to that awareness. Part of the purpose of this book is to highlight the implications of reformism, and to suggest how it might be countered not by grand schemes and visions but by a straightforward attention to the class needs of the movement's basic constituency – its rank-and-file membership.

UNION AS INSTITUTION, UNION AS MOVEMENT

The question of internal trade union democracy is pivotal to this analysis. Maintaining a connection with the membership base is the most effective barrier to the only-too-common slide of militant activist into obstructive bureaucrat. Correspondingly, membership education and mobilisation are essential to maintaining class-independent resistance which may otherwise be diluted by rank-and-file members' susceptibility to management threats and persuasions.

Both arguments for union democracy relate to a key distinction made in this book between 'unions and unions': union-as-institution, enshrined in formal, official structures prioritising institutional survival, and union-as-movement, an organisational form rooted in the class needs and demands of the rank and file. The distinction between these two separate and often directly contradictory facets of trade unionism parallels a second distinction between member-led, participative, direct democracy and its formal, bureaucratically structured 'representative' counterpart. The notion of *direct* democracy emphasises the link between the issues members actually care about – pay, work, job security – and collective membership involvement and action. In this approach, trade union democracy becomes a crucial component of union effectiveness, rather than an abstract ideal; rank-and-file membership involvement is recognised as a central and indispensable force in rebuilding the strength of the movement.

RAMPARTS

This focus on rank-and-file union organisation and its roots in issues-based 'direct democracy' draws attention to the distinctive organisational forms built by workplace representatives, which work horizontally across sectors, industries and the class as a whole, rather than vertically within separate unions. These forms include workplace-based multi-union joint shop steward committees, combine committees, and rank-and-file union reform caucuses; their delegate-based, essentially accountable structures echo the forms universally created in 'spontaneous' working-class struggles, from soviets to factory occupation committees.

Whether in times of 'upsurge' or 'downturn', such networks are rooted in the ongoing bedrock of workplace organisation and resistance, the 'ramparts' which continue to pose a frontier against the undiluted demands of capital. The wider solidarity and unity so valued, rightly, by advocates of 'social movement unionism' has its roots here – in the everyday, unromantic, but necessarily collective struggles by workers against the demands of capital.

This focus does not suggest the confinement of organisation and struggle to the narrow remit of the workplace; most major workplace-based struggles immediately affect 'the community' and work to enlarge, rather than restrict, the horizons of working-class consciousness. An everyday revelation for workers involved in such struggles is that only now do they see their experience in a wider context: 'It's happening all over the country but everyone thinks it's just them', as one American striker eloquently put it.

One important way of increasing workers' awareness that it's not 'just them' is the development of classwide rank-and-file networks. This is not a new idea. In more promising times, activist involvement in left-based rank-and-file initiatives demonstrated workplace trade unionists' serious interest in building movement-wide links. Even now, the actually existing organisational forms described above themselves contain, at least potentially, the raw material for reactivating the movement. One central strategic implication identified in this book is the need to link rank-and-file activists together.

WHY WORKERS LOST THEIR POWER ...

A reasonable objection to invocations of 'workers' power' or, indeed, the need for a rank-and-file movement based on such grass-roots struggles, is that the upsurge is no longer with us. The statistics on union density and strike incidence need no spelling out; it is dismally clear that the movement is in an era of extreme defeat. If workers ever had 'power', they seem to have lost it now.

Why? Leaving aside relevant but restricted explanations of economic restructuring and political change, the answer seems to lie in the lack of recognition, by both union leaders and some of their most militant opponents, of the real value of what they held – sheer, gut-level, class-based resistance. If such resistance is ever easy, it was so in a period of postwar boom and full employment. Yet the organisational structures and movement dynamics it created could have been consolidated and developed, preserved to fight another day, used to study the lessons. Even at the height of the upsurge, and certainly in the brave mass struggles of the neoliberal era, these same lessons recur over and over: workers' misplaced faith that the justice of their cause will prevail; capital's no-holds-barred aggression and strategic superiority; the ever-present threat of bureaucracy and class collaboration. Despite attempts, no ongoing rank-and-file structure was built out of the struggles of the upsurge which could study and spread those lessons; perhaps they can be studied now.

... AND HOW TO GET IT BACK

How to combat the ever more monstrous Goliath of capital with what seems an ever shrinking David? Again, by starting from the ground up. The continued presence of rank-and-file resistance and organisation provides the bedrock for a 'critical mass' of activists able and willing to revive the movement, while retaining links with the base. Both the history and the theory presented in this book point to the need to build an *in-class* rank-and-file movement prepared to provide grass-roots leadership in the event of another 'upsurge'. Those who see such a prospect as unlikely may be reminded of the many previous periods of defeat and fatalism out of which apparently impossible resurgence has arisen – only to be once again conquered by the cycle of strategic confusion and bureaucratic compromise. This time, like the ruling class, we need to be ready. Encouraging a turn in the direction of such readiness is one of the central objectives of this book.

Part I

What Happened

1

The Upsurge: 1968–74

This book begins at the postwar peak of 'trade union power', though few who used that phrase took much interest in what this 'power' consisted of, or who held it. To examine in detail one of the most tumultuous and even revolutionary times in living memory is to discover that this whole question of power was central in a way that the media pundits and Conservative speech-writers could scarcely recognise or understand. It is to the detriment of the movement that few trade union leaders – few even of the most militant of the rank-and-file activists at the front line of the upsurge – recognised or understood it either. To explore what was really going on in the first half of the 1970s, in Britain and America, this chapter will describe the actual events of the period, wherever possible from the standpoint of those who took part in them. We can then try to understand why what happened, and how it might have been different.

MILITANCY

In many ways the workplace and wider trade union organisation of the late 1960s and early 1970s presented the features found in trade unionism of any other period – sectionalism, economism, sudden explosions of conflict triggered by last-straw pressures among previously passive workers, national or companywide struggles by more experienced and militant trade unionists. But above and beyond the standard fabric of trade unionism, the 1968–74 period demonstrated at least three key features that differentiate most of these years – and the 1970s in general – from subsequent decades.

The first and most obvious was the untrammelled militancy of the period, which has often been compared, at least in Britain, to the quasi-revolutionary strike wave of the World War I years.[1] In the 1968–74 upsurge 'The number of strike days rose from less than five million in 1968 to 13.5 million in 1971 and 23.9 million in

1972 ... [It was] the greatest wave of industrial struggle Britain had seen since the 1920s ...'.[2] A similar picture was evident in the US: between 1967 and 1976 'the average number of workers on strike each year rose 30 per cent ... while the average number of days lost to strikes increased by 40 per cent'.[3]

The story in these pages will take us a lot further than statistics in examining the real fabric and 'smell' of this militancy, but for the moment it is simply noted as a central and historic feature of the late 1960s to early 1970s in both Britain and America. The militancy of the 1968–74 period, although in few cases guided by explicitly class-conscious ideology, raised the objective question of a significant revolt against capital through its very explosiveness, unpredictability and rank-and-file subversion of union bureaucracy. Until the latter part of the 1970s, at least in Britain, this was a decade in which the issue of 'trade union power' reversed itself to a significant and unprecedented extent in the direction of grass-roots union struggle rooted in the workplace.

Rank-and-file representation

One of the central features of the 'rank-and-file rebellion' was, by definition, its distance from union leadership control. By the late 1960s, 95 per cent of all strikes in Britain were unofficial,[4] expressing a dynamic of grass-roots organisation and resistance which became the central motive for anti-union legislative efforts by both Labour and Tory governments. A key factor in this 'unconstitutional' action was the production system itself; the piecework payment system still widespread in manufacturing was now used by stewards as a basis for enhancing earnings through setting work-group production norms. This led not only to a marked increase in small sectional walkouts, but also to the notorious 'wage drift' – a growth in earnings well above the levels set by industrywide agreements. Such dangerous inroads into profitability attracted the attention of the Labour government and led to the setting up of a Royal Commission whose findings (the Donovan Report) were presented in 1968. Yet at the end of the 1960s British workplace organisation still retained an almost frontier-style character in which the mysterious character of shop steward activity, though probed and prodded,[5] remained elusive to government or managerial strategies of control. The loyalties of most shop stewards were firmly with their members; they worked alongside them and, in the relatively rare cases where they were given time off for trade union duties, returned to (typically) the assembly line rather than to a separate office. In fact very few stewards had offices, or any kind of facilities at all.

In this context probably the strongest sustained workplace organisation in decades was combined with an unusually high level of grass-roots trade union democracy. Although members could by no means always be relied on to support their stewards – adding to the fluidity of the representational process – there was an essential match between stewards' and members' concerns and interests which spoke of a direct, participative form of democracy strongly distinct from the representative form favoured by the ruling class and the state under capitalism.

Pushing the boundaries

Another factor which allowed grass-roots struggle to expand and move forward to significant levels of 'upsurge' in the late 1960s and early 1970s was the increased confidence of organised workers in an era of postwar full employment. As with the higher level of workplace union democracy, this confident mood had the potential to enrich and advance class struggle. The 1968–74 upsurge in Britain has been compared to the 'New Unionism' of the late 1880s, when organisation and struggle among many previously unorganised sections gave the movement a renewed class character.[6] In both Britain and America, the 1968–74 upsurge displayed a clear political component in its tendency to push against the boundaries of the system. The renewed confidence of the movement led to greater challenges to the economic structure through the extension of 'ordinary' trade union demands. During a period of resistance to the Labour government's pay policies, a contemporary journalist wrote: 'As the mass wages movement grows here ... the struggle deepens ... No longer is [it] directed only to prevent the effects of the incomes policy and the policy itself. It begins to attack the causes'.[7]

This impulse beyond the 'economistic' came from the rank and file rather than the union leadership, which tended to reduce such 'qualitative demands ... "to an economic core" ... in order to facilitate compromise in negotiations with employers'.[8] In the US, also, despite the meshing of basic workplace organisation with highly political demands in plant-based movements like the autoworkers' DRUM (Dodge Revolutionary Union Movement), 'rank-and-file struggles did not succeed in reorienting the unions to "qualitative" demands'.[9] Yet widespread resistance to ever more onerous working conditions showed that 'large numbers of industrial workers are simply no longer willing to tolerate the conditions under which they are expected to produce the goods and services that ... maintain this society'.[10]

Extension of organisation

Along with this broadening of class demands went an extension of class *organisation* into sectors which had previously been unorganised or 'out of the loop' of active trade unionism; public sector workers, 'professionals', white-collar and service workers, along with increasing numbers of black workers and women. This broader spread of organisation also brought the expansion of workplace representative structures previously most typical of manufacturing. Many new groups began to adopt the organising methods of more experienced workplace activists, consciously extending the 'shop steward' model to public sector areas. In particular, the National Union of Public Employees (NUPE) and the National Association of Local Government Officers (NALGO) in Britain began to introduce shop steward structures in their workplaces from the early 1970s. In 1970, 38 per cent of NUPE branches lacked stewards; by 1974 almost half had five or more.[11]

These organisational changes were part and parcel of growing levels of union density and strike propensity among white-collar and manual groups in the public sector and beyond, including semi-'professionals' like technicians, civil servants, nurses and teachers. In 1969, the National Union of Teachers (NUT) made an unprecedented call for industrial action; in 1970 it broke with 'professional' tradition by affiliating to the Trades Union Congress (TUC). The growing trend towards once despised trade union organisation among groups like clerical workers and technicians was shown in the rapid growth of unions like the Association of Scientific, Technical and Managerial Staffs (ASTMS) and the TGWU's Clerical and Supervisory Group (ACTSS).

Not surprisingly, dipping a toe into the waters of 'industrial' organisation led to a new propensity towards industrial action, making 'the strike an increasingly common experience for an increasingly broad section of the labour force'.[12] Such sections included local authority manual workers, who entered 1969 on a wave of strikes commemorated as 'the revolt of the lower-paid'; they provided inspiration to equally low-paid and inexperienced hospital manual workers who 'had thought their industry would never strike. Now they had been on strike for the first time in their lives'.[13]

Nor was the rebellion confined to the public sector. Traditionally 'deferential' workers in rural outposts like the South West of England plunged into action with a spate of strikes culminating in the three-year Fine Tubes strike; at the paternalistic, long-quiescent Pilkington's Glass Company, last on strike in 1870, workers walked out almost 100 years later in an explosion of anger over pay, local news about a £4 a week settlement just gained at the nearby Ford Halewood plant undoubtedly contributing to their determination.

THE WILDCAT YEAR

The unpredictable explosiveness of rank-and-file resistance, the roots of struggle in concrete experience rather than abstract ideology, the class dynamic which thrusts workers, however briefly, into history; all these elements were part of the 1968–74 upsurge in both Britain and America. The year 1968 itself was a seminal one not only for the Prague Spring and the Paris cobblestones. In Britain, a strike by women sewing-machine workers at Ford sparked government moves towards a 'historic', if ultimately toothless, Equal Pay Act; more prosaically, the 1968 Donovan Report on industrial relations, which highlighted the 'informal' currents at the base of the movement, signalled the government's alarm at the extent and potency of workplace-based resistance.

In the US, a strike by black sanitation workers in Memphis weary of ceaseless racist exploitation launched a wave of struggle culminating, tragically, in the murder of Martin Luther King; in Detroit the same year, black autoworkers poured their anger into the formation of DRUM (Dodge Revolutionary Union Movement), soon part of a League of Revolutionary Black Workers which, while short-lived, was an inspiring example of the potential of linked class- and race-based resistance. But the action didn't end there. In particular, the US strike wave of 1970, crested by postal workers' and Teamsters' national wildcats alongside an official, but highly conflictual, General Motors strike, continued to pose compelling evidence of the significance and potential of mass struggle.

They can't fire everybody ...

The remarkable national US postal workers' strike of 1970 was, like its companions, prosaic in its beginnings but highly political in its implications. In this case, the 'political' nature of the dispute was clear from the start; US postal workers, whose terms and conditions were set by Congress, were legally prohibited from going on strike. When postal workers in New York walked off their jobs on 18 March 1970, the action presented a challenge not only to the economy but to the American state.

The central issue which triggered the New York wildcat was pay, which was so low that many postal workers, particularly in the high-cost area of New York, were eligible for welfare – a factor lending irony to the media's sob stories about welfare recipients missing their cheques because of the strike. Almost as soon as the New York City workers walked out, their colleagues throughout New York State, New Jersey and Connecticut joined them; within a few days almost a quarter of a million postal employees in over 200 towns and cities had brought the US Postal Service to a halt.

Such action was unprecedented. The government moved swiftly, declaring a National Emergency and ordering the Army and National Guard to New York to 'scab' against the postal workers. Yet the soldiers themselves, 'infected by the militancy of the strikers ... sabotage[d] the mail they were supposed to move'.[14] Just as danger-ously for the government, the strike mood began to spread to other unionised federal workers. As one member of the American Federation of Government Employees put it, 'We've learned from the postal workers that if practically everybody strikes, then nobody is going to be hurt ... After all, they can't fire everybody'.[15]

Unfortunately, postal workers' leaders were less impressed by their members' intransigence. While soldiers were sabotaging the New York Post Office in support of the strikers, the letter carriers' presi-dent Rademacher and union officials were urging the strikers back to work. New York postal workers voted en masse to defy their leader-ship, 'branding their national union leaders "rats" and "creeps" ... Signs behind the rostrum ... read "Hang Rat-emacher" and "We won't take rat poison" ...'.[16] The New York strikers' fury at their lead-ership's betrayal extended the fight. Their rejection of the 'back-to-work' demand spurred action throughout the country, causing so much disruption that the government was rapidly forced into con-ceding a settlement which awarded workers an immediate 6 per cent pay rise, rising to 14 per cent within the next four months. 'The 1970 Post Office strike won in two weeks what postal workers couldn't get in years of begging'.[17]

The risks the strikers took were considerable; striking against the government was a felony punishable by fines and imprisonment. At times their action, particularly combined with support from soldiers and government workers, posed a serious threat to the state. Yet the strikers had not taken this objectively subversive action out of any explicitly 'political' stance; they were propelled into it by their material circumstances. 'When postal workers struck in 1970, when they risked fines, jail sentences, loss of jobs, seniority and pensions, they did it because they had no choice'.[18]

'Open warfare': the Teamster wildcat

At almost the same moment, thousands of rank-and-file Teamsters walked off the job after their National Master Freight Agreement (NMFA) contract expired without agreement on 1 April 1970. Within a day, wildcat strikers shut down trucking companies across America. When Teamster president Frank Fitzsimmons agreed a disappointing $1.10 per hour increase, truckers began preparing to go back to work. But in Chicago, a crucial hub of national freight movement, two groups of workers held out – the members of dissident Local 705 and the independent Chicago Truck Drivers Union (CTDU).

This reversed the back-to-work trend; the wildcat strike spread across the country to San Francisco, where Teamsters followed a parallel air traffic controllers' action and organised a massive 'sick-in'.[19] Meanwhile, the ongoing action in Chicago stopped shipments to cities all over the country. When the Fraternal Association of Steelhaulers (FASH), a dissident rank-and-file caucus, started its own wildcat on 6 April, the truckers' action was strengthened by thousands of drivers refusing to carry steel.

Like the FASH strike, the truckers' wildcat was almost completely based on rank-and-file initiative, coordinated and led by local activists. Predictably, the Teamster leadership saw sinister forces at work, claiming the strikers were influenced by 'outside goons' and 'Communists';[20] but the tens of thousands of Teamsters who stormed out of their 'barns' did not give the impression of having been indoctrinated; there were simply too many of them. Two thousand Toledo truckers who shouted down the officials ordering them back to work on 10 April were hardly the dupes of outside agitators; nor were the 16,000 Ohio Teamsters who defied a similar order, 500 of them marching through Cleveland in an anti-leadership demonstration. By this time even Fitzsimmons' own local, Detroit 299, had joined the wildcat, which ended in clear victory that July.

Employers and the government were well aware of the political implications of the action: 'Coming on the heels of a successful Postal wildcat, a totally successful Teamster wildcat might have sparked off a long period of worker militancy throughout the country'.[21] Lamentably, the labour movement failed to make the same connections; as in Britain, no effective cross-class leadership arose to coordinate such struggles. Yet a lasting gain of the 1970 wildcat was its outcome in the dynamic, member-led reform caucus Teamsters for a Democratic Union (TDU), which eventually unseated the union's corrupt and undemocratic leadership. While TDU was not fully established until 1976, its industrywide, grassroots network of activists was clearly rooted in the 1970 wildcat strike.

'The union don't do nothing'

In contrast to the wildcats, the 1970 General Motors (GM) strike was a formal, union-approved dispute, part of the standard industrial relations procedure which accompanies the expiration of an American pay contract. However, the GM strike took on an enhanced meaning in the context of the changing dynamics of both capital and labour; one report christened it 'America's most important strike in a decade, perhaps the most important strike in twenty-five years'.[22]

Why was such epochal importance attached to otherwise run-of-the-mill pay negotiations accompanying the end of a contract? The main factor was the joint determination of both company and union to bring about (they hoped) irreversible changes in worker and membership behaviour. In the company's case, the spur was the urgent need to reverse declining profit rates through increased productivity; for the United Auto Workers (UAW), it was the resolve to suppress an over-militant membership 'once and for all'. Throughout the 1960s, postcontract wildcat strikes which had erupted over working conditions in the plants had dogged the union; while crucial for the rank and file, the issue of plant conditions was regarded as an exasperating irrelevance by the union as much as by the company. As one worker put it, 'On the question of conditions, the company ain't done a motherfucking thing about it, and the union don't do nothing'.[23]

With this 'problem' in mind, the leadership invited locals to submit their workplace-based grievances at the beginning of the dispute; but this reversal of the usual negotiating order did not reverse its attitude to the membership. Instead, the union cooperated with management in working out a joint strategy aimed at undermining the rank and file. Rather than opposing strike action, both sides agreed that a long strike would be useful in gradually wearing down members' militancy and expectations; it would create an 'escape valve' for workers' built-up frustrations over ever increasing labour intensification while at the same time 'foster[ing] union loyalty ... by uniting [workers] against a common enemy'.[24]

In the event, however, this strategy almost backfired on the two 'partners' through the very factor they were trying to destroy – rank-and-file militancy. The strike lasted 67 days, far longer than expected; even after six weeks, only 52 of the 155 local agreements had been settled. When the UAW settled nationally on 10 November, a number of locals were still refusing to return to work. One dispute in Georgia prevented full resumption of production at GM's Pontiac division until the following February. Rank-and-file workers had had enough impact on a strike aimed at undermining rank-and-file organisation to take it far beyond the limit their leaders had originally planned.

And then there was Lordstown ...

In 1972, a rather more notorious GM strike took place in a newly built GM plant 'in the heart of the heart of the country'[25] – Lordstown, Ohio. Here a white, almost entirely young workforce, many of them embittered veterans of the Vietnam War, took wildcat action over exactly the same issues which had mobilised dissident locals in the 1970 strike: deteriorating working conditions, particularly speedup and labour intensification. Since 1971, line speed had risen from a bearable 60 to an impossible 100 cars an hour; from this point onwards an already combative workforce launched escalating actions against the speedup, from basic sabotage and 'doubling up' to outright refusal to do extra work. Essentially, 'the workers were conducting a strike inside the plant'.[26]

Since these workers happened to be young and white, many sporting long hair, bandannas and other hippy regalia, the strike garnered national attention as a symptom of what was christened the 'Blue-Collar Blues'. The catchphrase suggested that what was pushing these workers into conflict was a romantic rejection of alienation, a generalised dissatisfaction with the uninspiring repetitions of assembly-line work. While this was of course true – for less media-worthy black workers as well as Lordstown's fair-haired rebels – the trigger for outright resistance, as in other workplaces, lay in less glamorous, more material issues of a highly intensified work-pace rooted in GM's incessant drive to reduce labour time.

Tightened work standards and harsher discipline across the industry worsened considerably over the next few years. The effects of the relentless pressure exploded in the summer of 1973, when workers stormed out of the plants in three major wildcats at Chrysler's Detroit plants. The first began with a dramatic action by two black workers who occupied a power cage at the Jefferson Avenue factory in protest at the systematic racism of their foreman. The cage was immediately surrounded by 150 cheering workers, with the rest of the workforce 'support[ing] us ... 95 per cent'.[27] That same evening, management surrendered to the demand that the foreman be sacked.

The second wildcat, sparked by appalling safety conditions in the Detroit Forge plant, erupted after two workers suffered particularly horrific accidents, but was crushed when the UAW backed a management decree that anyone refusing to go back to work would be immediately sacked. The union played an equally repressive role in a third wildcat, also over safety, at the Mack Avenue plant, when UAW officials joined police in a 1,000-strong cordon outside the plant to crush the strikers' picket-lines. It was a symbol of the UAW bureaucracy's determination 'to end wildcats like this one, once and for all'.[28]

The harsh punishments dealt out by management in the wake of the 1973 wildcats, along with the UAW's decisive part in crushing shopfloor protest, broke both the morale and organisation of the dissident workers. Yet the 1973 rebellion again reflects the tempestuous nature of the period, even in the ideologically conservative environment of the United States. Once again, like the actions of British workers who mobilised to defeat the anti-union legislation of the same period, it raised questions of political potential rooted in 'ordinary' workplace resistance – questions which, then as now, remained largely unrecognised.

BRITAIN'S SUMMER – AND SPRING – OF DISCONTENT

The British labour movement of the time displayed a number of contradictions. It was seemingly unaware of basic necessities like the coordination of strikes, which would have pulled workers together as a class and provided a far more potent challenge to the Tory (Conservative) government. The movement appeared itself to be unaware of the true 'trade union power' in the face of which a frightened state called on union leaders to control their members. Despite the high levels of both militancy and solidarity, the trade union movement remained absurdly disorganised. A disastrous defeat for postal workers in 1971, which could have been prevented with the support of telephone workers, took place the same year those workers were due to settle; joint action would have strengthened both parties. A rail strike began almost immediately after the postal workers' strike was over, whereas 'had it coincided with the earlier stoppage, [it] could have blocked the major alternative channel for parcel distribution'.[29]

And yet, during the same period, workers mobilised massively to defeat successive governments' attempts to bring in anti-union legislation. Political action and opposition on a grand scale were combined with strategic inadequacy and lack of class awareness in a mix that was eventually to lead to defeat in the face of the far more focused attack led by Thatcher. For the moment, though, the period seemed to possess its own irrepressible impetus, a class struggle dynamic seen at its strongest in the legendary 'Saltley Gates' and 'Pentonville Five' revolts by miners and dockers in 1972.

'We don't want your pound notes ...'

Despite their historic reputation as working-class leaders, miners had seen their pay decline steadily since the mid 1950s; between 1967 and 1971 they had experienced a 3 per cent cut in real wages. The miners' anger at their deteriorating position had resulted in two earlier, localised strikes in 1969 and 1970 which had strengthened the left and enabled militants to develop tactics like the famous 'flying pickets' commonly credited to Arthur Scargill, though used by a range of activists since the 1940s.[30] In November 1971, miners voted for national action for the first time since 1926; the strike began on 9 January 1972.

The militant Yorkshire left of the National Union of Mineworkers, headed by Arthur Scargill, began almost immediately to use flying pickets to block the most vulnerable points of coal production and transport, like power stations, coke and coal depots. Only weeks into the strike, the Yorkshire pickets were drafted into a national effort to stop movements of coal across the country; by early February only three weeks' supply of coal was left in the power stations. However, some large depots were still relatively unscathed, including Saltley coke depot in Birmingham, where over 1,000 lorries a day were transporting coke unhindered.

As soon as Scargill became aware of the situation, coachloads of pickets headed down to Saltley. Yet, four days later, with the police 'kicking hell out of our lads',[31] reinforcements were urgently needed. In desperation, Scargill appealed on television for more miners to get to the area as fast as possible. Within hours, 200 arrived. By this time the local TGWU had already backed the miners by forbidding its members to drive through picket-lines, as well as supplying mounds of steak pies which were both consumed by hungry miners and used as missiles against the scab drivers.[32] Unfortunately, although the TGWU succeeded in persuading its own members to turn their lorries around, the non-union 'cowboys, inspired by greed, brought Alsatian dogs, iron bars and sticks to force their way through the picket'.[33]

In the context of this continued assault, to which local police gave their full backing, it became obvious that the miners could not win on their own. In an eloquent appeal to the local engineering union to lend more than financial 'solidarity' in the increasingly desperate battle at Saltley, Scargill pleaded: 'We don't want your pound notes ... Will you go down in history as the working class in Birmingham who stood by while the miners were battered or will you become immortal? I do not ask you – I *demand* that you come out on strike'.[34] Despite their largely conservative history, the engineers unanimously agreed support, as did the local National Union of Vehicle Builders. Two days later, on Thursday 8 February, this class solidarity came into its own at the Battle of Saltley Gates.

The usual lines of the picketing skirmish – striking miners at the gate, mounted police confronting them with truncheons – were established by 6 a.m. that day. But this time, the outcome was different. Coachloads of Welsh miners walking to Saltley during the morning rush hour 'called on the Brummies: "Come and join us". Building workers on sites joined them and soon the ranks were swelling'.[35] Thousands of carworkers from plants across Birmingham began to march in, moving slowly to allow workers from the massive Rover factory six miles away to catch up.

'No traffic moved, only bodies blocking the road chanting: "Close the Gates". Then they came over the railway bridge with banners and cardboard placards made that morning ... From the other side of the city workers from Lucas GKN and others were still on the road to Saltley. The roads were blocked with workers ... The human sea was too strong to hold back'.[36] And it was too strong for the forces of law and order: 'The roads all around the depot were jammed, and the police ... were surrounded and simply couldn't cope. "Close the gates, close the gates", the crowd chanted. At about ten forty-five that Thursday morning, an official from the Gas Board walked across the yard, and locked the padlock on the gates of Saltley'.[37]

Through the united power of sheer numbers, rank-and-file workers had overwhelmed the forces of the state in the form of the government, the National Coal Board and the police. From his perch on top of a white-tiled public lavatory outside the depot, Scargill told the victorious workers: 'This will go down in trade union history ... as the battle of Saltley Gate. The working people have united in a mass stand'.

While disdained by some writers as 'lavishly romanticised',[38] the fundamental truth of such statements did not escape Margaret Thatcher, who recounts in her autobiography, 'For me, what happened at Saltley took on no less significance than it did for the Left. I understood, as they did, that the struggle to bring trade unions properly within the rule of law would be decided not in the debating chamber of the House of Commons ... but in and around the pits and factories'.[39] By contrast, Edward Heath's relative ineptitude in the face of 'trade union power' ensured his own effective political execution two years later – again at the hands of the miners.

'Why Aren't You Out?'

The story of the Pentonville Five, five dockers imprisoned by the Conservative government in the summer of 1972 and released after mass action by the organised working class, sums up the mood of resistance and solidarity that reached its highest peak in that episode. Like the miners, dockers were traditionally strong and determined fighters, yet had not received the riches that their media image suggested. Even after the 1967 Devlin reforms replaced casual labour with a dockers' 'register', earnings continued to fall and job insecurity to increase. While registered dockers technically could not be sacked, they found themselves increasingly relegated to the pool of labour known as the Temporary Unattached Register, where the fallback rate was approximately half average earnings.

In this context of insecurity and hardship, the threat posed by containerisation – the packing of goods into enormous boxes which can be moved by crane directly on to inland transport – was explosive. The new technology threatened more than a reduction in the number of dockers; it also meant the wholesale transfer of dock work into non-unionised, unregulated container depots established just outside the dock area, where employers could legally take on low-paid casual workers to 'stuff and strip' containers. Capital was not slow to take up the advantage. Between 1967 and 1969, containerisation more than doubled in London and almost tripled elsewhere.

From 1969 onwards, dockers began staging strikes and boycotts of container terminals in London and Liverpool. With the passing of the 1971 Industrial Relations Act, these actions began to pose a challenge not only to employers but to the state, which had now outlawed 'secondary' picketing, that is, picketing not directly aimed at the workers' own employer. In March 1972 Heatons, a container company near Liverpool, was granted an injunction under the Act against the TGWU for its stewards' continued refusal to allow container lorries into Liverpool docks. The union was fined £50,000 for defying the injunction; the following month, it was fined a further £50,000 for contempt.

Caught in these legal entanglements, the TGWU tried denying responsibility for the action of its shop stewards, opening up the prospect of the stewards themselves being fined or imprisoned. In July, Heatons struck again; this time five stewards from Tilbury docks were arrested and taken to Pentonville prison in North London.

Between 22 July, when the Pentonville Five were imprisoned, and 1 August, when they were released, at least 170,000 workers came out in their support, creating what could have been – and almost was – a TUC-led general strike. Engineering workers, printers, bus drivers, carworkers, building workers, miners, workers in London's wholesale markets, and, significantly, the container drivers who only a few days before had been pitted against the striking dockers, joined the huge march of workers from every section of the movement which surged up the dingy moat of Caledonian Road to the embattled castle of Pentonville. Images from the video *The People's Flag*[40] show turbanned Sikh workers grinning broadly on either side of a placard reading 'Five Trade Unionists Are Inside: Why Aren't You Out?'; marching workers shouting 'We are the working class'; the seething of the crowds around the freed dockers as each was lifted shoulder-high and the whole mass of workers exploded in victory. A previously unheard-of 'Official Solicitor' had miraculously appeared to secure the Pentonville Five's release. The pride and confidence of organised, united workers who had defeated a government in less time and with more force than any 'constitutional' action could dream of doing still emanates from these now decades-old images.

At the time, the effective destruction of the Industrial Relations Act by this wave of rank-and-file resistance seemed little more than a logical next step in the unstoppable advance of an apparently invincible working class. After all, a national building workers' strike had escalated from selective to all-out action at roughly the same time as the dockers' victory; a rank-and-file rail workers' revolt over pay had also called the bluff of the Industrial Relations Act with an overwhelming ballot for strike action; and a stream of quasi-revolutionary plant occupations, including the Manchester engineering sit-ins, had followed the relatively respectable 'work-in' by shipyard workers at Upper Clyde Shipbuilders in 1971.

REVOLT FROM BELOW

In the US, oppositional rank-and-file trade union caucuses, based in concrete issues of pay and workplace conditions while simultaneously challenging an often stifling bureaucracy, offered a different kind of challenge to the status quo. Such caucuses were not confined to the Teamsters. The late 1960s and early 1970s were the era of a widespread 'revolt from below' in which a range of rank-and-file groups – autoworkers, longshoremen (dockers), steelworkers, airline mechanics, transport workers, seafarers, miners – rebelled, almost entirely on the basis of working conditions, against both company and union. Such workplace-based groups were 'the power base for the insurgencies from below that in the last three years have ended or threatened official careers of long standing ... Almost without exception the revolts were conducted primarily to improve the conditions of life-on-the-job'.[41]

Among rank-and-file miners, explosive wildcats broke out in 1969 and 1970 rooted in anger over both scandalously inadequate safety regulations and the corrupt autocracy of the union leadership. By the late 1960s, the callous and autocratic regime of miners' president Tony Boyle had pushed his membership to breaking point. Boyle had made almost a cult of cosying up to the bosses, assuring a government committee that 'The UMWA will not abridge the rights of mine operators ... We follow the judgment of the coal operators, right or wrong'.[42] The last straw came in 1968 after a mine explosion in Farmington, West Virginia which killed 78 miners; in a speech 'commemorating' the dead, Boyle remarked that the mine owner, Mountaineer Coal, 'was one of the better companies to work with as far as cooperation and safety are concerned'.[43] In response to this outrage, and to the continuing lack of action over pneumoconiosis ('Black Lung'), rank-and-file miners began organising across the industry, starting with the formation of the Black Lung Association (BLA) in January 1969.

Not long afterwards, one West Virginia miner, sickened by the continuing lack of progress on health and safety conditions, 'spilled his water out on the ground ... the traditional appeal to other miners to join a strike'.[44] Within five days the wildcat spread to 42,000 of West Virginia's coal miners. As one of the founders of the Black Lung Association recalled, 'I don't know exactly how the strike began or started spreading ... It just spread. And then we all decided to march on the [state] Capitol'.[45]

That strike, which lasted 23 days until the miners' demands were met, resulted in a state law offering compensation to victims of Black Lung disease. But the basic problems remained, and the surge of rank-and-file militancy continued, filling the mountainous mining areas with roving bands of angry miners; continuous sporadic wildcats obeyed 'roving pickets' who moved from mine to mine calling the workers out. The movement was 'heavily populated with angry Vietnam vets', one of whom summed up the mood: 'I took it in 'Nam because I had to, but I'm not about to take it here'.[46]

Up to this point strike action had been coordinated, if at all, by a network of local leaders which formed the backbone of an incipient rank-and-file movement in the UMWA. This essentially localised organisation changed in 1969, when a former UMWA executive member, Jock Yablonski, decided to run as a reform candidate for the presidency. Local strike networks, along with organisations like the Black Lung Association, became linked nationally in a joint effort to elect Yablonski and oust Boyle. Tragically, Boyle reacted to the rival candidacy with a response typical of US 'business unionism' – violence. In late December 1969 Yablonski, his wife and daughter were found murdered, literally, in their beds.

This crime, for which Boyle was later convicted, did not destroy the reform movement; on the contrary, the rank-and-file responded by forming Miners For Democracy (MFD), a nationwide movement which united wildcat strikers, veterans of the Yablonski campaign, the Black Lung Association, and the newly formed Disabled Miners and Widows. Over the next two years, these groups 'welded together and began to operate almost like an opposition political party inside the United Mine Workers'.[47]

In June 1970, rank-and-file miners' anger again came to a head, with 40,000 coal miners across three states walking out over the continuing failure to enforce mine safety legislation. In the words of the *Wall Street Journal*, 'The nation's coalfields are seething with anger and disappointment over the new law … Rebel miners … charge that the [government] is acting in concert with the Boyle leadership and coal operators'.[48] Finally, in the early 1970s, the MFD succeeded in ousting Boyle and establishing its own leadership, which unfortunately proved weak and undemocratic, cutting off its links with the MFD. Yet the contribution of the MFD in democratising the union remained in many ways crucial. In the late 1970s, despite the record of the leadership, it could still be said that 'this democratisation of the union has tended to strengthen the position of the local versus … management'.[49] Once again, it was organisation from the grass roots which had brought about fundamental change by taking on union bureaucracy, employers and the state.

Also in the early 1970s, rank-and-file steelworkers mobilised to overturn the almost equally collaborative leadership of their president, I.W. Abel, forming a dissident caucus, Steelworkers Fight Back, to overturn Abel and force the union to take more note of workplace issues. In the UAW, rank and filers built a United National Caucus rooted in the same combination of workplace and internal union grievances; and 1970 saw the founding of TURF (Teamsters United Rank and File), the precursor of the combative and successful TDU.

Whatever each group's achievements or failures, one underlying problem with this impressive wave of rank-and-file organisation was, again, the lack of coordination between different sections and waves of activity: 'Symptomatic of the limits of the rank-and-file upsurge of this period was the virtual absence of any contact or cross-fertilisation between the massive strike movements of 1970 and the organisations of the era such as MFD, TURF and UNC'.[50] As in Britain, the period saw huge eruptions of grass-roots working-class activity which expressed the potential of class struggle for mobilisation and democracy. But, also as in Britain, few of even the most militant US workers took the step towards envisaging a 'class for itself'.

'SPECTACULAR EVENTS ...'

Nevertheless, the era continued to display a stunning predisposition towards dramatic forms of working-class organisation and revolt. In Britain, the early 1970s saw a new form of resistance – a wave of plant occupations sparked by the UCS 'work-in'. This action, taken by workers at Upper Clyde Shipbuilders, a Scottish shipyard threatened with closure, was a form of occupation in which the workers continued to produce under their own self-direction. Though the tactic eventually succeeded in saving UCS, neither the 'work-in' concept nor its practical expression in the takeover of the yards – from July 1971 to October 1972 – came anywhere near a revolutionary 'expropriation' of the yards, despite (or perhaps because of) its leadership by the Communist Party. The cautious position taken by the UCS stewards was clear at their first press conference: 'We are not going on strike ... We are not strikers. We are responsible people and we will conduct ourselves with dignity and discipline ... We want to work'.[51]

Yet the response to the UCS battle by workers across the movement showed a mood of rather more conflictual resistance. Along with one-day strikes and huge demonstrations throughout Scotland, the best endorsement of the Clyde workers' action came from the wave of worker occupations which paid it the tribute of imitation – yet imitation which stopped short of replicating the 'work-in' tactic and confined itself to occupation per se. Less than a month after the beginning of the UCS work-in, Plessey workers (also in Scotland) occupied their factory to prevent equipment being transferred. This was followed swiftly by occupations at the River Don steelworks in Sheffield, Fisher-Bendix at Kirkby, Sexton Shoes at Fakenham, BP Chemicals at Stroud, the Meriden motorcycle plant and many more. As late as 1973, occupations were continuing at Cole Cranes in Sunderland, CAV in Liverpool, and Bryant Colour Printing in South London.

These workers' refusal to accept such standard attacks on their livelihoods and job security posed a significant challenge to the power and ownership of capital, demonstrating the growing class confidence of the times; any of these initiatives 'before the advent of the UCS occupation ... [would] have been considered most spectacular events'.[52]

Two of the most notorious sit-ins were those by women leatherworkers at Fakenham, who went on to a long-term experiment in self-management, and by motorcycle makers at Triumph at Meriden,

which along with the *Scottish Daily News* became a workers' cooperative under the auspices of Tony Benn. Not surprisingly, the road to
'worker ownership' in the midst of a still trenchantly capitalist economy became mired for these and similar experiments in a demoralising rut of self-exploitation and pressure from 'worker-managers'
which uncannily resembled that of their capitalist predecessors.

One particular group of occupations, however, was proof against
such diversions: the Manchester engineering sit-ins of 1972. The
difference was that these occupations were primarily *offensive* – in
support of engineering workers' 1972 wage claim – rather than
defensive (in response to the threat of plant closure and job losses).
Yet the Manchester sit-ins failed – largely, it seems, due to the familiar syndrome of lack of coordination, sectorwide strategic cohesion,
or, more bluntly, class unity.

Even when 1,650 engineering workers were occupying their factories, there was very little systematic effort to extend the occupation.
In some of the better organised areas, joint shop steward committees
were set up to link plants together, but these initiatives were limited;
the local union bureaucracy appeared incapable of coordinating the
action. In spite of all the obstacles, an impressive number of occupations continued; over Easter 1972 an additional 14 sit-ins began,
involving 8,000 workers and amounting to a total of 27 by 18 April.
However, the lack of official coordination and support meant large
numbers of workers being 'left in limbo to move either forward into
the unknown, or to retreat. As experienced, practical shop stewards
with little penchant for martyrdom, they retreated to more familiar
ground'.[53]

What could have been an effective, powerful movement for shared
class interests was thus left to wither in the limbo of official union
indifference, incompetence or perhaps fear of a coordinated class
response. The lesson can be taken forward to the ultimate analysis of
why the whole 1968–74 upsurge left few definable traces on the
future development of the movement. On the plus side, however, the
apparently inexhaustible class energies of the period had already
been harnessed to defeat two sets of government anti-union legislation, and were now about to defeat an entire government.

'WHO RUNS THE COUNTRY?'

For some writers, the events of 1973–74 came closer to revolutionary
upheaval than even the 'glorious summer' of 1972, dismissed as

'nothing like as serious as the [crisis] with which Heath had to deal in 1974'.[54] As one experienced industrial journalist reflects, 'I do not – cannot – underestimate the significance of that extraordinary year of 1974'.[55] It was a period of widespread ruling-class paranoia. An eminent British civil servant buttonholed the same journalist in late 1973 to say, 'I have to tell you that we must prepare for a possible revolution in this country'.[56] One 'leading businessman' predicted that Britain was 'heading for a slump and food riots';[57] a politician from the Ministry of Labour thought the country could well be 'on the brink of revolution';[58] even Margaret Thatcher comments in her memoirs that 'As the effects of the miners' industrial action bit deeper, the sense that we were no longer in control of events deepened'.[59] As has now been proved, after years of denial, army officers 'seriously considered the possibility of a military takeover' in 1974–75.[60]

What caused the panic? Once again, worker action rooted in concrete issues of living standards and working conditions. The miners' strike which led to the downfall of the Heath government in 1974 was preceded by a wave of protest against the government's wage freeze by healthworkers, civil servants, gasworkers and others in the public sector in early 1973. On 1 May 1973, a TUC-backed strike against the government's wage controls was 'the biggest political stoppage yet';[61] two million workers went on strike, and huge demonstrations took place in all the major cities. Miners themselves, despite their 1972 victory, were now well down in the pay league, and their anger was shared by the now left-controlled NUM executive.

By mid 1973, however, the wave of militancy appeared to have died down, and by mid July Heath was confident enough to initiate a meeting with the NUM to preempt (he hoped) another large pay claim. However, the Prime Minister 'operated from a very limited understanding of the miners' demands [and] their intensity ...'.[62] In October 1973, when the Coal Board offered a 16 per cent increase, which Heath expected to go through with no trouble, the union turned the offer down and began an overtime ban in preparation for strike action. Combined with the simultaneous oil crisis of late 1973, this led to the notorious three-day-week shutdown of industry, along with regular electricity blackouts, prompting the famous exhortation by the Energy Minister to 'clean your teeth in the dark'. The oil shortage further shifted the balance of power in favour of the miners; unable to buy oil to burn in the power stations, the government was forced to use coal, thus burning up its coal stocks.

Nevertheless, Heath remained stubborn, refusing to make the miners a 'special case' under the incomes policy. Criticising the dispute as 'political', he proclaimed that the miners were not interested in settling a pay dispute but only in 'smashing' the incomes policy and 'get[ting] rid of the elected government of the day'.[63] This logic led directly to Heath's ill-fated decision to call an election on the theme of 'Who runs the country?'.

The miners voted by more than 80 per cent for a national strike, which began on 10 February 1974, already backed by pledges of solidarity from engineering, transport and other workers. On 28 February, Heath's question was answered by his defeat at the hands of Labour from an electorate with no confidence in his ability to run the country, 'the unions' or anything much else. The stage was set, ironically, for the beginning of the trade union movement's long-term defeat through its incorporation into an apparently benevolent Labour government.

2
'How Little It Asked' (The Working Class):[1] 1974–79

By 1975 or 1976 at the latest, the party was over. At least, this is the verdict of a number of commentators on the mid 1970s industrial scene in both Britain and America. The heady struggles of 1968–74 were forgotten as strike figures fell, workers suffered a disastrous drop in earnings, unemployment and inflation soared in concert, and government approaches to 'the unions' turned either dismissive (America) or dangerously collaborationist (Britain).

For many commentators, both radical and mainstream, these changes indicated a bulk-standard diagnosis of 'downturn' for the mid to late 1970s. The potential for class politics raised by the 1968–74 upsurge was, according to this argument, somehow lost at the beginning of the mid 1970s. Yet the apparent lull in class struggle after 1974 becomes, on closer inspection, a many-stranded and often contentious response to the continued – mounting – pressures of capitalism on the working class.

THE REALITY OF RECESSION

There is no dismissing the brutal external economic factors which assaulted workers in the mid 1970s. The danger signals had begun to emerge even before unemployment and inflation soared simultaneously in 1974–75; the impact of the 1973 'oil crisis' and profit slump immediately affected terms and conditions as employers moved, as always, to solve the crisis on workers' backs. The reduction in pay was widespread and severe. Real average earnings for US workers fell from $327 a week in 1973 to $305 in 1975 and $285 by the end of the decade.[2] In Britain, workers experienced a cut in real take-home pay of 6 per cent between 1974 and 1975, with a further 2 per cent and 3 per cent over the next two years.[3]

The 'Social Con-Trick'

This decline in earnings was the result of two factors: a massive rise in inflation, on the one hand, and direct wage restraint on the other. By the end of 1974 inflation in Britain was running at 23 per cent, by March 1975 the annual rate had reached 27.7 per cent, and by April it was 33 per cent; in the US, where the annual rate of inflation had averaged only 1.3 per cent over the period 1960–65, it rose to nearly 11 per cent in 1974. While conservative commentators blamed 'inflationary' pay rises, in reality wages soon began to fall well behind inflation, considerably damaging workers' spending power in both countries.

The more direct attack on pay was, by the mid 1970s, the result of explicit government policies. In the US, politicians began to listen to corporate calls for spending cuts and wage restraint, President Ford responding with the felicitously named 'Whip Inflation Now' campaign.

In Britain, pay restraint took a more convoluted form – the infamous, incorporationist 'Social Contract', or, as it soon became universally known, 'Social Con-Trick'. In sharp contrast to American 'business as usual', the new Labour government seemed to be speaking the language of class war – on the workers' side. In the orgy of radicalism that accompanied Labour's March 1974 victory, the Chancellor had promised to 'squeeze the rich until the pips squeak', a stirring vow accompanying Labour's overall commitment to 'a fundamental and irreversible shift in the balance of power and wealth in favour of working people and their families'.[4] The most radical Labour election manifesto since 1945 included an Industry Bill backed by the radical MP Tony Benn which promised the extension of 'social ownership' and 'industrial democracy' through shop steward-based planning agreements. These, and more immediate benefits like food subsidies and price controls, higher pensions and improved healthcare and education, embodied the new Labour government's rhetorical commitment to its side of the ill-fated 'Social Contract'.

Given such government generosity, where was the workers' contribution? The initial side of the bargain was that the trade unions should exercise some kind of (unspecified) wage restraint. From the official side of the movement at least, this policy was loyally supported; the AUEW backed down from pressing a major wage claim in April, while the TUC agreed a 'zero real income growth' policy in the summer of 1974.

This official cooperation, however, sidestepped the unofficial action which continued unabated as Labour came into office. Strikes and occupations continued throughout the early months of the new government, provoked at least in part by Labour's bizarre decision to maintain the previous government's 'Phase Three' wage freeze. Resentment at this decision triggered a wave of strikes among nurses, council workers, public transport workers, teachers and BBC staff, joined by factory workers and others in the private sector. By the summer of 1974, the Labour government was fighting 'a sustained pay revolt ... at the base of the unions'.[5] As Labour sought and regained power by a fragile margin in October, unofficial strikes by thousands of Scottish workers again challenged what was still one of its main election planks, the Social Contract.

Yet this was not politically conscious defiance of a 'labourist' bargain; for most workers, the strikes were motivated simply by the need to make up for the fall in living standards under the previous government's wage restraint. The groups of public sector workers most lambasted for 'inflationary' pay settlements were the same that had struggled under the previous government to improve unacceptably low pay levels; this was a much-needed catching-up exercise. By April 1975, wage rises were rapidly falling behind price rises, with every indication that this gap would grow in the months ahead.

In this context it seems bizarre, to say the least, for TGWU leader Jack Jones to invoke 'the self-interest of trade unionists' in 'stemming price inflation' by wage restraint.[6] Nevertheless, invoke it he did; in April 1975, when inflation hit its highest level yet, Jones took the initiative in proposing a year-long across-the-board £6 limit in pay. The suggestion was gratefully taken up by ministers; support for pay restraint by a leading 'left' union representative allowed the government to break through the labour movement taboo against incomes policy dating from the defeat of Labour's 1969 attempt at anti-union legislation, 'In Place of Strife'.

What might be seen as a betrayal of that rank-and-file victory against pay restraint was thus neatly set in place by the very TGWU leader who had revitalised shopfloor trade unionism in the late 1960s and early 1970s. Yet the appearance of fairness given by a flat rate of £6 seems to have silenced protest. Not long after the pay limit was brought into play on 1 August, the striking (with notable exceptions) stopped. Between 1975 and 1976, strike levels fell to their lowest levels for over a decade. Working days lost, well over 14 million in 1974, dropped to just over six million in 1975 and only a little over three million in 1976 – the lull which, for most commentators, signifies the 'downturn' following on the 'upsurge' of 1968–74.

The 'Magnificent Seven' – and more

What was behind this relative acquiescence? Rapidly rising unemployment was clearly a basic factor. In February 1976 over a million workers were unemployed, and by 1977 it was one and a half million. Clearly, this was likely to have a severely dampening effect on workplace-based resistance. Other aspects were ideological; when called on to submit to 'equality of sacrifice' by union leaders like Jack Jones to whom millions of workers still retained enormous loyalty, union members were prepared to make sacrifices they would refuse to any Tory government. The continued credibility for rank-and-file workers of reformist ideology, along with the lack of any apparent alternative, prompted workers to 'pull together' for the sake of a 'national interest' assumed to be common to all classes.

Yet even during the full flush of support for wage restraint between 1975 and 1976, there were a number of exceptions to the overall acquiescence. Healthworkers staged strikes and occupations against cuts and hospital closures in 1975 and 1976; in late 1975, junior hospital doctors took unofficial action against excessive hours. In the summer of 1975 a sit-in was still in progress at Imperial Typewriters, where 500 Asian workers had struck over pay in 1974, and in the autumn of 1976, 'muscle power proved more effective than the law'[7] when a long strike by male and female workers at the Trico engineering plant won the women's claim for equal pay despite its dismissal by an Equal Pay Act tribunal.

Carworkers continued to resist not only incomes policy but also management's continuing workplace offensive. In late 1975, intransigence by one militant section at British Leyland's Cowley plant, led by a group known as the 'Magnificent Seven', defeated a repressive management campaign against 'restrictive practices'. Ford workers were also involved in ongoing guerrilla warfare against management, whose draconian layoff policies sparked blockages of production lines and a plant occupation in April 1975, resulting later in a 'prolonged strike ... in which parts of the factory were occupied'.[8]

Skilled workers entered the fray; in March 1976, 32 tool makers at SU Carburettors in Birmingham struck against the erosion of pay differentials brought about by the £6 limit. The AUEW forced the strikers back to work, but in early 1977 the SU action was followed by a Leyland-wide strike of toolmakers, led by an unofficial committee established after the earlier strike. Hardly class warriors, the toolmakers carried signs declaiming 'We are not challenging the incomes policy'; but this, as Leyland activist Thornett remarks, 'did not make the government feel any better about it'.[9] Not long afterwards, steel industry electricians, seafarers and Heathrow Airport workers were also on strike. Rumblings of discontent among workers in all sectors had begun to arise from the impact of Labour's insistence on introducing further phases of incomes policy in mid 1976 and 1977, while prices were rising by 15 per cent and the purchasing power of the average worker had fallen by 7 per cent in the two years of pay restraint.

As the TGWU's 1977 conference began, Jack Jones was given warnings by even his most moderate officers that they couldn't 'keep the lid on any longer'; Jones' own Midlands area was 'in open revolt' against the policy.[10] In a spectacular defeat, delegates voted down Jones' recommendation of yet another pay limit; immediately afterwards dockers and still more carworkers walked out. By the autumn, firefighters and power workers were on strike, and a hysterical flood of headlines – 'Callaghan Warns of Winter Strikes'; 'Lights Stay Off'; 'Blackout Threat to Kidney Patients' – gave some indication of what was to come.

The unrest was hardly groundless. As early as mid 1975, it had become increasingly obvious that what might at first have been thought of as a social contract without an incomes policy was turning into an incomes policy without a social contract. Most of the reforms Labour had introduced in its first few months were now withdrawn; after the introduction of the £6 limit in mid 1975, statutory price controls and food subsidies had been weakened and phased out. The sweeping reforms of industry that had so excited Benn's constituency of activists had been shredded by a determined alliance of business and right-wing Labour leaders almost as soon as the Labour government took over; Benn himself was forced to resign as Industry Secretary in mid 1975.

The mass of workers had clearly been prepared to continue with some notion of 'equality of sacrifice' to aid the survival of a Labour government – but only as long as it seemed to make any sense. And after mid 1976, when the government insisted on imposing a year-long 5 per cent limit, it clearly was not. By late 1976 and early 1977, working-class militancy had burst from its restraints in a resurgence of resistance, and a legacy of bitterness, which culminated in the 1978–79 'Winter of Discontent'.

CORPORATISM, AMERICAN-STYLE

American union leaders must have looked on with envy at British unions' cheek-by-jowl relationship with the Labour government. Although the US union bureaucracy once enjoyed what now seems an astonishing degree of influence – in 1970, Richard Nixon invited 200 labour leaders to the White House in order to 'woo ... labor for the coming election'[11] – it had never achieved the degree of corporate inclusion represented in the trade union–Labour Party relationship in the 1970s.

But the mid 1970s was the beginning of the end of any 'wooing' of unions by either employers or the state. Far from being drawn into a 'Social Contract'-style alliance with government, American unions were beginning to be rudely rejected by it. Though the Democratic Congress backed a labour law reform bill during Ford's presidency in the mid 1970s, the President vetoed it at the behest of business. Even under Carter's Democratic administration in 1977, the labour leadership's dreams were shattered; the Democratic Congress turned down union proposals for reforming the minimum wage, and in 1978 another attempt at labour law reform also failed.

During the same period, American employers became increasingly aggressive on their own account. The anti-union offensive often associated with the 1980s can be traced back as far as 1973, when employers came together to form an organisation known as the Business Roundtable. Along with tax cuts and deregulation, on the Roundtable's agenda were 'reforms' of labour law and a general offensive against union organising. By the mid 1970s, a damaging sign of the growing employer aggression was a major increase in the number of contested union recognition elections. While union recognition was legally backed by the National Labor Relations Act (NLRA) and overseen by the National Labor Relations Board (NLRB), management was beginning to challenge nearly every election. The number of 'unfair labour practice' charges against employers, most involving workers sacked for supporting the union, grew from 3,655 in 1957 to 20,311 in 1975.[12]

Employer hostility to union organisation was backed by widespread layoffs and 'rationalisation' which swelled the insecurity of the workforce; unemployment, more than any other aspect of

recession, underlay the retreat from struggle shown in sharply
falling strike figures after 1975. Resistance began to ebb dramatically
as workers' confidence evaporated. The 1974–75 recession 'was the
great divide between the insurgent world of the early 1970s and the
new economic order beyond'.[13]

Nevertheless, in the US as in Britain, any blanket assumption of a
ceasefire in class struggle during the recession years would be misplaced. Once again Teamsters and miners were in the forefront, with
two more major national wildcats in 1975–76; nor were they alone
in resisting the ruling-class onslaught. In 1975, faced with the
impact of a fiscal crisis, militant public sector workers 'tied up New
York City' with 'wildcat strikes against layoffs'.[14] As late as 1976,
'collective action on the part of ordinary workers shook virtually
every major US industry – mining, steel, auto, communications,
trucking, post office, longshore and many more'.[15] One vivid
description of the mid 1970s miners' wildcat poses the question, 'If
I were to say ... that for two years in the middle of the 1970s almost
all the coal miners in America were engaged in a strike against the
US government, would you believe me?'.[16] Not if you accepted the
widespread assumption that, from 1974 onwards, the American
working class was defeated, inactive and in retreat.

'War for the end of the world'

Once again, the issue which had miners 'marching up and down the
back roads, tossing away helmets, lanterns, etc., as in some war for
the end of the world'[17] was safety. The ongoing conflict between
productivity and miners' lives came to a head when, in mid 1976,
miners at Gateway Coal walked out because the company refused to
fix some faulty wiring. The Supreme Court ruled that the miners
were to keep working; but the Gateway miners stayed out, and other
miners came out on 'illegal' strike in their support. The Court
responded by issuing an injunction a day, so that by August 1976
miners throughout the area were subject to contempt fines or
prison; yet the strikes continued.

A semi-anarchic miners' revolt began to 'rage all over
Appalachia ... The federal courts would issue injunctions, impose
contempt, etc., but the miners kept walking out'. Rank-and-file
miners' fury against a federal justice system which found their lives
disposable was unstructured by any formal negotiations; the UMWA
'didn't call the strikes, or approve of them. They were simply
happening ... a "wildcat" would start ... at a single mine, and then

go like a forest fire from state to state. Soon it would be a national strike, burning wild and out of control ...'.[18]

In late 1977, the conflict over safety resurfaced in a 14-week-long strike against cuts in health benefits and measures against rank-and-file organisation – including the right to fire anyone engaging in unofficial action, or even refusing to cross a picket-line – which reflected the determination of the coal employers' organisation to 'come to grips with the cancer of the wildcat strike'.[19] Yet rank-and-file activists still linked in the union reform caucus Miners for Democracy (MFD) defied the employers with historic tactics like 'stranger pickets' in which squads of miners would travel hundreds of miles to mobilise their fellow-workers in the struggle. The coal employers were faced with 'hundreds, perhaps thousands, of experienced local leaders willing to use those traditions ... That is why the miners were not defeated in 1978'.[20]

Two things kept the strikers going during the dispute: their own determination ('We'll eat the bark off the trees before we'll accept enslavement') and massive support from the rest of the movement. Steelworkers, Teamsters, dockers, autoworkers, builders and others across the country sent money, held rallies, and built solidarity. Machinists at Lockheed and Boeing, wildcat strikers at Detroit's Chrysler plants, steelworkers on strike for seven months against Latrobe Steel, iron ore workers concluding their own five-month struggle, came forward to support the miners. One rank-and-file activist, leader of 200 women parts-plant workers on strike for the first time in their lives, declared, 'I think we ought to be behind the miners 100 per cent. They can turn all my lights off'.[21]

A Detroit Teamster echoed the sentiment: 'Most of us are ready to use candles until the miners win their strike, if necessary ... We say strike until you win; our hearts are with you'. When, in desperation, President Carter invoked the Taft-Hartley Act to get the miners back to work, West Coast longshore workers voted to walk out on a coast-wide general strike; the miners themselves simply ignored the threat of any injunction and remained as solid as before. The most powerful piece of anti-union legislation in the government's armoury was rendered powerless because, as one striker wrote on his placard, 'Taft-Hartley Can't Mine Coal'.[22]

A remarkable harvest ...

Much of the mid-1970s wildcat action was fuelled by burgeoning rank-and-file caucuses like MFD and Teamsters for a Decent

Contract (TDC), precursor of Teamsters for a Democratic Union. TURF (Teamsters United Rank and File), an earlier caucus founded after the 1970 wildcat, had largely fallen apart by 1973, but was succeeded by PROD, an organisation of 'professional drivers', UPSurge in United Parcels Service, and other 'loose networks of active union members who, though they had no group or newspaper, had informal organisations among their coworkers and fellow union members'.[23] From early 1975, some of the better organised of these groups had begun to contact each other, leading to a national meeting in Chicago which established Teamsters for a Democratic Contract (TDC).

In the runup to the 1976 negotiations, TDC activists threw their leaflets into tractors, cabs and truck trailers; 'the harvest was a remarkable collection of union activists'. When Teamsters across the country, backed by the TDC, voted ten to one to strike if their 1976 contract was unsatisfactory, Teamster president Fitzsimmons called the first national strike in Teamster history. In June 1976, TDC and UPSurge activists met to transform TDC into Teamsters for a Democratic Union: 'TDC had existed solely to fight for a better contract ... TDU would take up the task of building a rank-and-file movement and a national organisation to reform the Teamsters union'.[24]

TDU tapped into a rich vein of rank-and-file rebellion focused not only on continuing concerns around pay and conditions but also on outrage at the corruption and anti-membership complacency of the union bureaucracy; a revolt also expressed in MFD, the United National Caucus in the UAW and Steelworkers Fight Back in USWA (United Steel Workers of America). These and similar groups represented a uniquely American form of internal union rank-and-file organisation rooted in workplace issues. They raised, and brought to life, crucial issues of internal union democracy relating not only to formal procedures but to the basic class issues that provide the working-class rationale of trade unionism.

'The eight hours you're in there ...'

Unfortunately, even these grass-roots organisations were often fatally undermined by activists' drive to transform their unions as institutions, a determination usually directed at overthrowing the current leadership. The early triumphs of MFD had ended in decline rather than development; in a lesson on the shortcomings of relying on change at the top, the MFD's own candidates 'let the MFD die, cutting off an essential link to the rank and file'.[25] By the late 1970s the leadership had become disastrously weak; UMWA president Miller was becoming notorious for bizarre behaviour like driving in circles around the Washington beltway to avoid negotiations.

Similar contradictions beset the once lively and workplace-rooted caucus in steel, Steelworkers Fight Back. In 1973, leaders of USWA had come together with employers to establish what was essentially a no-strike deal, the Experimental Negotiating Agreement (ENA). In direct response to ENA's anti-strike provisions, rank-and-file activists formed a Right to Strike committee which elected 'avowed reformer' Ed Sadlowski as leader of a key local in the Chicago-Gary area, District 31. It was here, at the heart of the industry, that leaders of a range of reform locals and caucuses came together to form Steelworkers Fight Back in 1975.

One of the original purposes of Fight Back was to form a national network of activists to press for shared demands, mostly rooted in workplace conditions. As one supporter observed, 'It's what goes on during the eight hours you're in there. That's what constantly aggravates people'.[26] Yet, although 'the eight hours you're in there' constituted the key source of resistance and activism within the movement as a whole, Fight Back, like many similar groups, became drawn into putting the election of its favoured candidate at the centre of its concerns. The organisation decided to run Ed Sadlowski as president, and from this point Fight Back became, rather than a rank-and-file network, an electoral campaigning organisation.

In fact, Sadlowski lost the 1977 election, although he received a 51.9 per cent majority in the large basic steel locals. Steelworkers Fight Back ceased to exist after the election. Yet the reform movement it had generated continued to provide a valuable base for committed activists to link up with others in the industry. As one put it, 'A lot of people from here, there and everywhere didn't know each other until they started coming in around Sadlowski'. The network gave activists 'an idea of what kind of problems ... guys ... are having ... and what kind of solutions they've found'.[27]

Nevertheless, the fact remained that the 'guys' making contact with one another were already experienced, committed and often politically aware union activists whose chief objective now became the winning of locals by reform candidates in order to continue the pursuit of change in the top leadership. What was left out of the equation was the relation of such leading-edge reformers to the basic workplace concerns of the rank and file, to which the electoral reformers paid little attention. Meanwhile, many local activists remained unaware of the political and union activities of other caucuses in nearby plants. The syndrome pointed to a deeper difficulty: 'The transformation of informal networks into a unionwide organisation would have taken a major change in consciousness'.[28]

The beginnings of that 'change in consciousness' seemed to be emerging by the late 1970s, when rank-and-file activists began actively seeking to overcome their isolation through reaching out towards other similar movements and sympathetic 'experts' like those involved in the Association for Union Democracy (AUD). During this period, 'unofficial labor publications and educational projects began to proliferate',[29] including *Labor Notes*, a monthly newsletter on labour struggles and workplace issues which rapidly took on a wider role as a rank-and-file project linking activists across the movement with day schools, conferences and publications.

A 'BUREAUCRACY THESIS'?

In Britain, by contrast, academics and radical commentators had begun to note an increasing tendency for shop steward organisation to become drawn into managerial objectives and structures. What became known as the 'bureaucracy thesis'[30] argued that the reforms proposed by the 1968 Donovan Report, with their emphasis on 'formalising the informal' had begun to be taken more seriously by management and were generating a bureaucratisation of the independent and combative workplace structures of the 1960s.

In concrete terms, this meant providing office space, time off and general facilities to shop stewards who had often, in previous years, enjoyed none of these privileges; at the same time management began to 'woo' senior stewards with negotiation sessions at luxury hotels far removed, geographically and culturally, from the workplace. The trend posed the twin dangers not only of workplace bureaucratisation but of more substantive cooption into managerial perspectives.

The 'bureaucracy thesis' was argued at a time when it seemed union organisation in Britain had never been stronger – 1979 saw a historic peak in trade union density to over 57 per cent of the workforce, and the battles of the 'Winter of Discontent' hardly augured bureaucratic ossification. Yet the beginning of the end of direct, workplace-based trade union democracy and workgroup resistance were crucial factors in what was to become, all too soon, significant trade union decline.

'Drowning in support ...'

A different dimension of the movement's growing weakness in the late 1970s was the development of a post-1960s radicalism which tended to substitute 'protest politics' for ground-up organisation and resistance. The notorious Grunwick dispute of 1976–77 illustrated some of these tendencies only too clearly. Initially a comparatively small strike by Asian workers who walked out in August 1976 over atrocious pay and conditions at a photo processing plant in Cricklewood, West London, the Grunwick strike was taken up as a cause célèbre by the left, leading to huge mass pickets outside the plant which, unfortunately, were never able to make any real impact on the company. The one group which could have won the dispute, and was prevented from doing so by its own union leadership, were local postal workers.

In November 1976, before the mass pickets hit the headlines, postal workers at the Cricklewood sorting office began refusing to handle Grunwick's mail, an action which its managing director described as 'cutting the jugular vein of Grunwick'.[31] Yet within only a few days Tom Jackson, leader of the Union of Postal Workers (UPW), called off the action on company promises of 'conciliation'. The workers threatened to renew their blacking, but were headed off by pledges of TUC support for the Grunwick strikers.

The dispute continued to simmer until June 1977, when the strikers themselves began calling on the movement to mount mass pickets in their support. Mobilised by the active, left-wing Trades Council in the area, the first mass picket of 13 June drew impressive numbers of engineers, dockers, seafarers, building workers and miners from across the country. The volatile mass pickets which followed throughout the summer continued to give enormous – but entirely symbolic – support. By this time Grunwick was notorious – the strikers received a standing ovation at the Labour Party conference in October – yet lack of effective support continued to dog the dispute. At one point strike leader Jayaben Desai commented in despair that they were 'Drowning in support, starving for action'. The TUC refused to give a clear lead on solidarity action (still within the law at the time), enabling union leaders to claim that 'their members would not have the confidence to stick their necks out'.[32] Yet postal workers in Oxford who backed a renewed Cricklewood boycott were immediately instructed to stop the action by the UPW leadership.

The strikers' final hope, that essential services to the factory would be cut off by local water and electricity workers, was crushed; despite its fervent support, the local Trades Council lacked any real influence over the local union leaderships. Later, the right-wing leader of the Electrical Power Engineers' Association explained his decision to withhold support to the strikers with the argument that 'Once started down this road we would indeed be on the highway to anarchy'.[33] Such 'anarchy' might have saved the dispute. As it was, the strikers finally had to admit defeat in July 1978; 'No union got into Grunwick'.[34] The tragic episode confirmed the ultimate symbolism of left support for trade unionism which continued to confound the movement through the late 1970s and beyond.

BENN'S DREAM

The impatience of many radicals of the 1970s with workers' pursuit of 'economistic' issues of living standards, jobs and working conditions found expression in contemporary arguments deploring the blindness of such 'narrow' struggles to 'alternative, let alone socialist, economic policies'.[35] The mid to late1970s saw the rapid growth of what became known as the 'Bennite' left, alongside and often in cooperation with the revolutionary groups of the time. Yet Benn's own central concern with 'industrial democracy' rather than basic forms of worker resistance had a disproportionate, and often destructive, impact on leading sections of the labour movement. The essentially left-reformist 'popular democracy' championed by Benn was enormously influential within the powerful layer of committed workplace-based militants emerging from the 1968–74 upsurge; the false hope it offered formed a kind of ideological wall between these militants and conscious awareness that the real source of their power lay in the workplace rather than in parliamentary policies or 'control' over 'investment decisions'. It served to divert them, sometimes disastrously, from straightforward class struggle and its extension and consolidation into a fantasy world of 'workers' co-ops', 'workers' plans' and other apparently radical strategies which relied heavily on denial of the brutal realities of capitalist production.

The fate of the worker cooperatives launched in the mid 1970s is symbolised in an extraordinary dream recorded by Benn himself after yet another cooperative, Kirkby Mechanical Engineering, failed to win government support: 'Last night I dreamt that I visited KME ... and found that all the equipment had been taken out, and there were wires hanging from the ceiling and gaps in the floor where all the basic machine tools had been torn out. There was just one candle, and by this candlelight fifty workers were trying to turn the rubbish, the old pieces of wood and stuff, into little objects to sell ... I burst into tears and put my hands over my eyes and wept uncontrollably ...'.[36]

Yet such self-reproach did not slow down the wave of diversionary strategies which studded the progress of a working class at the height of its receptiveness to alternative politics. One such strategy, backed even by the government for a brief spell, was 'workers' participation'; more influential among the radical shop steward leadership of the time was the strategy of 'workers' plans' for industries under attack from the onslaught on manufacturing that began in the late 1970s. Examples of shop steward committees where such plans were investigated included those at Vickers, C.A. Parsons, Metal Box, Thorn EMI and, most notoriously, Lucas.[37]

The late 1970s were the heyday of one of the most class-oriented of rank-and-file organisations, the combine committees which linked together stewards or convenors from different plants within the same company – a process central in bringing together activists from different parts of the movement. All the major shop steward committees attracted to 'Bennism' were part of these combines. Yet at no time did the left make the connection between the potential of this rank-and-file organisational form and the political advance they so desperately craved. The process of formulating 'socially useful', 'democratic' alternatives to capitalist production was seen as of far more political importance than rank-and-file organisation and its strategic and political potential. Socialists were more focused on 'prefiguring' socialism than on working out how it might be achieved via a working class largely scorned for its economistic proclivities.

The Lucas Plan itself derived from a suggestion by Benn, then still Industry Minister, after the Lucas Combine Committee approached him in 1974 to present the case for nationalisation when the company threatened to cut its workforce. Benn, dubious about the possibilities of government support, proposed instead that the Combine draw up an 'alternative strategy' for Lucas Aerospace. Initially sceptical, the Combine Committee became fired with enthusiasm for producing its own, socially responsible 'corporate plan', producing highly detailed blueprints of products like kidney machines, heat pumps and road-rail vehicles in contrast to Lucas' standard fare of RB211s and Sting Ray Missiles.[38] The Lucas workers' proposals were enormously impressive both technically and socially, as might be expected from a group of highly experienced, skilled and politically conscious workers. Yet, true to form, corporate management remained unimpressed with any 'alternatives' which dented its bottom line.

After the company rejected the plan in late 1978, the stewards were stonewalled by what was left of the Labour government, which refused further grants for the project. When they approached Benn, now Energy Minister, he was unable to help; 'We may as well not have met him', one of the chief architects of the plan commented later.[39]

Benn's powerlessness was rooted, of course, in a socioeconomic structure which rendered 'workers' plans' little more than fantasies. The Lucas Plan was drowned in the corporation's 'major rationalisation'; Vickers workers, whose stewards had enthusiastically subscribed to the notion of 'industrial democracy', suffered a worse fate when they called off a strike against plant closure on the assurances of left MPs that Labour 'could exert control over the big corporations'. Two weeks later, Vickers reneged on its promises to the government and closed the plant. As one commentator pointed out, 'The alternative would have been for the workers to direct their energy to building up the shop stewards' combine committee ... to exert power *directly* on Vickers to keep the factory open'.[40]

Unfortunately, this insight came too late to change the political direction of a stratum infatuated with working out 'alternative economic strategies' rather than working with the highly promising material then available – an impressive rank-and-file leadership deeply rooted in effective workplace structures. Rather than using its theoretical and political skills to build a concrete, class-based counteroffensive against the growing ruling-class assault, the left relied on the power of its *ideas* alone to change things. The irony that the very combine committees which supported these 'alternative' plans could have mobilised far more effectively on a cross-class workplace basis to challenge capital went unnoticed. For the radical reformist sections who mobilised behind Benn, the rhetoric of politically correct but abstract 'demands', 'programmes' and 'campaigns' held more attractions than the rough and tumble of actually existing class struggle. While they dutifully turned out on anti-cuts demonstrations and cause célèbre pickets like those at Grunwick, the radicals who eagerly touted 'workers' control' and 'industrial democracy' remained largely uninvolved with the enormous class potential of the workplace resistance and organisation going on, so to speak, under their noses. Even during the mass strikes of the 'Winter of Discontent', any intervention along the lines of linking activists and struggles together for a classwide approach failed to surface on the left's agenda.

'HOW TO SCREW YOUR EMPLOYEES ...'

While British workers howled on the picket-lines of Grunwick and geared up for their 'Winter of Discontent', labour organisation in the US went into freefall as the full force of neoliberal policy bore down on the working class. Despite union leaders' hopes that the rebuffs they had suffered would prove temporary, the reverse was the case; Carter was, if anything, more pro-business than his predecessor, with a background in the anti-union 'New South' uniquely suited to business's new agenda in promoting what was euphemistically termed the 'right to work'. In sharp contrast with the faltering illusions of the union bureaucracy, US capital was up and ready to defend its class interests. In the late 1970s, US employers developed a number of dangerous new strategies to destroy union organisation; first and foremost was simple deunionisation, or 'union-busting'.

The growing weakness of the National Labor Relations Board in the late 1970s permitted an 'astronomical rise' in election delays (the main strategy for avoidance of union recognition);[41] this simple evasion of the law was reinforced by a mushrooming industry of commercial anti-union consultancies which moved away from the violence-based 'goon' tactics of the 1930s towards more subtle psychological advice: 'We will show you how to screw your employees (before they screw you) – how to keep them smiling on low pay ... how to hire and fire so you always make money'.[42] By the end of the decade such consultancies had become a growth industry, with an estimated 7,000 offering the 'new science'.[43]

The race to the bottom

The relentless attack on basic union organisation undermined labour's ability to fight yet another employer offensive – the introduction of 'concession bargaining', in which union leaders accepted cuts in pay and benefits in return for enhanced job security. One major early example was the New York City public sector unions' acceptance of pay cuts during the 1975 fiscal crisis; but it was the

1979 'Chrysler bailout' which fully established this extraordinary reversal. In return for a $1.5 billion government loan, hailed as the salvation of the ailing Chrysler corporation and thus of 85,000 jobs, the UAW accepted a freeze on wages and sick pay, pension deferments and other losses. In contrast to some later concessionary deals of the 1980s, the Chrysler worker's 'give-backs' seem almost mild. Yet 'These concessions would alter the course of collective bargaining to a degree that not even the Business Roundtable ... had dreamed of'.[44]

How could union leaders be persuaded to negotiate *cuts* in the living standards of their members? The answer, of course, was that old enemy of working-class unity, competition. Union leaders' – and workers' – acceptance of the ideology of corporate 'competitiveness' was a useful weapon in the hands of employers peddling the myth that the plant down the road was more 'cooperative' and thus more likely to be 'saved' than their own. Known as 'whipsawing', this adroit introduction of competition into labour was the first step in a long road of decline for workers' living standards, a race to the bottom not only for American workers but workers worldwide.

'Whipsawing' was aided by deregulation, another growing trend of the period. While not publicly owned in the US, sectors like transport, telecommunications and utilities had been governed by regulations which prevented open competition and guaranteed safety and service standards. In 1978, deregulation was introduced into airlines and 'trucking' (road haulage), followed by energy, banking and telecommunications; the removal of government restraint saw the sudden appearance of low-wage, non-union competitors who savagely threatened the wages and conditions of unionised workers.

'Poisoning the spirit'

The promotion of competition between workers clearly stood in direct contradiction to their solidarity as a class – never a foregone conclusion in a society weighted against class struggle, but focused on unerringly by a combative ruling class. As one union-busting consultant put it: 'The enemy was the collective spirit. I got hold of that spirit while it was still a seedling; I poisoned it, choked it, bludgeoned it if I had to, anything to be sure it didn't blossom into a united workforce'.[45] Workers' collective spirit began to suffer some of its most serious, and subtle, damage with 'employee involvement' schemes like Quality of Working Life (QWL) which gained momentum in the late 1970s.

Job enrichment experiments with carworkers in Europe had begun to gain some notoriety in the 1970s, but US unions remained unconvinced. However, by the late 1970s many 'progressive' leaders were becoming drawn to European initiatives which reportedly gave workers a say in the organisation of their work. In 1978, UAW vice president Irving Bluestone declared in favour, arguing that 'A persistent and historical goal of unionism is to bring democracy into the workplace'.[46]

Eventually the chief factors persuading both union leaders and corporations of the democratic virtues of QWL programmes were economic rather than ideological. During the economic crisis of the late 1970s, 'competition from foreign producers … led corporations to turn to QWL. Massive unemployment caused the labor unions to accept it'.[47] Such schemes, in fact, were less about 'quality' than about raising productivity and undermining the union. QWL programmes, which had great initial appeal for many workers, were in fact tailored towards appropriating workers' detailed knowledge of their jobs in order to increase managerial efficiency and reduce supervision, and the apparent recognition of workers' experience and tacit skills was also aimed at undermining collectivism in favour of an individual identification with company goals.

Yet, as always, even the concerted efforts of capital failed to entirely slay the dragon of rank-and-file-based class struggle. The 1977–78 miners' strike, in which action by 'ordinary workers' brought a government and a militant employer organisation to their knees, had seen the beginning of new forms of 'solidarity unionism' which maintained resistance in the face of the growing ruling-class offensive. The courage and determination of US rank-and-file workers who took action in the 'downturn' years, despite being largely unsupported by their officials, presaged that of the carworkers, lorry drivers and low-paid public sector workers who created a never-to-be-forgotten 'Winter of Discontent' in Britain between 1978 and 1979.

THE WINTER

Despite enduring stories of uncollected rubbish and unburied dead, the 'Winter of Discontent' was not only a rebellion of public sector workers. It was carworkers at Ford who finally killed off Labour's faltering 'Phase Four' with the first in what became an uninterrupted wave of strikes throughout the autumn and winter of 1978–79. In

September 1978, a total shutdown of UK Ford plants was reinforced by solidarity action from dockers and seafarers; a convenor noted that widespread resentment of the pay policy explained 'the speedy and unprecedented degree of external support Ford workers received from the outset'.[48] By late November, after nine weeks of solid strike action, the Ford workers 'had driven a coach and horses through Phase Four'[49] with a 17 per cent settlement.

The 'Ford effect' was felt in a wave of strikes. Workers at British Oxygen, technically the first to break the pay norm, had won an 8 per cent rise in October; 26,000 bakery workers, novices to industrial action, walked out in November and won 14 per cent. And in December another crucial private sector group, oil tanker drivers, began an overtime ban in preparation for strike action.

The diaries of Tony Benn, then Energy Minister, provide some interesting minutiae on the realpolitik of these strikes. In December 1978, he noted: 'There are two options: to mobilise troops before Christmas, which would of course be very provocative to the unions; or wait till after Christmas, which might be too late to prevent a serious oil shortage ... If an emergency arose, we would ask the unions themselves to maintain essential services ... It is very exciting because, if you call in the trade unions to help you allocate oil, then you are getting to a situation of joint government'.[50]

What was being proposed was not exactly a situation of 'dual power'. Benn's efforts were focused on agreeing a list of emergencies which would justify breaking the strike. However, while TGWU officials went along with the exercise, the 'men' were more obdurate. On 22 December, Esso drivers rejected a 12.8 per cent offer, and on 4 January 1979 the Texaco drivers went on all-out strike. However, even then it was clear that the action was beginning to fragment. Workers at Esso and Shell had voted in favour of 12–15 per cent rises, and although for about a week all three groups were striking at the same time, by 11 January the dispute was over. In the words of one critic, 'the oil tanker drivers were "bought off" after merely flexing their muscles'.[51]

The lessons seemed clear; yet the next major dispute, by lorry drivers employed by the private sector Road Haulage Association (RHA), revealed no obvious awareness of the need for coordinated action, although the leaders used flying pickets to spread the strike throughout the country.

The 7,500 drivers had presented their claim for a 22 per cent rise on 19 December; on 3 January, over a week before the Texaco strikers returned to work, 7,000 drivers were out, with picketing of docks and factories threatening to bring industry to a standstill. It remains a puzzle why, given the enormous 'muscle' of two groups of workers without whom the country could not function, these strikes were conducted separately and almost in ignorance of one another, like ships passing in the night. Yet the bargaining power of lorry drivers alone was demonstrated by their victory at the end of January, when most of the drivers achieved their target, a 20 per cent increase.

The 'Peasants' Revolt' begins

As the lorry drivers departed the industrial stage, on came the public sector workers in whose name the 'Winter of Discontent' is normally commemorated. The Labour government's failure to reduce differentials had by this time reversed the once favourable ratio between private and public sector earnings. And so the public sector workers staged their 'Peasants' Revolt'.[52] On 22 January a one-day strike brought out over a million public sector workers, of whom about 80,000 marched through London: 'It was biting cold. There were gravediggers, dinner ladies, caretakers, ambulance drivers ... '.[53]

From this time on a variety of public sector groups began coming out on strike in pursuit of their own pay claims. School caretakers and maintenance workers struck at the beginning of February, supported in many cases by teachers; the maintenance workers' withdrawal of labour meant that in any case most schools had to be closed because of lack of heating in the freezing weather. Water workers broke through the pay code at the end of February with a 16 per cent increase; on 23 February, civil service unions began national action for a substantial claim. The public workers' struggle continued to stampede through almost every sector; picket-lines appeared in front of hospitals, ambulance stations, refuse depots, schools, colleges and a host of other workplaces. The impact of the stoppage revealed to a shocked middle class 'a whole Mayhew subclass of occupations we scarcely know exist – the rat-catchers and drain-cleaners and grave-diggers ... '.[54] The rebellion of workers whose provision of essential services would in 'normal times' remain decently invisible triggered media tirades against 'Rats on the Rampage', 'Cancer Ward Torment', 'Sick Children Dragged into the Firing Line' and 'Outrages Against Human Decency' as 'The Dead Pile Up'.

'Little Soviets'

Rather than coming to the strikers' defence, much of the labour movement leadership seemed equally horrified by the sight of uncollected rubbish and other reminders of their members' indispensability. Labour Prime Minister Callaghan argued that 'the industrial actions which left the dead unburied and the sick out of hospital were not in fact examples of trade union activity ... real trade unions should only be equated with officialdom';[55] TUC leader Len Murray was 'near to despair: this was not trade unionism, this was "syndicalism"'.[56] Yet stentorian condemnations did nothing to stem the quasi-revolutionary dynamic. Not only 'syndicalism', but elements of 'dual power' began to characterize the dispute: 'Within a short time strike committees were deciding what moved in and out of many of the ports and factories. Passes were issued for essential materials ... but supplies for industry were halted ... In some cases strike committees controlled the public services of whole cities'.[57]

Echoing the 'dual power' theme, Thatcher records in her memoirs that 'the Labour government had handed over the running of the country to local committees of trade unionists'.[58] Her fellow Tory James Prior complained in January that Britain was now being run by 'little Soviets' – local strike committees of lorry drivers, train drivers and other public sector groups beginning to come into the strike movement.[59] Denis Healey, Labour's Chancellor, complained retrospectively, 'Each night the television screens carried film of bearded men in duffel coats huddled around braziers. Nervous viewers thought the revolution had come'.[60]

Yet the outcome of that struggle was not 'revolution', not the triumph of the 'little Soviets', but victory for the emissaries of neoliberalism. On 3 May 1979, Labour surrendered, in what should have been 'an easy win', to Thatcher and all that she stood for.

'WHAT WENT WRONG'?

Despite what now seems its historic inevitability, the victory of Thatcherism in 1979 was by no means a foregone conclusion. During the election campaign itself, opinion polls ricocheted too sharply to promise uncontested victory. As the future Prime Minister herself records, the beginning of the campaign found her 'neck-and-neck with the Labour Party in the opinion polls', while just over a week before the election, 'the opinion polls suggested that Labour might be closing in on us'. Two days before voting, 'a further opinion poll ... showed Labour 0.7 per cent ahead'.[61]

In the event, the Conservatives won by 7 per cent, more than enough to authorise Thatcher's mission to destroy social democracy. The conventional explanation for the loss was the electorate's disgust with 'trade union power' as symbolised in the industrial chaos of the 'Winter of Discontent'. Yet even the undoubted 'unpopularity' of the strikes only accounted for about 1.5 to 2 per cent of the swing.[62] In fact the Tories' policies on industrial relations were not even at the top of voters' agendas; 'law and order', tax cuts and the sale of council houses were preferred reasons for voting in the new government.[63]

The fact that the 'Winter of Discontent' was followed almost immediately by the triumph of Thatcherism, however, led most analysts to lay the blame for the one upon the other. While Thatcherites might be expected to revel in their triumph over 'trade union power', it is less predictable that the leadership of the labour movement should adopt more or less the same arguments. Yet almost the entire labour movement leadership took it for granted that it was 'the unions' who had let in Thatcher. The question of what, or who, was lumped together in that formulation was not considered, any more than was the question of who held the 'trade union power' she promised to vanquish.

Yet there was a form of power in the land during the 'Winter of Discontent' – workers' power. It was shown only embryonically, but it was based not on 'greed', not on the satanic motives with which the press embellished their tales of evil, but on the usual reasons – incursions by capital on workers' lives which go beyond the bounds of the tolerable. As one post-mortem pointed out, those who blamed Labour's defeat on 'union intransigence' might be hard put to it to explain 'what it was that turned the social contracting trade union saints of 1975–78 into the demonic fiends about whom we read in the *Daily Mail* of last winter'.[64]

Those 'demonic fiends' did the only things that workers in struggle can do – they struck, they picketed, they stopped the movement of goods, they disrupted services. In that sense, these prosaic struggles of tanker drivers, gravediggers and dustmen also displayed the only power that workers can have; they withdrew their labour, with a force and to an extent that seriously challenged the organisation and structure of society. What they did not do was to display 'trade union power' in the monolithic, dictatorial way which the press, aided by politicians of right and left, sought to depict it.

Strike statistics show the number of working days lost in 1979 at 29,474,000, higher even than the 1972 peak of 23,909,000; the number of workers involved again beat the 1972 figure, at 4,608,000 as opposed to 1,734,000. The wave of action swept up almost every section of the working class, from civil servants to carworkers. Though one brave struggle followed another during the prime years of Thatcherism, none came close to the range and combativity of the strike wave which took place between late 1978 and early 1979. The 'Winter of Discontent' represented the last mass struggle of the postwar working-class movement in Britain. Yet neither this raw, uncoordinated militancy, nor even the more conscious rank-and-file caucus perspective of a minority of American activists, could withstand the icy blast of the 1980s.

3
Gone With the Wind: Thatcher, Reagan and the Early 1980s

The 1980s in Britain was the decade of Thatcherism. The 'Iron Lady' had come to power only months before the decade began, and she lost it only months after it ended. British workers, of course, bore the full brunt of this new and ominous 'ism'; but in many ways 'Thatcherism' became a catch-all term for the policies of untrammelled free market capitalism that the decade launched across the whole world. 'Reaganism' – or 'Reaganomics' – existed too, in a country far more powerful than Britain, and American workers suffered, if anything, a still more damaging neoliberal onslaught. Yet the politics of social democratic consensus had always been more dominant in Europe, and Thatcherism represented a more complete and conscious break from their comparatively benevolent embrace. 'Welfare state capitalism' would never be restored; but there were times, during the early 1980s, when its departure appeared to open up some very different perspectives.

'A KIND OF TORPID SOCIALISM ...'

Thatcherism was, without doubt, a disaster for the British labour movement. But when the new Prime Minister first ascended to her throne on 3 May 1979, the scale and totality of that disaster were by no means obvious. Thatcher had become leader of the Tory Party in 1975, so the electorate knew by this time what Thatcherism looked like; and for those not subscribing to the 'saloon bar' philosophy to which her speeches most appealed, it was not a pretty sight. Yet to many union activists at the time her election victory 'looked like a temporary setback'.[1] To understand this, the first term of the Tory government needs to be placed in its contemporary context. The corporatist ideology associated with 25 years of Keynesian welfare policies was not lightly shed by even the most radical of governments. As Thatcher complained in 1977, 'A kind of torpid socialism had become the conventional wisdom in those years ... it was increasingly difficult for anyone ... to challenge the prevailing orthodoxy'.[2]

It was also taken for granted that 'the unions', however maligned, were a power in the land. The election itself had come on the ebb tide of the 'Winter of Discontent'; the associated press hysteria assumed the movement's continuing strength, rather than its prospective decline. Despite Thatcher's widely canvassed determination to 'take on the unions', neither she nor her inner circle was entirely sure, initially, of how to go about it. In 1977, she mused: 'It would still be necessary to frame the measures to reduce trade union power. And so far we had not seriously considered what those measures should be'.[3]

Nevertheless, on gaining leadership of the Tory Party in 1975, Thatcher had commissioned a series of studies to address the problem. The first of these, the Carrington Report, argued (astoundingly in retrospect) that 'The power of the state confronted with strong unions ... had historically diminished' and called for 'alternatives to simply trying to face down'[4] strike action. A second document, 'Stepping Stones', lived up to its name with a gradualist approach, beginning with a propaganda offensive 'to make trade unionism dirty words [sic] with the electorate ...'.[5] Finally, the infamous Ridley Report, leaked to the *Economist* in 1978, laid the groundwork for the defeat of the1984–85 miners' strike with its recommendations for strengthened policing of strikes, increased reliance on alternative energy sources such as nuclear power, and the build up of bigger coal stocks.[6]

At a time when leading Tories were united in fearing outright confrontation with organised labour, Thatcher was at first only able to reveal the true extent of her plans behind the scenes. This caution, and its generally more strategic approach, led the government to proceed in a far more sophisticated and calculating manner than Thatcher's hapless predecessor as Tory leader. In contrast to Heath's confrontational approach, a programme of gradually accumulating legislation was developed which stealthily but remorselessly bound the bemused Gulliver of the trade union movement head and foot.

The government's 'salami tactics' effectively concealed, at the time, the real seriousness of the Thatcherite threat. Yet, from the beginning, its effect was deadly. Some of the provisions of the 1980 Employment Act, like government funding for union postal ballots, seemed almost benign to those unaware of the implications. But the Act's restrictions on picketing and, still worse, its attack on 'secondary' (solidarity) action, began the long process of nailing strikers to the ground.

Red-hot air

In a 1980s remake of the old ASE slogan 'Defence not Defiance', the TUC protested much against Thatcherite economic policy and the early anti-union laws, but supplied enough 'compliance' – 'it became increasingly clear after 1981 that compliance was not a major problem'[7] – to give the Tories a solid start in launching their Falklands-style offensive against the working class. The TUC's effective collapse in the face of the Thatcher anti-union laws combined naivety – 'We didn't believe a lot of what she was saying ... We just didn't believe it ...'[8] – and false hope – 'The TUC hoped and prayed ... that Thatcher would do a U-turn ... just as her predecessor Heath had done'[9] – with its usual ineffectuality.

Certainly the TUC huffed and puffed with all its might against the legislation and the government's generally anti-working-class policies. At its September 1982 Congress, 'the air was red hot with militant declarations'.[10] Delegates passed a resolution condemning the Thatcher legislation and pledging to express its opposition 'without regard for legal consequences'.[11] Yet it was already too late. Six months earlier, the TUC had convened a special conference at Wembley to discuss the 1982 Employment Bill, the most damaging slice of the anti-union legislation yet; along with other highly destructive measures, it removed British unions' historic immunity to being sued for strike action. But even as union leaders condemned the government's 'emasculation' of the unions and trumpeted the 'historically unique step' of coordinating movementwide resistance, the escape clause was being slotted neatly into place.

Clause 5 of the 'Wembley Principles' announced that the TUC would organise united action in support of any union threatened under the law. But the pledge was diluted by a careful amendment: 'That cannot mean ... that a union encountering legal difficulties should automatically receive support from the TUC ...'.[12] Given the TUC's professed reluctance to leave itself open to an injunction, the likelihood of TUC-led solidarity with any 'illegal' strike was, to put it mildly, slight; and so it proved within 18 months of the Wembley Conference. In two major disputes, British Telecom workers' strike against Mercury and the fatal *Stockport Messenger* debacle, employers used the 1980 and 1982 Acts with ease against workers fighting on crucial class questions.

The Thatcher government had been active on many fronts other than that of its battle against organised labour, including opening up nationalised industries and utilities to privatisation; when British Telecom (BT) was ordered to open up its telephone networks to the private corporation Mercury Communications Ltd, BT workers promptly refused to carry out any work related to the linkage. In October 1983, their Post Office Engineering Union (POEU) was served with an injunction to end the boycott. Despite its left-wing majority, the POEU executive voted to obey, a disastrous decision directly encouraged by TUC 'advice' that compliance would be in line with its policy. Only a few months later, equal faintheartedness from the movement's leadership would be shown, with even more damaging consequences, in the keynote *Stockport Messenger* printers' dispute.

The spectre that frightened the government ...

The TUC's reluctance to take effective action did not stem from any lack of combativity within the working class. As in the mid-1970s Social Contract, both the rhetoric and reality of the 'official movement' bore little connection with what was happening on the ground. Civil service and engineering workers' strikes had continued blithely through the upheaval of Labour election loss and Thatcher victory, suggesting that the subversive strength and meaning of such struggles was rooted in material class experience rather than overt 'politics'. Yet that experience sustained a level of solidarity and consciousness more reminiscent of the 1970s than of the dejection and demoralisation of the movement ten years on.

Occupations like those at Garner's Engineers in 1980, Lee Jeans in 1981 and Laurence Scott in 1982, alongside recognition strikes by black workers and Asian women at Chix Confectionery and Aire Valley Yarns, accompanied determined fightbacks by more traditionally well-organised shipbuilding, car and dock workers. A strike by 60 women workers at the Rulecan clothing factory, supported by clothing catalogue workers from Kay's and Grattan's who 'blacked' their products, provoked one of the first uses of the 1980 Employment Act.[13] As well as factory struggles, the period saw a series of disputes within the National Health Service (NHS) against government cuts, deteriorating conditions, and incipient privatisation. While the action was weakened by union leaders' insistence on one-day strikes rather than all-out action, it attracted wide support: 'The hospital workers caught the imagination of the working class ... If the angels of mercy were badly paid, then other workers had to help them ... There was ... a stirring of class feeling'. Union activists at bus garages, docks, building sites and post offices called on nurses to speak at their work sites. The NHS strikers served as a kind of travelling class caravan, inspiring workers too cowed by growing unemployment to do much about their own situation: 'We may not be able to do anything about the mess in this office, but by God we can come out for the hospital workers'.[14]

This still formidable 'class feeling' was taken more seriously by the ruling class than by the leaders of the labour movement. When, in 1981, miners went on strike over pit closures in a clear prelude to the Great Strike of 1984–85, the Energy Minister pressured the Coal Board to withdraw its plans, claiming, 'I did not come into politics to act like a kamikaze pilot'.[15] What constituted the 'spectre that frightened the government' was 'the very clear evidence that there would be massive strike action'[16] in support of the miners; the closures were withdrawn. Similar restraint was practised with striking water workers in 1983 and even rail workers during the 1984–85 miners' strike, with the aim of avoiding any possible formation of a public sector alliance[17] – in which context it is interesting that union leaders apparently made no attempt to form one until just after the defeat of the 1980 steel strike, when it was too late.

Yet, despite their clear threat to Thatcherism and all it represented, the numerous disputes of the period did not arise directly out of opposition to her by now widely unpopular government. Even the more openly political nurses' strikes of 1982 originated in Thatcher's failure to come through on a pay deal promised them, and the inadequacy of the eventual 6 per cent offer in the context of 12 per cent inflation.[18] In the same way, the 1980 national steel strike was in no way undertaken as an outright challenge to Thatcher's rule; it is just that, objectively, that is what it was.

A ST VALENTINE'S DAY MASSACRE?

The 1980 steel strike was a massive event. Though both the British Steel Corporation (BSC) and the Iron and Steel Trades' Confederation (ISTC) expected it to be settled in two or three weeks, it became the longest national strike in Britain since the Second World War and possibly the biggest in British history. Nearly 100,000 workers, most of whom had never been on a major strike, stopped work for three months, from 2 January to 3 April 1980.

Even the highly moderate ISTC leader, Bill Sirs, described the BSC's double insult to steelworkers' pay and jobs as 'nothing less than a declaration of war'.[19]

And the strikers? The strikers were united, militant and determined. From the beginning, the rank-and-file strike 'reads' almost as a different dispute from the one at national level. Rank-and-file strikers pushed demands never taken up by the leadership: a 20 per cent pay rise without strings, more than twice the leadership's demand, and the urgent need to stop all movement of steel – a central strategic requirement never voiced by the leadership. Despite the leadership's undoubted anger at the colossal provocations, in the enclaves of the bureaucracy outrage was converted into a 'campaigning' mentality, centred on the media and sporadic, mostly ineffectual contacts with management.

With the rank and file the case was different. It was rank-and-file steel strikers who organised mass pickets at private steel companies like Hadfields and Sheerness, extended picketing to steel stockholders and the docks, and fought to stop production at major users like Metal Box, Ford and British Leyland. From the beginning, the chief method adopted for stopping steel movement was the picket, and there was no shortage of volunteers; in the Rotherham area the proportion of manual workers picketing was 94 per cent. These were not experienced militants; 75 per cent of those picketing on the first day of the strike were on strike for the first time in their lives. Despite repeated requests, ISTC officials failed to provide training, leading to 'chaotic' early pickets in which groups of strikers massed around plant gates 'without clear organisation or leadership, and uncertain how to behave'.[20]

The police had no such uncertainties. The first arrests of Rotherham and Sheffield pickets were made within the first week of the strike. In early February, a mass picket at the British Leyland plant in Castle Bromwich, Birmingham, was 'met and defeated by an unprecedented display of SPG [Special Patrol Group] force'.[21] The government was now sponsoring a much more aggressive police role in picketing, training paramilitary squads like the SPG which confronted unarmed and unarmoured steelworkers with batons and riot shields.

Only days after the Castle Bromwich debacle, however, a united and determined strike force staged a mass picket of over 2,000 outside one of the most intractable private steel producers, Hadfields, where strikers had voted to return to work only days before. Despite the massive police force – 'Coach after coach of police vehicles lined the street … Two hundred police officers ploughed straight into the mass of pickets'[22] – the biggest mass picket of the whole strike ended in victory. Faced with the police display of force and the strikers' strength of feeling, the Hadfields workers voted to come out again on strike. Taking place as it did on 14 February, the picket and its associated violence became immortalised as the 'St Valentine's Day Massacre'.

Unfortunately, this success was not repeated in the case of Sheerness Steel in Kent, where the nationally organised mass picket was repelled by both a still better prepared and drilled police force and by the hostility of the private sector workforce. Presumably demoralised by this failure and the ISTC's general vacillation over picketing – union president Sirs had granted, withdrawn, and then restored 'dispensations' to private steel plants – the Hadfields workers returned to work on 24 February, along with those from four other major private companies.

'Punitive militancy'

Ironically, the strikers' very dedication to picketing may have been one of the factors weakening the strike. The equally important strategy of building solidarity with private sector steelworkers and key external groups like transport workers received relatively short shrift. In discussions at the Rotherham Strike Committee about stopping private steel production in Birmingham, two craft worker representatives argued that, given the large number of plants in the area, this would be difficult to achieve through picketing alone. They argued that 'picketing should become almost redundant if we use the existing trade union organisation' and suggested that the strikers should approach private sector steelworkers to encourage sympathy action; private sector steelworker representatives should be invited on to the strike committee. The representatives' suggestions were politely listened to, but ignored. The focus on picketing was so 'central to the RSC's supremacy and self-image that criticism … was difficult to incorporate or discuss'.[23]

The steel strikers' model, and ideal, appears to have been the Saltley Gate mass picket, instrumental in winning the 1972 miners' strike. Although they achieved far higher numbers than at Saltley, however, the steelworkers' pickets never considered mobilising the crucial worker solidarity which had been the key to the miners' success. This task became more and more essential by the middle of the strike, particularly in the case of private steel; yet strikers tended to adopt an 'If you're not with us you're against us' approach. Rather than directing their strategies toward the need to build and mobilise a united front of all steelworkers, the activists' convictions tended to encourage a kind of 'punitive militancy'[24] in which private steel-workers were condemned rather than addressed. In part this obsti-nacy on tactics stemmed from the moral certainty of the strikers that their cause was just, a crusading 'right is might' spirit which – as in the later miners' strike – tended to blind the workers to the brutal realities of a capitalism, and a government, to which moral justice was immaterial.

Nevertheless, it can hardly be argued that picketing was unimpor-tant, central as it was to stopping the movement of steel. That this crucial objective was never effectively attained during the entire length of the strike is almost certainly due to the national leader-ship's failure to take it seriously. Not only did the ISTC leadership issue picketing dispensations to key private steel producers, it wavered over whether the dispute was with the BSC alone or included the private sector, thus delaying the calling out of private steelworkers until three and a half weeks into the strike.

'The bureaucrats were terrified ...'

This reluctance to take effective action over either picketing or soli-darity was matched by other union leaderships whose support was crucial to winning the steelworkers' battle. Despite the usual prob-lems caused by 'rogue' lorry drivers, the TGWU dragged its feet in issuing a clear instruction not to cross picket-lines until mid March, the ninth week of the strike. Even more damaging was the approach of the Confederation of Shipbuilding and Engineering Unions (CSEU) which obstructed efforts to picket engineering plants by pushing for constant dispensations. In the case of one of the most imaginative solidarity initiatives of the strike, when rank-and-file British Leyland (BL) workers in dispute offered joint action with the steel strikers, the response of the local TGWU bureaucracy was equally unenthusiastic. Stewards at BL's Cowley plant had contacted the steel strikers and organised a mass meeting in Sheffield, where they 'got a tremendous reception' from steelworkers for the sugges-tion that 'we could be fighting side by side with them. We were all fighting the same battle. It was all obvious'.[25]

Not so obvious to the local BL union officials. As two coachloads of Yorkshire steelworkers joined BL workers from Cowley and

Longbridge to lobby a 7 March convenors' meeting, the Longbridge convenor responded to a leaflet urging joint action with a curt 'You've got no chance'. On the contrary, the convenors refused even to set a strike date on the BL pay dispute until after the steel strike was over. 'We were to remain divided and isolated whilst facing employers and government which were united and determined'.[26]

Similar rank-and-file attempts at solidarity were spurned by other union leaders, again including workplace officials. Steel strikers fighting to prevent the closing down of the Ford plant at Dagenham met consistent opposition from the convenor, who insisted on the CSEU policy of limiting picketing to basic 'strip steel' plants only; the strikers succeeded in shutting down this huge steel consumer only in the last week of the strike. When Liverpool dockers walked out in solidarity with steelworkers in the last week of the strike, the TGWU leadership refused to spread the action nationally or make it official; and the ISTC leadership itself, despite urgent telegrams from strike committees, made no attempt to change the TGWU's mind.[27]

Was this absence of solidarity rooted in a simple lack of awareness of the implications of a steelworker defeat? Not at all. As a steelworker convenor noted, 'The TUC and all the unions involved were very aware of the Ridley Report and knew exactly what was at stake. The TUC knew the battle plan of the enemy well in advance, yet sat back and allowed the enemy to fight based on that plan'.[28]

Why? It was clear to rank-and-file steelworkers that their leadership 'was just as afraid as the government and the employing class … of a drift into a general strike. The bureaucrats were terrified of what the results would be if the strike had continued …'.[29] Ironically, this fear was exacerbated by the fact that the private steel companies were by now also in the middle of negotiations. As usual, the employers and the state knew who their enemies were, and had prepared accordingly, weakening the overall effects of the steelworkers' picketing-based strategy.

Faced with this abdication of leadership, and the reality that even after three months' strike action 'steel was still being transported and management's position was almost unchanged',[30] rank-and-file strikers saw no point in continuing. When a hastily appointed government commission made a 15.5 per cent pay offer (11 per cent basic, 4.5 per cent productivity-based), they voted, fatalistically, to accept. Speaking in the wake of a battle not lost, but not won in a way that could have made any difference, the Rotherham convenor concluded, 'The strike ended not because union members lacked the will to fight ... the officials of the labour movement allowed it to happen'. This view was echoed by the members; a mass meeting held on the final day of the strike was 'marked by passionate speech-making which laid the blame for the strike defeat firmly on the national leadership'.[31]

Was it a loss? The general opinion is that the ending of the steel strike was a kind of draw, with nothing achieved on the jobs front, but a much higher pay increase than would have been won other-wise. The fact that the productivity 'strings' would cause still more job losses, and that the BSC's projected plant closures would go ahead, are sufficient reasons for reservations. However, the result was much more serious even than that. Because the first major (and invited) class confrontation of its reign was won by the government, Thatcher was encouraged to pursue 'the lesson the Government wished unions everywhere to learn: that the market must rule, and let the devil take the hindmost'.[32]

The 1980 steel strike should have been the beginning of the end for Thatcherism. As 'the first setpiece confrontation between the forces of the Thatcher Government and the forces of labour'[33] the strike most certainly posed the possibility of early defeat for Thatcherism and all it represented. But the fact remains that Thatcher was not stopped at the starting post of the steel strike. The union leadership was only too aware of the outright class implica-tions of organising a solidarity-based victory; the rank and file, despite far greater courage, tenacity and commitment, were unable to overcome the parochial and moralistic ideology common to so many groups of workers effectively struggling alone. Thatcher was to achieve her first push down the rapidly accelerating slope of British workers' race to the bottom.

THE BEAST OF THE APOCALYPSE

The obvious similarities between the Thatcher and Reagan regimes of the early 1980s concealed important differences. While Thatcher very much controlled her own pro-capitalist version of government intervention, Reaganism tended to 'enable' business to get on with what it wanted and needed to do. Part of this difference, of course, was connected to the two leaders' very different degrees of personal ability; asked whether Reagan himself could 'do' economics, an adviser mused, 'In my experience, he fails the essay questions but gets the multiple choices'.[34] Luckily for the student, capital was considerably better organised in America than in Britain. Employer associations like the Business Roundtable kept the process of industrial and economic reorganisation on course as 'Like some shaggy beast of the Apocalypse, Reaganism hunkered out of the sunbelt, devouring liberal senators and Great Society programs in its path'.[35]

Ironically, one of the first acts of this decidedly neoliberal regime – generous corporate tax cuts – created a 'Keynesian'-style deficit, causing a major recession in the early 1980s whose main effects fell, predictably, on the workforce. By 1982, US unemployment had risen to almost 11 per cent, its highest level since the 1930s. The rate began to fall within two years, mainly due to an explosion of growth in the service sector, but the basic problems facing the American workforce grew steadily. The expansion of the service sector itself saw the creation (or more accurately, recreation) of the 'working poor'; an ever increasing labour force of part-time, low-paid, highly vulnerable workers of whom the vast majority were women, ethnic minorities and illegal immigrants. By the mid 1980s, it could be said that 'Low wage employment, far from being a mere "periphery" to a high-wage core, has become the job growth-pole of the economy'.[36]

All the tendencies emerging in the mid to late 1970s – deregulation, deunionisation, concessions, 'team concept' – came fully into their own under Reaganism. The National Labor Relations Board (NLRB), already considerably weakened under Carter, was handed over to business through Reagan's appointment of representatives from bodies like the National Right to Work Committee, the Business Roundtable, and the highly conservative Heritage Foundation. Not surprisingly, the new regime enthusiastically recommended a series of further 'reforms' which weakened workers' collective rights. Given the blessing of the 1947 Taft-Hartley Act, a set of cooling-off provisions and bars to solidarity action which had never been decisively beaten by labour, Reagan had no need to introduce specific 'anti-union laws'. However, the regime did everything else.

One of its most damaging measures was to revive a long-buried legal right to hire 'permanent replacements' to take over from striking workers. A 1938 Supreme Court decision giving employers the right to hire alternative workers in order to maintain production had remained largely dormant until that point, when it became a standard employer tactic central to the defeat of many of the pitched battles of the early 1980s and beyond. The aggressive revival of a neglected employer opportunity to undermine the strike weapon was symbolic of the loss, with Reaganism, of even the most basic tolerance of labour's right to organise.

The concessions snowball

This undermining of collective organisation took place against a background in which American workers' earnings had been falling in real terms since 1973. The causes were various: inflation, 'pay pauses' and 'wage guidelines' under Nixon and Carter, pay deals stretching for years while prices rose, weak or non-existent organisation. But, from the early 1980s, concessionary bargaining – 'collective bargaining in reverse'[37] – was a major factor. The 1979 'Chrysler bailout' had set rolling a 'concessions snowball';[38] after Chrysler won still further concessions in January 1980, 'light bulbs seemed to appear over the heads of executives at many major corporations'.[39] The number of companies slavering for concessions, whether or not they were suffering from any significant crisis in profits, escalated; in a May 1982 survey, 19 per cent of corporate executives agreed that 'although we don't need concessions, we are taking advantage of the bargaining climate to ask for them'.[40] That year, 44 per cent of workers negotiating new agreements agreed to no wage increase in the first year of the agreement, and more than a third took a wage freeze for its entire duration, usually at least three years. Other workers suffered wage cuts – in one case, Wilson Foods, of up to 50 per cent. Not surprisingly, in 1982 'the overall rate of wage increases *decelerated* for the first time in forty years'.[41] The trend continued into 1983, when in the first quarter over half the workers covered by new pay agreements had taken wage cuts. Another third took pay freezes, and the rest got the smallest wage increases on record.

Nor was slashing wages the only avenue to enhanced profitability. In the 'second round' of concessions, beginning in 1983, the emphasis began to switch to working conditions. A *Business Week* survey found that 57 per cent of company executives would rather win concessions on work rules than wages; the article listed eleven industries in which unions had granted major changes in work rules.[42] Although these changes included, as of old, speedup and increased workload, there was a new emphasis on utilising the whole of the working day – as Marx puts it, 'filling in the pores of the labour process'. This meant shortening or removing breaks, eliminating 'washing-up' time, employing fewer relief workers and banning 'job and finish' practices. A major objective was the removal of 'rigid' work classifications, thus increasing the number of jobs each worker was expected to do: 'Employers would like every worker to be a "renaissance man" – able to do every job – and would like them all to be completely interchangeable'.[43]

PUNISHING THE PEOPLE OF THIS COUNTRY

In the face of this relentless assault on their legal rights, living standards, working conditions and job security, what did American workers do? Like British workers, they went on strike, and like British workers they – largely – lost. In tune with his British counterpart – radicals mischievously drew Rhett Butler/Scarlett O'Hara comparisons – Reagan was committed at national level to undermining trade unionism as a central blockage to the free play of market forces. As with the 1980 British steel strike, one early keynote dispute demonstrated the American government's stop-at-nothing determination to stamp out strike action. In this case, the action was taken by 12,000 government-employed air traffic controllers, members of the Professional Air Traffic Controllers' Organisation (PATCO).

This strike, which began in 1981, was rooted in long-term grievances surrounding extended hours and falling wages. The government was well aware of its employees' pent-up anger, but its response was to preempt resistance by forming a Management Strike Contingency Force within the FAA (Federal Aviation Authority). It was this force which developed and, a year later, implemented the plan to run air traffic without the controllers.

When the 15,000-strong workforce finally walked out at the beginning of August, Reagan went on television to warn PATCO members that if they failed to return to work within 48 hours 'they would have forfeited their jobs and will be terminated'. When only 700 crossed the picket-line, Reagan was as good as his word; the strikers were indeed 'terminated' and replaced by supervisors, military personnel, non-union controllers and newly hired workers.

This action was unprecedented in postwar industrial relations. It was only too clear that the intent was to declare outright war on the ability of workers, particularly government employees, to withdraw their labour. Reagan's move indicated a 'public sanction of replacement workers',[44] placing the regime's seal on the draconian strategy that had surfaced a few years earlier.

So ... a strike that was over before it began? Far from it. Undeterred by the instant transformation of their strike into a lockout, striking PATCO members set up picket-lines across the country. Almost immediately, the rank and file mobilised, activists from unions throughout the movement joining the PATCO pickets. Widespread support for the strikers was expressed in unofficial acts of solidarity, as when 300 building workers refused to cross the PATCO picket-line at an airport construction site in Florida.

However, caution and back-tracking was the equally immediate response of the union leadership. Early in the strike, AFL-CIO president Lane Kirkland sent a letter to affiliated unions attacking the idea of nationwide action in support of PATCO: 'I personally do not think that the trade union movement should undertake any-thing that would represent punishing, injuring or inconveniencing the public at large for the sins or transgressions of the Reagan administration'.[45] Even more damagingly, the leadership of the International Association of Machinists (IAM), 'whose members could have closed down the airline industry overnight',[46] refused to provide solidarity, citing the risk to their financial reserves should they sanction a sympathy strike.

Nonetheless, the AFL-CIO gave at least symbolic support, organising a major 'Solidarity Day' event on 19 September 1981 in Washington which was echoed across the country by huge marches and rallies. In Washington, bizarrely, the AFL-CIO refused to ask PATCO to lead the march, arguing that this honour should go to whichever union had brought the largest contingent. The decision seemed symbolic: 'The real reason the air traffic controllers were buried, it seems clear', one contemporary article commented wryly, 'is that the AFL-CIO Executive Council has written off the strike as lost'.[47]

Within the next month or so this seemed to be borne out. Union leaders who had refused to fly during the strike now began to with-draw their boycotts; rank-and-file actions received no leadership backing. When union members attending an AFL-CIO rally at Boston's Logan Airport spontaneously blockaded traffic, tying up the airport for the day, their action went unsanctioned by officials at the rally.

Yet rank-and-file support remained strong. AFL-CIO leader Lane Kirkland admitted that he had 'never gotten as much mail on an issue in my life'. Of the letters, 90 per cent supported the strikers and '50 per cent ... denounced me for not calling a general strike'. Yet Kirkland commented primly, 'I find it hard to see what con-structive end would be served by an action that would punish the people of this country for the actions of an administration'.[48] At its

November 1981 convention, the AFL-CIO leadership evaded expressions of support for the strikers by preventing solidarity resolutions reaching the floor; in the same month, PATCO was decertified, sending the union into financial crisis. A year later, the strikers remained fired. The government had won its first round, hands down.

PATCO on wheels ...

Yet at least two more keynote disputes took place in Reagan's first term, both in response to the concessionary attacks which gained even more momentum in the wake of the PATCO defeat. July 1983 saw the beginning of a two-year stand-off in Arizona between women miners and the copper-mining giant Phelps Dodge; in November 1983 Greyhound bus drivers took month-long strike action which drew support across the movement.

Perhaps because of its location in a remote corner of Arizona, this magnificent saga of resistance received little more than token support from the movement. The strike, in which women played a major role as strikers and pickets,[49] provoked a classic mobilisation of state and corporate force against a tiny, inexperienced band of intransigent fighters. Despite the strikers' courage and determination, the forces mobilised against them were probably just too massive for them to win. Determined to show the miners who was boss, the company moved replacement workers into the mines even though, given falling copper prices, there was little incentive to continue production. State power, in the form of troops brought in to protect the scabs, backed Phelps Dodge to the hilt with a full-scale armed occupation of the tiny mining towns. The scale of corporate power and aggression was far beyond the reach of unarmed, isolated workers.

The Greyhound bus drivers' strike, by contrast, was taken up as a movementwide cause by the rank and file, prompting the question 'Will it be a PATCO on Wheels?'.[50] The drivers walked out after the Greyhound Corporation – at the time a profitable concern – announced its fourth year of concessionary demands, signalling deep cuts in wages and benefits. When Greyhound announced it would run its buses with replacements, rank-and-file members and activists from across America converged on 'the familiar downtown bus station'. Hundreds of pickets in Philadelphia and Boston managed to stop the buses for the first two days; rallies, picket-lines and fund-raising events continued until the strike ended on 20 December with acceptance of a modified package of concessions.

Although the settlement could not be called a victory, it was not a demoralising defeat; and its aftermath saw continued cross-union organising by the strike's supporters. In a number of cities, activists worked to organise permanent, multi-union solidarity committees which could act quickly to generate support in future disputes. While solidarity for the Greyhound dispute had been impressive, it had been organised at the last minute – too late to muster the kind of force needed to defeat a huge corporation like Greyhound. But networks bred in the dispute, like the Toledo Area Solidarity Committee (TASC) and the Boston-based Massachusetts Labor Support Project, now stood ready to fight the second time around.

These organisations signalled a more hopeful turn within the labour movement – the further development of the kind of 'solidarity unionism' signalled in the miners' strike of 1977–78. When workers at a small Toledo autoparts plant struck against concessions in May 1984, TASC acted to spread word to other workers; at a plant rally against replacement workers, 'something happened that no one had dreamed of. With only two hours to organize, three thousand workers showed up ... to help stop the scabs'.[51] It was a small, but immensely promising, gesture in the direction of classwide solidarity.

'RUNNING THE PLANT BACKWARDS'

Yet the PATCO debacle, alongside the Phelps Dodge and Greyhound defeats, lent weight to the argument that 'traditional' strikes were becoming increasingly ineffective in the piranha-like atmosphere of the 1980s. Committed rank-and-file organisers began to look around for other methods; one of the most successful – at least until employers got wise to it – was the 'inside strategy' developed by local UAW official Jerry Tucker in the early 1980s and first used successfully at Moog Electronics, an autoparts supplier in St Louis, Missouri. In 1981, Moog demanded significant concessions, including a wage freeze and the ending of the cost of living agreement (COLA). Aware that its workforce might walk out in response, the company had already prescreened 400 people to act as strike-breakers. Given the level of unemployment in the area and the workers' lack of experience, any conventional strike action would, Tucker argued, 'simply have destroyed them'.[52] Instead, the local decided to fight the concessions by staying in the plant and adopting various subversive job actions, based on workers' own detailed knowledge of their jobs.

Armed with this unique weapon, Moog employees immediately began the work-to-rule and slowdown actions comprising what Tucker famously termed 'Running The Plant Backwards'.

A crucial strength of the 'inside strategy' was that it relied on grass-roots membership involvement to be successful, eschewing the run-of-the-mill remoteness typical of 'business unionism'. One of the workers' first moves was to elect a 100-strong Solidarity Committee to run the dispute; those not on the committee were fully involved, reporting back on production levels in their departments and taking part in regular strategy discussions. In a rather more concrete sense than the wistful fantasies of 'workers' control' advocates, the workers were taking complete charge of production.

After almost six months of 'guerrilla warfare', Tucker received a management phone call which stated simply: 'You've won'. In effect, the company was offering the bargaining committee anything it wanted. When Tucker relayed the workers' original demands, with the addition of increased job security and a total amnesty for workers sacked in the early stages of the dispute, the company spokesman said, 'Is that all you want? I can get you more'. Bemusedly, Tucker comments, 'And he meant it, the bastard'.[53]

The Moog workers' success with the 'inside strategy' was repeated in a number of other disputes, including actions at much larger companies like Bell Helicopter and LTV. Its effectiveness began to decline somewhat in the mid 1980s, by which time the element of surprise had been lost, and employers could block the strategy from the start by locking out workers and hiring temporary replacements.

In the meantime, another new idea for fighting corporations without using strike action – the 'corporate campaign' – had been developed by another activist, Amalgamated Clothing and Textile Workers' union official Ray Rogers. The central strategy of 'Corporate Campaigning, Inc.' (CCI) was to expose particularly scandalous corporate activities and thus undercut support from banks and business institutions. The strategy was at its most successful in the case of J.P. Stevens, a giant textile corporation in North Carolina where Rogers was a union full-timer. A 'corporate campaign' which lobbied banks and insurance companies and pressured their representatives to resign from the company's board, alongside a series of rallies at shareholders' meetings, finally won the right to organise the savagely anti-union company in October 1980. However, while workers involved in major struggles took up this strategy enthusiastically, its perspectives tended to play down more grass-roots tactics;

ultimately, its lack of direct impact on production rendered the approach increasingly symbolic.

BACK TO THE FUTURE: ENTER 'TEAM CONCEPT'

Employers were less easily diverted from the workplace as the fundamental axis of production and thus profit. This focus was at the heart of renewed moves towards 'employee involvement', 'jointness' (labour–management cooperation) and 'team concept' schemes, all of which took their logic and meaning from the day-to-day minutiae of the organisation of work at the point of production. Yet a crucial difference between these schemes and capital's traditional means of intensifying labour was the ideological incorporation of union organisation through a systematic assault on the 'adversarial' concept of worker–management relations. Capital rapidly learned the lesson that ideology was as important a weapon as work reorganisation in securing workers' cooperation and thus enhanced productivity. With the recession and job losses of the early 1980s triggering eager cooperation from union leaderships, the whole perspective of cooperative, 'non-adversarial' management–union relations now took a huge step forward (or backward, depending on one's point of view). The essential logic of 'team concept', that management's interests were the workers' own, was expressed most clearly in the top-down doctrine of labour–management cooperation, formally adopted at an early stage by the UAW in the form of 'jointness programs', particularly at General Motors. While, as one activist critique puts it, it is 'almost unbelievable that a union could buy into the notion that job security is primarily dependent on corporate competitiveness',[54] this was exactly the notion that the UAW bought into, in more and more determined fashion, from the early 1980s onwards. The priorities were those of the company; the means to achieving them, and thus 'saving jobs', was the acceptance of cooperation, 'team concept', the end of them-and-us. In practice, such moves failed to save jobs and meant huge setbacks in workplace union organisation and democracy.

EUNUCHS RESTORED

In Britain, a more insidious but equally dangerous process of identification with corporate objectives had begun with the increasing bureaucratisation of shop steward organisation in the mid to late 1970s. The 'growth of professional shop stewards',[55] associated with increasing office and secretarial provision, time off for union duties and direct access to management, continued in the early 1980s to accelerate a dangerous trend away from the member-led, grass-roots steward organisation of the 'upsurge' period.

Management strategies focused on drawing previously rebellious workplace activists closer not only to themselves but to full-time union officials. At Ford Halewood, a plant with a long tradition of shopfloor dissent against trade union officialdom, the admission of all 21 convenors onto the previously officials-only National Joint Negotiating Committee (NJNC) 'demonstrated how far the company was prepared to go in its attempt to incorporate the senior full-time shop steward leadership in the plants'.[56] Yet these benevolent invitations to share in corporate problems and responsibilities coincided with an era of what was widely referred to as 'macho' management, symbolised in the axe-happy regime of Michael Edwardes at British Leyland and encouraged, of course, by the government. As one business-friendly writer noted during Thatcher's first term, 'All over British manufacturing industry, managers are celebrating their return to life and power, like eunuchs miraculously restored to wholeness and potency'.[57]

At one level, then, management directly confronted workplace organisation on issues of plant closure, labour intensification and job mobility, frequently employing the Edwardes-inspired technique of going over stewards' heads to appeal directly to the workforce; at another, the same representatives were invited into the spider's web of collaboration with capital. Rather than commandants of trench warfare, to be cautiously approached by managers hoping to broach the barriers workers had put in the way of capitalist production requirements, workplace representatives started to become the anxious guardians of corporate 'competitiveness'. Under Edwardes' regime, senior stewards at British Leyland were increasingly pushed into accepting job losses and intensive working practices in the interests of company 'viability'. And like the Leyland stewards, experienced shopfloor representatives across British industry swallowed the kindly myth of cooperation with those happy to destroy their lives and livelihoods, seemingly without knowledge of the ingredients or side-effects of that bitter medicine; or, if they jibbed at the taste, persuaded to force it down by the ever present mantra of 'saving jobs'.

An empty facade ...

Equal lack of resolution was shown, with even more damaging consequences, in the keynote *Stockport Messenger* strike. The dispute began in July 1983 when newspaper tycoon Eddie Shah opened up two non-union print shops in Warrington, Lancashire, near the unionised plant which produced the local paper, the *Stockport Messenger*. When members of the printers' National Graphical Association (NGA) objected to handling non-union work, Shah sacked six *Stockport Messenger* printers and built up his Warrington press to a level where it could take over all the *Messenger* titles. The NGA responded with a series of pickets outside the plant which, while they appeared to have little impact on Shah's operations, allowed him to issue injunctions against the union for 'secondary picketing', now outlawed under the 1980 and 1982 Employment Acts.

By November, growing frustration led to escalations of the pickets to 500-strong mass demonstrations, evoking cries of 'bullyboys' and 'Nazism' from the press but still failing to stop the 'scab' papers from leaving the plant. The NGA, faced with a £50,000 fine for ignoring Shah's injunctions, was by now desperate to extend the fight to the rest of the movement and convinced that the movement in its turn would respond; 'there was a genuine belief that "this was it", the fight from which the TUC could not walk away'.[58] The union approached the TUC for support under Clause 5 of the 'Wembley Principles'. The response proved the melancholy truth, already demonstrated by the Mercury dispute, that the Wembley rhetoric was empty. Just as he had 'advised' the POEU, Len Murray insisted that the TUC must stay within the law. Arguing along classic self-ful-filling prophecy lines that 'other unions would not answer a call for supportive action', the TUC invoked the loophole in the 'Wembley Principles' that it 'had to be satisfied that assistance from the Movement is justified'.[59] Even when the TUC's Employment Committee supported the NGA's call for a 24-hour national print strike, Murray refused to endorse the action. It was the final nail in the coffin for the print workers' struggle, which ended in defeat early in the New Year. The TUC leadership's failure to back this cru-cial dispute – print workers, like miners, were in the vanguard of the organised working class – conclusively demonstrated that 'the Wembley Principles were an empty façade ... That was the message sent out to the government. The NGA affair ... represented a turning point'.[60]

The same turning point also marked the end of what had at least been the rhetoric of class struggle from the TUC. Confronted with the nightmarish tenacity of Thatcherism – which had secured a triumphant return in the 1983 election after the jingoistic Falklands War – the TUC abandoned even its pretence of resistance, adopting a policy of 'new realism' which, rather than regretting its failure to defend workers against the relentless assaults of the new regime, blamed the old-fashioned philosophy of class warfare for its defeat. With a sigh of relief, the leadership sank back into its comfort zone, while Thatcher rudely demonstrated her lack of concern for the TUC's 'moderation' and 'responsibility' by continuing with still more vicious anti-union policies, symbolised in January 1984 by the derecognition of civil service unions at the government's GCHQ 'spy' headquarters. The ban shocked the movement, forcing the TUC to make 'its clearest gesture yet. If the government withdrew the ban, they promised a voluntary no-strike agreement'.[61] Yet Thatcher turned down the offer and held fast to her refusal to reinstate union recognition, while simultaneously, like her union-busting counterpart across the Atlantic, smiling upon the 'anti-Communist' Solidarnosc initiative in Poland. Meanwhile, though the GCHQ workers themselves mounted a trenchant campaign based on a call for strike action, they failed to get any more robust support from the TUC than being put at the head of yearly protest demonstrations.

In this way, leadership vacillation continued to combine with a rank-and-file ideology unable to consciously challenge the parameters of capitalism to undermine both workplace organisation and the grass-roots life-force of trade union resistance. In both Britain and America, at exactly the historical moment when it was clear that the formal basis of trade unions' postwar 'power' – the social democratic state – was the target of a determined assault by capital, the essentially reformist ideology of even the most militant activists kicked in. Full-time union leaderships clearly led the trend; but from national bureaucracy to workplace shop steward committee, the inability to explicitly recognise, and clearly combat, the ideological offensive of 'company viability' was the key element in rendering workers defenceless against the depredations of a profit-hungry capitalism.

Within the next decade, 'lean production' – an outgrowth of 'team concept' concerned less with team togetherness than with lean-and-mean, increasingly intensive working patterns – was to become the dominant mode of work organisation, spreading far beyond the auto industry to the service and public sectors of employment. The ideology of 'team'-style common interests between workers and management was the foot in the door. More than anything, the willingness to accept corporate goals of 'competitiveness' over their own members' class interests was at the root of trade union decline in both Britain and America in the 1980s. The defeat of crucial class battles like the 1984–85 miners' strike did the rest.

4

Against the Stream: 1984–89

For organised labour on both sides of the Atlantic, the mid to late 1980s seemed to signal a final defeat. It was a period of huge, courageous mass struggles and long-term lost causes; a David-and-Goliath struggle in which David was, this time, the loser. In the years between 1984 and 1989, mass battles by miners, printers, Caterpillar workers, seafarers and dockers were pitched, and lost, in Britain; in the US, Hormel 'P-9' meatpackers, International Paper workers and, more successfully, Watsonville canning workers and Pittston miners waged battles of equal length, numbers and sometimes desperation. To many, the lesson of defeats like those of miners in 1984–85 and P-9ers in 1986 was that 'the strike was a casualty of the changed climate of the 1980s'.[1] Yet, by the end of the decade, the 'bad old days' of traditional – and successful – industrial action were back.

MAGNIFICENT MINERS

The 1984–85 British miners' strike has often been termed the Great Strike, a title which acknowledges the true greatness of the rank-and-file miners and supporters who experienced daily struggle, violence and hardship for almost a year. But the 'greatness' of the strike lies in the strikers rather than in its contribution to the morale of the labour movement or the undermining of Thatcherism. On both these counts, the defeat of the miners' strike was an unmitigated disaster.

Why did the miners lose? The strike's inauspicious timing (the end of winter) and the built-in split in the strike force, are answers enough. But to understand fully how these came about, and why even the vanguard of the labour movement was unable to slay the dragon of Thatcherism, we need to go back as far as the historic victory at Saltley Gates, and forward to Thatcher's prudent withdrawal from confrontation in 1981.

Saltley Gates, the mass picket which essentially won the 1972 miners' strike, acquired immediate mythological status within the movement. But it was the sheer numbers at Saltley, rather than the solidarity of workers in the area, that seemed to stick in the collective memory of the working class. The tactic of the mass picket began to dominate in struggles like the 1980 steelworkers' and 1983 printers' strikes as workers began the battle against the tank-like assaults of Thatcherism.

Unfortunately, it was not only the working class that had taken note of Saltley. From the moment of the police defeat both Tory and Labour governments began mobilising to ensure that this particular piece of history would not repeat itself. In March 1973 the Conservative government established a National Security Committee and 'Intelligence Bureau' to exchange information about flying pickets; in 1974, Labour set up a paramilitary police force, the SPG (Special Patrol Group), aimed at combating future Saltleys. By 1984, fuelled by fighting inner-city riots, and tested on the useful training ground of Northern Ireland, the SPG and its companion Police Support Units (PSUs) had become well honed and deadly weapons on the battlefield of the mass picket.

What about 1981?

This new balance of power between police and pickets was one crucial factor shaping the relative positions of miners and government in 1984. The determination and strategic clear-sightedness of the ruling class was another. It was well known that the Thatcher government had 'run away' in February 1981 only to fight another day. Its avoidance of confrontation at this stage was based almost entirely on the miners' enormous popularity; even the moderate leaders of the railway and steelworkers' unions had said they could not rule out a general strike[2] if the government went ahead with its proposed pit closures. The miners had three years, under Scargill's openly militant leadership, to consolidate that support and prepare for that confrontation. Yet by 1984 not only was the trade union movement less united behind the miners, but the miners themselves were fatally split. What had happened?

Even before 1981, the seeds of the fatal division between Nottingham and the rest of the workforce had been sown by the 1977 pit incentive scheme, opposed by the NUM left on the accurate grounds that it would 'set miner against miner' by automatically raising earnings in coal-rich areas. The membership opposed the scheme on a national ballot, but union president Joe Gormley had the ballot declared 'null and void' and gave the different mining areas the go-ahead to negotiate their own local schemes. In the light of the 1984 furore over the decision *not* to hold a national ballot, this story is rich in historical irony. However, the outcome was less entertaining; the 'stampede to sign incentive schemes' opened up large gaps in pay between different groups of miners, sowing the seeds of the divisions of 1984.[3]

Added to this, the strong relationship with the rank and file which had made the left so effective in the 1972 and 1973–74 strikes was beginning to fade. The Barnsley Miners' Forum, which had been a centre of left rank-and-file organisation in Yorkshire, held fewer meetings after the left won control in 1973, and by 1976 these had stopped altogether. Despite Scargill's status as a symbol of militant unionism, he appeared reluctant to mobilise his members: ironically, there were fewer strikes in Yorkshire under his 1974–83 presidency than before.

The Cripple Alliance

By the early 1980s, the divisive effects of the pit incentive scheme began to emerge in miners' reluctance to take action on behalf of those threatened by pay loss or pit closure: one miner admitted that strike ballots were becoming 'the way you stabbed your mates in the back in secret'.[4] Rather like a figure in a fairy tale, Scargill had tried three times to bring the miners out – in January 1982, October 1982 and March 1983 – and each time had failed. Whether cause or symptom, NUM members' caution suggested that 'The rank and file organisation which had created the flying pickets and led the strikes of 1969, 1970 and 1972 was becoming atrophied'.[5]

It was not only internal militancy which had been undermined, but the cross-movement support which had so alarmed Thatcher in 1981. The early 1980s had finally seen the creation of a Triple Alliance of steel, rail and mining unions, seen by Scargill as crucial to a successful strike. Yet by 1984 the alliance had 'come unstuck', having failed to do much that 'actually brought together workers from the pits and the steel mills'.[6] Later in the strike, miners' renaming of the ill-fated initiative as the 'Cripple Alliance' expressed their contempt for the failure of steelworkers' leader Bill Sirs to deliver on his promises.

In contrast with the growing vacillation of the trade union movement stood the Thatcher government, its single-minded determination to defeat the miners evident in two seriously disabling measures: the build up of coal stocks, and the timing of the strike – or its provocation. The infamous Ridley Report of 1978 had explicitly called for the building up of coal stocks as key to a final confrontation with the miners. Faithful to its advisers, the government had rapidly built up supplies from 42.25 million tonnes in 1981 to 57.96 million in 1984. Meanwhile, the timing of the strike was decided by the announcement on 1 March 1984 that Cortonwood, a traditionally non-militant pit in Yorkshire, was to be closed. In its lack of logic or warning – 'Management had always spoken of another five years' life in the pit'[7] – the announcement looked like a clear government provocation. Yet Cortonwood was the spark that ignited the 'Great Strike'. When, only days later, the National Coal Board (NCB) announced that it was considering the closure of a further 20 pits, eliminating 20,000 jobs, the NUM had little choice but to fight. Despite its inauspicious timing at the very end of winter, the 1984–85 miners' strike was on.

'A running sore'

The strike began on an area-by-area basis, with spontaneous walkouts in Yorkshire and Scotland followed by official area ballots. Scottish president Mick McGahey declared, 'Area by area will decide, and in my opinion it will have a domino effect'.[8] But ballots in the first week were disappointing. Lancashire, Derbyshire and Nottinghamshire (Notts) voted against strike action; of the three, coal-rich Notts was by far the most crucial to the success of the dispute. Insisting that 'miners would not be given the right to vote other miners out of a job', Scargill signalled the stubborn refusal to call a national ballot which drew the media furore of the first few weeks and beyond.

The unrelenting assault on Scargill focused on the 'lack of democracy' of his decision, a critique which conveniently ignored the media's fervent support for exactly the opposite stance in 1977. But the real issue it raised was almost forgotten by both the left and the Scargill-hating right: the defection of Nottinghamshire.

As the truly fatal flaw in the strike's hopes of success, this issue demanded urgent attention from the leadership. Yet, preoccupied with the 'political' defence of his position on the ballot, Scargill neglected the opportunity to use his enormous influence to rally support in the region. The leadership apparently did little to mobilise, failing even to adequately inform members in the area; one Yorkshire activist reported, 'I've been appalled by the ignorance I've found. Men quite obviously haven't heard the arguments against pit closures at all'. Where information was presented, it was in the form of 'bureaucratese', complained an activist, when 'we want plain-speaking truths'.

Scargill, who excelled in 'plain-speaking truths', had received a rapturous reception in the Notts pit village of Calverton only weeks before the strike: 'All the people who are scabbing now were standing up at the meeting shouting for more'.[9] However, it seems he took the NUM Executive's dictates of regional autonomy too seriously to speak in the area once the strike had begun.

Striking miners were less hesitant than their leaders. Yorkshire militants flooded Nottinghamshire to 'picket out' the pits, gaining significant success with the help of fellow-activists in the area. At the start of the dispute, hundreds of Notts miners were out; one pit, Creswell, was shut down completely for several weeks. Given this base, it is reasonable to argue that the Nottinghamshire miners could have been won over to the strike, if the area executive had given its support. But the Notts executive voted 8 to 5 *not* to instruct members to respect picket-lines, and did nothing to mobilise the thousands of Notts miners who refused to cross during the first weeks of the strike. By May 1984, 'the battle for Nottinghamshire was effectively over';[10] the split had become permanent. The fissure between the areas on strike and those still working, most of all Nottinghamshire, created a 'running sore' at the heart of the strike, weakening the huge, doomed conflict at its very roots. From the beginning, the union was fighting with one hand tied behind it.

Solidarity – or not?

The bad news was compounded, according to doleful union leaders, by lack of solidarity from the rest of the movement. Yet closer inspection reveals a very different story; in the autumn of 1984 at least, the government came close to defeat[11] due to daring and committed acts of unofficial solidarity. Power workers, in particular, almost clinched victory for the miners by refusing to handle coal, raising the risk of massive power cuts; the head of the Electricity Board dissuaded Thatcher from using troops to move the coal because the power workers 'would have gone on strike immediately and the lights would have gone out within a week'. Years later, Thatcher ally Norman Tebbitt confirmed that, at this point, the strike had been 'a close-run thing'.[12]

The power workers were not alone; oil tanker drivers refused to take oil into power stations, and struck after the work was given to scabs, while many lorry drivers, despite the lack of clear advice from the TGWU, respected picket-lines. Printers at the *Sun* refused to set up a front page portraying Scargill with his arm raised under the headline 'Mine Fuhrer'; in September, they again closed the paper by boycotting an editorial calling miners the 'scum of the earth'.

Most of all, courage and solidarity were found on the railways. Railway workers from Coalville in Leicestershire prevented the movement of coal throughout the area for months; in Nottinghamshire, drivers, guards and signal workers were threatened with the sack as they stopped the flow of coal to Trent Valley power stations. Members of the National Union of Seamen, closely allied with the rail workers (the two unions merged in the 1990s), stopped coal being shipped from Durham and Northumberland pits until almost the end of the strike.

But these workers' loyalty could have relatively little effect; well aware of rail workers' support, the government moved from the start to switch coal transport from rail to road. The cooperation of lorry drivers, often non-unionised and working for small, low-wage private contractors, was easily bought. Meanwhile, an unstoppable flood of cheap imported coal came in through unregulated ports outside the government's National Dock Labour Scheme, worked by non-union dockers.

The truly disastrous failure, however, was with steel. Preventing coke and coal from getting into steel plants was a crucial requirement of victory; yet getting support from the steelworkers was 'like asking for a blood transfusion from a corpse'.[13] The defeat of the steel strike in 1980 had almost literally drained steelworkers of the energy or morale to support other workers in struggle; an outcome defined cautiously at the time as a semi-victory now revealed its true meaning as a fatal blow to class morale and solidarity.

Defeat from within

Union leaders' crocodile tears over their 'inability' to bring their members out in support of the miners, however, demand more detailed scrutiny. At the September 1984 TUC, leader Len Murray told delegates, 'Our purpose is to bring the concentrated power of this movement to bear on the NCB and the government, to get the Board back to the negotiating table'. Yet even this prosaic objective was undermined when the TUC agreed to request affiliated unions not to cross NUM picket-lines, but specifically repudiated sympathy strike action: 'The purpose of the TUC statement ... wasn't and couldn't be a blueprint for spreading strike action in the coal-using industry ...'. As the right-wing *Economist* put it, 'The TUC may be an ironic weapon for Mrs Thatcher to wave in the face of union militants. But at the moment it is the best she has'.[14]

In fact, the only two chances the strike had for victory – and they were serious chances – came precisely from 'spreading strike action'. In July 1984, dockers across the country struck over the threat posed by unregistered container ports to the National Dock Labour Scheme, which still regulated working conditions and employment for most dockers. The scab coal pouring into the country through non-registered ports like Wivenhoe in Essex and Immingham in Hull symbolised the joint interests of miners and dockers. When Immingham's registered dockers walked out, the TGWU leadership called a national dock strike.

Now the Thatcher government was seriously on the alert. Unlike the mass pickets smashed by the police and vilified in the media, a dockers' action in conjunction with the miners' represented a catastrophic threat. As the *Financial Times* reported on 16 July, the 'big fear' was that the dock strike would 'escalate ... bringing the whole of the TGWU into the fight' and thus preventing all movement of oil. This in turn would cripple the power stations, now mostly using oil to sideline the miners' strike.

The dockers' strike was solid, closing all 71 registered ports and halting traffic through unregistered docks. The crucial need was now to involve the unregistered dockers, which could only be done by raising the demand to extend the Dock Labour Scheme to all ports. In 1973, unregistered dockers at Dover had spent 13 weeks on strike demanding precisely this; the TGWU had refused to call a national strike in their support, and the dockers had been defeated. Now, in 1984, the leadership demonstrated the same almost inexplicable weakness, failing either to demand the extension of the scheme or to organise picketing of unregistered ports.

Not surprisingly, the strike faltered. On 19 July lorry owner-drivers stormed strike bound docks demanding to be let on to the cross-channel ferries. Local union officials called off the pickets, and soon afterwards the strike collapsed. An invaluable opportunity for miners and dockers to act together in action with the potential for bringing down Thatcherism had been lost.

'Losing everything'

The second, even more dangerous blow to the government came with the NACODS dispute at the end of October. The National Association of Colliery Overmen and Deputies was a semi-managerial union which had shown few signs of militancy in the past. Now, however, NACODS members' fury was aroused when the National Coal Board cancelled an agreement which guaranteed pit deputies pay when kept out of the pit by NUM picket-lines. The NACODS executive launched a ballot; deputies voted by 82.5 per cent to strike.

Since, legally, pits could not be opened without deputies present, the NACODS dispute presented an unparalleled opportunity for winning the miners' strike. The government was certainly aware of this: 'Whitehall was awash with fears'. As Thatcher later recalled, 'We had got so far and we were in danger of losing everything because of a silly mistake'.[15]

The government and its supporters were instantly involved in frantic efforts to prevent the pit deputies' strike, with hastily arranged late-night meetings between eminent politicians and individual members of the NACODS executive.[16] The machinations were successful. Only 24 hours before NACODS was due to close down the first working pits, the government persuaded the deputies to accept a hastily cobbled deal offering an 'independent' pit closures review, but no guarantee that the NCB would reconsider the overall pit closure strategy. Even Thatcher later declared herself unclear as to why the deputies had 'saved her skin'[17] by accepting such a worthless compromise.

Speculation about backhanders aside, the probable explanation for the NACODS backdown was fear of the seismic implications of their action. A group of conservatively minded pit supervisors would have been responsible for a potentially revolutionary victory over the massed forces of neoliberalism, and, consciously or otherwise, they shied away from that place in history. If anything, a more important question is why the *NUM* did not, as Thatcher had on her side, move heaven and earth to ensure that the deputies stayed on strike. Not only is there no record of Scargill's intervention, but NUM strikers remained apparently uninformed and unmobilised, their family and neighbourhood connections with NACODS members – many themselves ex-miners – neglected. One rank-and-file account poignantly conveys strikers' mingled hope and bewilderment as the NACODS episode unfolded:

> In early October there was talk that the pit Deputies would go out on strike ... It seemed that if they did come out the strike might be over and we might have our victory ... we started to let ourselves hope, against our better judgement ... [Then] it was announced that the Deputies had settled ... Over the next few days a despondency started to creep into the [strike] Centre, people actually started talking about going back to work'.[18]

The settlement with NACODS in late October 1984 marked a turning point in the strike, which staggered on until 5 March with first a trickle and then a flood of miners returning to work. Veterans of the strike marched back to the pits with heads held high, affirming their moral victory, but there is no question that the outcome was a massive defeat – not only for the miners but, as Thatcher knew well, the whole of organised labour.

'The legions of hell'

Against the formidable obstacles of government-sponsored scabbing, police violence and internal dissension, 80,000 striking miners held the line between victory and defeat for the working class in 1984–85. Stone-throwing pickets in jeans, pitched against Darth Vader-style mounted police wielding batons and riot shields in a direct confrontation with the overwhelmingly superior force of the state, were justly hailed as heroes: 'Like their forebears in 1926, the miners had ... fought the "legions of hell". They, and the women who had endured with them the longest major strike in British history, were all heroes, every one of them. They were magnificent ...'.[19]

Yet fighting the legions of hell requires full recognition of the diabolical nature of an enemy deaf to moral appeals and blind to justice. Rather than a focused, strategic approach, identifying from the start the crucial goal of defeating Thatcherism, the Great Strike evoked a defiant moral crusade, a struggle of right against might defenceless against the infinitely stronger, more brutal, more devious forces of capital. As striking miners recalled, years later: 'They had a strategy for everything that you were doing, but you didn't have a strategy for anything ... They had 10 years to plan for another miners' strike ... We went into it and we hadn't a clue'.[20]

THE MYTH OF PICKETING

Unfortunately, the movement seemed unable to learn the lessons. Wapping, the next mass battle in the war against Thatcherism, featured mirror-image scenes of pickets battling with paramilitary police forces. Even more than the miners, the printers struggling at Wapping had recent history staring them in the face; only three years earlier, mass pickets at the gates of the *Stockport Messenger* had signally failed to thwart the triumphant progress of the anti-union entrepreneur Eddie Shah. Yet the Wapping strikers showed little sign of connecting this grim outcome with their own situation.

The Wapping dispute, so named after the bleak riverside area in East London where Rupert Murdoch set up his anti-union enclave, represented the culmination of the newspaper war against 'restrictive practices' in the printing industry. Media mogul Murdoch, purveyor of opium for the masses in the *Sun* and ruling-class reassurance in the *Times*, took the print unions on with a carefully planned strategy culminating with the triumphant opening of his high-technology 'fortress' at Wapping in January 1986. Far from the strife-torn enclaves of Fleet Street, the traditional bastion of 'hot-metal' print methods and craft restrictions, the new enterprise was staffed by Electrical, Electronic, Telecommunications and Plumbing Union (EETPU) members schooled in high-tech methods after their leadership concluded a behind-the-scenes 'sweetheart' deal with the tycoon.

The print unions called their members out; but the year-long dispute, like so many of the era, was lost before it began. The National Graphical Association (NGA), Society of Graphical and Allied Trades (SOGAT) and other print union members who had seen their jobs usurped by electricians fought passionately but hopelessly on the nightly picket-lines; meanwhile, their union leadership 'tried to capture the electricians' ground ... by offering Murdoch an EETPU-style strike-free package',[21] while projecting a propagandistic, 'reasonable' approach aimed at winning 'public support' for the dispute. Naturally, this was no match for the shark-like aggression of Murdoch's News International.

The 5,000 printers and 'refusenik' journalists who had seen their jobs swept away in a less than 'reasonable' manner were contemptuous of their leaders' conciliatory approach. But, imprisoned by their geographical and strategic isolation, there was little pressure they could put on Murdoch. Thatcher's latest employment legislation allowed picketing only at the sacked workers' place of work – in this case Fleet Street rather than Wapping. An extended definition of 'secondary action' meant that the few attempts union leaders made to get Murdoch's operations boycotted brought a rain of injunctions down on their heads. The main print union, SOGAT, finally gave up the ghost in January 1987, officially ending the strike when Murdoch threatened yet more contempt proceedings against the union.

Rank-and-file strikers fought on, but the battle increasingly took on the features of a symbolic protest; it was as though the sacked printers and their supporters saw the issue in terms of a physical confrontation between themselves and the police which if successful would bring them victory. Yet, more than anything, the Wapping dispute illustrated yet again 'the impotence of mass picketing ... confronted with a strong state'.[22] On average, police outnumbered the pickets six to one; wading into the fray with their usual vigour, they mounted road blocks and patrolled with batons to prevent frustrated pickets from getting anywhere near the gates of the plant.

The true value of Wapping, as of so many of the lost disputes of the period, lay in the transformed consciousness of its participants. The Wapping dispute took place at the height of Thatcherism; the printers who literally fought for their jobs on the picket-lines were amongst those most excoriated for their racist, sexist, homophobic 'white working-class' conservatism. They were stereotypical C2s,[23] clones of the 'Essex Man' to whom Murdoch's own *Sun* tabloid most directly appealed and on behalf of whom Thatcher had taken up the cudgels against the 'loony left'. Yet, through a struggle over something as basic as the need to make a living, these workers had been transformed into campaigners, into subversives who brought upon themselves the full force of state and employer opposition and who, as a result, learned what 'the forces of law and order' were really about.

P-9ers AND PAPER WORKERS

Many of the features which most undermined miners' and printers' chances of victory were replicated in the mammoth struggles of US workers during the same period. In their scale, desperation and class reach, these strikes raised the possibility of a deeper, cross-movement 'solidarity consciousness'. Yet even after the serious defeats of the early 1980s, a general awareness of the real intransigence of state-supported corporate aggression, and of the uncompromising stance needed for any chance of winning, was slow to spread amongst the working class.

The roots of the 1985–86 'P-9' strike, so named in honour of the local which organised it, reached back to the summer of 1982, when meatpacking conglomerate Hormel opened up a new plant in Austin, Minnesota which 'turned out more meat with fewer workers than any other plant in the industry'.[24] Production had been reorganised and intensified, with speeds on the cutting machines set so high that workers often stumbled into one another as they fell behind. Adding insult to (literal) injury, in 1984 Hormel sought concessions in line with those of the other meatpacking giants, slashing rates from $10.69 to $8.75 an hour. The meatpacking workers' union, the United Food and Commercial Workers (UFCW), offered little resistance to this onslaught, calling for an 'orderly retreat' in the face of the companies' demands. But the Austin workers' local, P9, signalled its opposition by electing a new leadership with a clear stand against concessions. In 1984, P9 members voted against Hormel's concessionary demands by 92 to 8 per cent and authorised strike action by a 93 per cent margin.

The local was confident that it could win. Not only would the company be hit in traditional fashion by the workers' withdrawal of labour, it would also be embarrassed by 'corporate campaigns' aimed at Hormel's bank and other financial institutions, and by the enormous support the P-9ers had already built among meatpacking workers and local radicals. The Austin workers were unusually prepared for confrontation, having built support and publicised their cause for well over a year before the strike date.

Unfortunately, these preparations proved blunt instruments against corporate ruthlessness and strategic advantage. In January 1986, Hormel announced its intention to recruit permanent replacements at Austin; though strikers scored a triumph when a huge counterdemonstration prevented its first attempt to bring in scab workers, within a few days the inevitable armed troops had come to the company's rescue. Still more damagingly, most of Hormel's other plants continued production throughout the strike. This gloomy picture was mitigated by the support of workers at Hormel plants in Iowa and Nebraska, where local activists honoured P-9's 'roving' picket-lines. But they paid a heavy price: 500 workers in the Iowa plant and 50 in Nebraska were fired, the UFCW making no effort to defend or reinstate them.

This incident illustrated perhaps the most disabling aspect of the dispute – the official lack of support for, indeed outright opposition to, the P-9 strikers. From the very beginning of the local's campaign against concessions, the UFCW had been actively hostile. The conflict emerged into the glare of publicity in January 1986, when union leaders condemned the strike on the nationally televised *Nightline* programme, publicly denouncing P-9 president Jim Guyette. In mid March 1986, union opposition culminated with a telegram to all P-9 members ordering an immediate and unconditional return to work. The P-9ers voted overwhelmingly to continue the strike, but the UFCW placed the local in trusteeship and informed Hormel over the strikers' heads that P-9 was making an 'unconditional offer' to return to work. In September 1986, the leadership effectively ended the strike at Austin and five other Hormel plants by signing agreements which conformed almost entirely to the company's original offer.

Yet the crusade of the P-9ers continued; the struggle had generated a unique constellation of rank-and-file fighters who had broadcast their own concerns to the wider movement and in return acknowledged, and became active in, that movement as a whole. As one activist recalled of a P-9 support event which featured guests from Groundswell, a farm workers' movement, and an ANC representative, 'If you said two years ago that this would have ever happened in Austin, you'd have been crazier than hell'.[25] As this comment implies, the P-9ers and their families had not started out as labour reformers or radicals; once again, a dispute over decidedly material issues had triggered unprecedented politicisation of a white, 'privileged', conservative group of workers. As strike leader Jim Guyette put it simply, in a statement that sums up the dynamics of struggle and organisation, 'The company was our best organizer'.[26]

Yet without concrete gains or lasting barriers against the corporate offensive, the P-9ers' 'victory' would remain symbolic. Like other struggles of the time, it was part of a prefigurative vision of what the working class – and society as a whole – could become, rather than an irreversible step towards attaining that transformation.

The 'greedy corporate hand ...'

Some of the same contradictions were evident in the 1987 paperworkers' strike led by workers at the Jay, Maine mill of the International Paper Company (IP). The papermaking industry, and

IP in particular, had always demanded a lot from its workforce. One worker – later a striker – 'would bring the work home, work at home, go in the mill, and be ready at 7 o'clock in the morning ... He actually worked 16 hours at a time ...'.[27] But the corporation's new demands were hard to take: the end of double time for Sunday working, abolition of the one holiday when the mill shut down – Christmas Day – and the elimination of 520 jobs through a mixture of outsourcing and multiskilling known as 'Project Productivity'.

In March 1987, workers at the Mobile, Alabama mill were the first to reject the proposed contract; IP's immediate response was to lock out the entire 1,400-strong workforce. In June, three other mills voted against the concessions and supported Mobile by coming out on strike.

Workers at Jay, the largest of the three, took the lead in the struggle, but the decision had not been easy; their United Paperworkers' Local 14 was well aware of the losses the movement had sustained since the early 1980s. Close to home in Maine, another paper workers' dispute had recently ended, after a long and bitter struggle, with the permanent replacement of all 300 workers. Local 14 knew the odds.

IP, however, left them little choice; the company's behaviour was 'like a declaration of war to the people'. These were not oppositional workers: their prime reaction was a deeply wounded sense of betrayal at IP's behaviour. 'It was like, I've worked all my adult life in this mill. Why are they doing this?'. Despite the relentless advance of cut-throat corporate neoliberalism in the 1980s, workers remained enmeshed in expectations of company benevolence and morality which left them ill prepared for a 1980s multinational determined to compete at all costs.

Such expectations wrong-footed union representatives who had assumed IP executives would listen to reason, or at least moral persuasion. When newly hard-nosed corporate representatives proved deaf to union eloquence, for the United International Paperworkers' Union (UPIU) it was 'a completely new type of negotiation. It caught everybody off base ...'.

Local 14 was indeed 'caught off base'. While negotiations were still in progress, the company began building a barbed-wire fence around the mill and moving trailers for replacement workers onto the site. Yet workers maintained a state of denial on the possibility that the company would contemplate the permanent replacement of their long-term employees. 'In all honesty I thought they would never do it', recalled one soon-to-be activist; another confessed, 'I was naive,

I thought things would work out'. The full-time UPIU official was equally trusting: 'I just didn't believe it and I said that publicly'.[28]

Yet within three weeks of the strike's inception on 15 June 1987, IP had permanently replaced over 500 of the 1,200 strikers, and by the end of the summer the entire workforce had been replaced. The speed and completeness of the action left the workers stunned; for one striker, it was 'unbelievable that a company would forget all of this service and dedication ... and would replace all of us with one swipe of their greedy corporate hand ...'.[29] Once again, the workers' own norms of reasonable human behaviour had led them to mistakenly assume the same outlook on the part of corporate capital.

'No balls McFalls'

Given the swift turn of events, the main strategy immediately available to the ousted strikers was, yet again, picketing. And, as with so many other disputes, this was often more effective as an outlet for the strikers' rage than as a way of gaining ground against the company. The strikers used every possible device to stop replacement workers crossing the picket-line, yet IP had more than enough desperate, unemployed workers to choose from, and the picket was unable to keep them out. As one striker sadly noted, 'After a while I still wanted to win, but I didn't want to picket ... What do you accomplish by standing on a picket-line?'.[30]

This time, an alternative to picketing was more readily available in the 'pool', a network set up before the strike by locals pledged to reject the IP concessions as their contracts came up. However, when the next two locals went to the vote, neither gave the 60-day notice required to end the contract and join the pool. While Local 14 activists had assumed that the UPIU was actively promoting the initiative, it became clear that this was not what was happening. As the weeks went on there were no noticeable signs of mobilisation: 'They always said they were working on it, having meetings and talking to folks ... But it was all so vague'.[31]

In August, the contract covering Pine Bluff in Arkansas – a key high-value-product mill like Jay – was due to expire. If the Pine Bluff local rejected the contract and joined the pool, it would be an enormous boost to the strike. At last, on 25 August, the union set up a meeting between a group of Local 14 activists and workers at Pine Bluff. Although the UPIU provided no publicity, and workers were worn out after working a 12-hour shift, about a quarter of the 1,200-strong membership turned up that night.

There was no air conditioning in the hall; the heat was over 100 degrees Fahrenheit, and massive floor fans competed with the speakers, who lacked a microphone; yet the meeting was a success. The Local 14 president received a standing ovation in response to his call for solidarity. Nevertheless, on 22 September the Pine Bluff local voted to accept the IPC concessions. Though the union leadership denied any responsibility, Local 14 activists were clear on where the blame should fall, naming Pine Bluffs official Tommy McFalls ('No balls McFalls') for his indifferent role in mobilising the local.

Whatever the claims and counterclaims, the Pine Bluff vote was clearly a crippling blow to the strike. Local 14, determined not to repeat the experience, presented a detailed proposal for early rank-and-file intervention at those mills yet to ratify their contracts. Yet the IPIU president equivocated, arguing, 'I don't think it is necessary to have groups travelling around the country. I think it would be much less expensive if we let our trained staff work on this problem in each location'.[32] Despite this, Local 14 began sending out activists to other locals, but trying to operate without the support of the national leadership was like moving through quicksand. The UPIU refused to supply contact information; union officials in the different areas reacted angrily when the local tried to go over their heads. Locals in New York State and Mississippi voted to accept IP's offer in the autumn of 1987, and by the winter, activists were forced to recognise that any prospect of activating the pool and extending the strike was over.

'Like the sun breaking through ...'

Early the next year, however, an entirely different opportunity arose to score a direct hit against the company. In February 1988, a major leak of the lethal gas chlorine dioxide occurred at the Jay mill, severe enough to close the mill and cause the evacuation of nearby residents. The entire population of Jay and surrounding areas was terrified by the episode; joint striker–community protests outside the mill put increasing pressure on International Paper, while environmental activists joined them to build a case against the company described by lawyers as 'absolute dynamite'. Ralph Nader agreed to hold a press conference on the issue. Pressure was gathering towards an exposé even IP's publicity machine would be unable to control. This, of all times, was the occasion when an acceptably 'broad' issue could have been used to blow IP out of the water and force the company to settle the strike on the workers' terms.

It was not to be. Only days before the March press conference, the union ordered the environmental campaign to be suspended 'so that national negotiations between IP and the UPIU could take place'. Finally, the company had offered the long-sought negotiations, but on one condition: the campaign must be put on hold. Local leaders reluctantly yielded to the UPIU's insistence; environmentalists cancelled the crucial press conference. For their part, the strikers were jubilant: 'I knew right then and there that was going to be the end of the strike'; 'We had IP on the run!'. Like the British miners, Jay Maine strikers and their wives were filled with hope: 'It's like the sun breaking through'; 'All this pain and trouble could finally be going to pay off ...'.

They were wrong. Throughout the talks, the union's conciliatory stance contrasted with the company's uncompromising hardball. IP's wondrously named Anne Silvernail insisted that 'The company still maintains that contracts must be negotiated on the local level and ... has not changed its position on keeping replacements'. In other words, everything the union sought was excluded from the talks. The Local 14 president later concluded that the so-called negotiations were 'the point at which the strike was lost'. Nevertheless, it dragged on until October, when the union leadership finally completed its betrayal of Jay Maine by agreeing, over the strikers' heads, a contract silent on the crucial issues of striker reinstatement and the removal of replacement workers.

To the very end, local activists refused to accept that the leadership's reluctance to support the strike would lead to defeat. The strike was the major topic at the IPIU's convention in September, where the Local 14 president got an 'overwhelming response'.[33] Yet the support of convention delegates, while undoubtedly genuine, was in itself powerless against an uncooperative union and intransigent corporation. Its only potential power lay in the same transformative process which had galvanised the Jay Maine strikers, in which workers who had never seen themselves as activists turned into eloquent speakers with a class message and an 'ordinary' working-class community learnt to sing 'Solidarity for Ever' at thousand-strong union meetings.

Yet ironically, the very transformation of Local 14 from company loyalty to worker solidarity became diverted into a path of 'vision' rather than class struggle: 'The paperworkers began to see the strike as an expression of solidarity *rather than* as an attack on the employer'.[34] For rank-and-file members of Local 14 as of P-9,

involvement in a battle against corporate might was an unforget-
table experience in which conservative white workers from small
'all-American' communities took a giant step towards recognising
the real structures of class and capitalism. Nor were they the only
ones. During the same period, workers at Clinton Corn in Iowa and
Colt Firearms in Hartford, Connecticut,[35] took part in very similar
struggles, with extraordinarily similar transformations in their view
of the world. But, in all these cases, there was the need to take one
crucial step further: the step from evoking an inspiring vision of
class unity and solidarity to consciously building for that solidarity
in a more concrete sense; from moral outrage at the deceit and
betrayal of corporations to a fierce, unbending identification with
the independent interests of the working class.

FORCING AND FOSTERING

Ignoring such irrelevant ephemera as worker resistance, the pendu-
lum of capital swung on in the mid–late 1980s, more often than not
scything labour down into near non-existence. Nor was it slow to
pursue its advantage at a more everyday level. Between strikes,
employers diligently continued with their workplace agenda, which
included 'a blend of forcing and fostering tactics ... that they hoped
would yield a competitive cost structure, a high-commitment workforce and a viable relationship with the union'. While recommended 'to bargain forcefully for the types of substantive changes
reflected in the economic package obtained by IP at Jay, Maine',
managers were also urged to 'learn how to foster ... employee commitment and union cooperation'.[36] In the wake of the wreckage of
lives that followed on the Jay defeat, it was an odd message, but no
doubt a heartfelt one. Either way, it was clear that workers were
going to be 'fostered' as well as 'forced', whether they wanted to be
or not.

Since General Motors (GM) and the UAW had been united in
labour–management cooperation since the early 1980s, it was
hardly surprising that one of the most prominent examples of
worker 'fostering' should be found in another GM factory, the
Saturn plant near Nashville, Tennessee, where the greenfield site
opened after two years of company–union preparation with the full
panoply of 'management-by-stress'[37] features. UAW workplace representatives, reviled as 'clipboard jockeys',[38] played a central role in
implementing 'lean production' at the heart of the labour process.

Nor were other employers slow to follow suit. By early 1988 Chrysler and Ford, as well as all the wholly or jointly Japanese-owned auto factories, had introduced 'team concept' of some kind, while other sectors as diverse as electronics, oil refining, telecommunications and education were taking up the approach. Originally associated mostly with the auto industry, 'team concept' had spread across industry, including the public sector, by the end of the decade.[39]

Yet capital did not have things all its own way at the workplace. US rank-and-file union reform movements received a boost in the mid 1980s with the founding of New Directions, a rank-and-file caucus in the auto industry. Rooted in workplace actions like the innovative 'inside strategy' of its director, Jerry Tucker, the caucus rejected a purely electoral model of union dissidence; while Tucker himself almost defeated the incumbent regional director at the 1986 UAW convention, he 'argued against depending on his candidacy as a panacea and continued to emphasize direct action and grassroots organisation'.[40]

In other sectors, such as the postal service, the realities beneath the rhetoric created activists out of initially cooperative union representatives. One National Association of Letter Carriers (NALC) local president became increasingly disillusioned with 'employee involvement' (E-I) as workers' suggestions were ignored by management and the scheme used to ratchet up productivity. In July 1989, the local voted to completely disengage from E-I, sending out its message to locals across the country. A highly successful forum on 'The Other Side of E-I' at the 1990 NALC convention led to the formation of a national rank-and-file coalition of postal activists.

WORKING WITH PRIDE?

British workers responded in less structured but no less hostile ways to the blandishments of 'team concept'. At British Leyland's successor, Rover, a 1986 initiative entitled 'working with pride' collapsed within a year; workers 'saw it as a waste of time and as a threat to the role of shop stewards'.[41] In equally subversive style, Ford Halewood workers refused to cooperate with West German-style cooperation initiatives until they received 'West German levels of pay',[42] while Post Office team briefings were 'a complete shambles, with indoctrinated local managers struggling to read out robotic style messages to staff who ... saw this as an unnecessary waste of their time'.[43]

At first, the initiatives also met strong official opposition. Ford's 'After Japan' initiative was opposed from the start by union leaders concerned that its 'quality circles' and 'employee involvement' measures 'threatened to bypass existing bargaining institutions';[44] TGWU officials at Rover took a similar stance. However, British management did not give up that easily. In 1987, Rover introduced a 'total quality' programme which this time apparently took root, paving the way for many of the company's later, more draconian changes in work practices.

A project that symbolised, above all, the entire team concept approach was the greenfield Nissan plant, constructed in 1986 to a chorus of approval from the government. The usual suspects – teamworking, JIT, kaizen ('constant improvement'), flexible working, and the keen pursuit of 'quality' – were built into the project from the start; opposition was precluded by the factory's location in the North East, an area blighted for years by unemployment. Finally, the initiative was sugar-coated in one of the early 'sweetheart' union deals now being pursued by the AUEW.

Though interviews revealed a workforce by no means blindsided by Nissan's 'team' ideology – 'Where we work it is quite bolshie ... we don't toe the company line ... we are pretty anti-Nissan really'[45] – the charade of 'union recognition' at the plant precluded resistance to the company's ferocious labour intensification. Even in better organised plants, 'flexibility'-style packages imposed by management increasingly aimed at a formal undermining of shop steward structures. At Norsk-Hydro in Humberside, a previous bastion of workplace organisation, management presented a 'new personnel package' to workers over the stewards' heads, wiping out negotiating structures and imposing a non-union 'advisory council' of management and worker representatives;[46] the package included, unusually, a single-union deal with the TGWU.

The more consciously 'business unionist' AUEW and EETPU in the 1980s had pioneered the single-union agreement at the UK plants of Toshiba and Sanyo in the early 1980s,[47] but the movement as a whole remained uneasy about the phenomenon, which became something of a curse for the movement in this period; one TGWU official complained of being made to 'parade before prospective employers like beauty queens'.[48] Unions like the print workers' NGA (for obvious reasons), along with the left-led National Union of Public Employees (NUPE), were clear in their opposition to single-union deals; the TUC formally ruled against them in December 1985, after a pre-Wapping coup by the EEPTU at Hitachi. But, as ever, the TUC's pronouncements were ignored by a cruel world.

'Back to the members'?

The TUC's own warmer, fuzzier version of union organisation now offered little more than credit cards and cheap rates on insurance as inducements to boost union membership, now dropping to alarming lows. Yet relentless government pressure on union organisation continued, the latest initiative further testing the TUC's mettle with an excursion into the sphere of trade union 'democracy'; the 1984 Trade Union Act opened up all union posts to election and ordained individual postal ballots for both these and strike votes. The proposal was billed as 'giving trade unions back to their members', suggesting a concern for rank-and-file union involvement clearly belied by its implications. The TUC fell easily for the government's trump card, the undeniable factor of shrinking attendances at branch meetings, to justify its lack of strong opposition. In fact, trade union branch meetings, organised on a geographical basis at places and times remote from the workplace, had never been a reliable indicator of the kind of active, direct union democracy signalled in mass meetings and show-of-hands strike votes – the last thing, of course, the Tories wanted.

In the ensuing years unions increasingly complied with the legislation, allowing for an inflated raft of bureaucratic procedures to stifle every strike initiative. Yet, ironically, the argument that the 'silent majority' would vote against hot-headed activist leaderships was proved to be false; now that strike votes were formally measurable, it could be shown that most members supported their leaders' recommendation to strike. Of 246 strike ballots held in 1986, almost 80 per cent went in favour of action.[49]

Our own grave diggers?

In fact, 'old-fashioned industrial action', as the media now delighted in calling it, continued, stubbornly, to exist. One particularly dramatic example, the Caterpillar dispute of early 1987, revived the tactic of occupation in an echo of what now seemed the faraway truculence of the 1970s. Perhaps the lessons of steel, mining and Wapping had finally been learnt; as one Caterpillar steward put it, 'there's only one way of preventing stuff coming out and in … a *mass picket*. And we all know what happens to mass pickets'.[50]

Yet the dispute resembled others of the mid to late 1980s in its mingling of inspiring struggle with a fatal trust in capitalist institutions.

When management announced the closure of the US-owned Caterpillar tractor plant at Uddington, Scotland, the 1,200 workers immediately occupied the plant. It was a powerful move; they found themselves in possession of enormously valuable amounts of highly capital-intensive equipment. The action 'terrified' the huge global corporation, but seemed to frighten its combatants still more. As one woman worker declaimed in a mass meeting, 'If we win, the whole country is going to be taken over by its workers ... They don't want us to win. We've *no* chance!'.[51]

No counterargument based in the enormous trump card of occupation was offered by its rank-and-file leaders, whose misplaced respect for 'the law' led them to retreat at the mere whisper of property rights. One of the more class-aware stewards pleaded, in a despairing twist on the Marxist conception of workers as the gravediggers of capitalism, 'We have got the occupation. We're not giving up the occupation. To do anything else is to *act as our own gravediggers!*'.[52] Unfortunately, his was a lone voice. Despite its commitment and determination, the joint occupation committee (JOC) was confused, unclear and unable to argue a forceful case to the workforce.

The weakness of the shopfloor leadership was compounded by the apparent determination of their union, the AEU, to put paid to the occupation. After misleading the JOC over a supposed campaign to boycott Caterpillar parts, the local AEU official effectively pre-empted resistance when he 'let the stewards know ... in no uncertain manner' that he was going to end the occupation; if they refused to cooperate, he would call a mass meeting of the by now decidedly ambivalent workforce and get a vote over the stewards' heads. The JOC leaders, neatly outmanoeuvred, were 'completely shattered'. As one sighed, head in hands, 'It's a helluva thing when you're not *allowed* to win'.[53]

However, the working class had not yet completely 'acted as their own gravediggers'. In 1987 British Telecom workers struck over the now privatised company's attempts to link pay, productivity and labour flexibility; once again, 'Essex Man' (a largely accurate description of telephone workers' origins) had gone on the streets against Thatcherism. Resistance reemerged in the seafarers' dispute of 1988, sparked by demands from the shipping companies for draconian changes in hours and conditions.[54] Predictably, the strike immediately ran into legal obstacles; at first the union defied the shower of injunctions, general secretary Sam McCluskie declaring that he would 'live in a tent on Clapham Common' (the location of the union offices) rather than submit. But the threat of sequestration of the union's assets was too much, and the strike was called off. The most militant section, Dover ferry workers, stuck it out until 1989, but they were heading for inevitable defeat.

The law proved the nemesis also for dock workers striking in 1989 against the proposed abolition of the National Dock Labour Scheme. TGWU general secretary Ron Todd delayed calling action for so long that the dockers' traditional, and initial, militancy was vitiated. The union ballotted for strike action in April 1989 and obtained a 3–1 majority, but delayed issuing a strike call while it waited for the results of a series of legal appeals. By 9 June, dockers in Liverpool had had enough and walked out; on 19 June, stewards from eleven ports met and agreed to call an unofficial national strike. But it was too late; the action fell apart when Liverpool and Tilbury dockers voted to return to work. Although a national strike was finally called on 8 July, it was supported by less than half the workforce.

Despite their tragic outcomes, the NUS and dock strikes were part of a spate of disputes in the late 1980s, many of which were more successful. Among these were the rail workers' strikes on London Underground Ltd (LUL) and British Rail (BR) in 1989. On the London Underground, unofficial action against one-person operation (OPO) of trains 'took off like wildfire' among rank-and-file members of both rail unions, the National Union of Railwaymen (NUR) and the Associated Society of Locomotive Engineers and Firemen (ASLEF), wiping out the traditional, and destructive, rivalry between the two. In the meantime the NUR and Transport Salaried Staffs' Association (TSSA), representing ticket-booth workers, voted overwhelmingly for an official strike over a simultaneous LUL job flexibility initiative, 'Action Stations'; the strike was, predictably, banned by the courts, yet workers at LUL managed to carry out a series of 24-hour strikes which boosted those striking at British Rail over a separate pay dispute. By late July, the actions brought an 8.8 per cent pay rise for BR workers, while LUL's 'Action Stations' plans were – for the time being at least – 'completely shelved'.[55]

These victories created a new awareness that organised workers could still successfully flex their muscles, even after ten years of Thatcherism. The feeling was renewed by an equally solid victory by white-collar local government workers whose series of rolling strikes and indefinite stoppages secured an 8.8 per cent increase – 9.5 per cent for the lowest paid – with no strings attached; the local councils' climbdown was seen as 'reminiscent of the bad old days of the 1970s'.[56] In the same year, the resurgent tendency for 'conservative' workers to become involved in subversive struggle was again illustrated with the 1989–90 ambulance workers' strike. Though fatally undermined by a leadership obsessed with public relations, the struggle drew unofficial solidarity action from council workers, construction workers and bus workers, and fundamentally challenged the outlook of many erstwhile Tory voters: 'It's shown me a side where politicians are prepared to lie and con the public'.[57]

The private sector saw a number of successful strikes by carworkers in which the 1988 Ford strike, in particular, was notable for its exposure of the vulnerability of newly introduced 'just-in-time' (JIT) systems, which streamlined production by limiting parts supply, as plants rapidly closed down across Europe. Ford workers also scored a success in preventing the opening of a new plant in Dundee, Scotland, on the basis of conditions which would have undercut the national agreement. Though denounced as an attack on jobs, the Ford workers' action was a crucial stand against the government's 'bargain basement' approach.

'CAMP SOLIDARITY'

In the US, a new, welcome dynamic of resistance had emerged in the 1986 Watsonville Canning ('WatsCan') strike in California. For the WatsCan strikers, almost all Mexican and Chicana women, illusions of capitalist morality were few. They had been made aware of corporate and state interests the hard way – through systematic discrimination against Mexican and Chicano workers throughout the area. When WatsCan and its main competitor, the Richard Shaw Company, announced wage cuts from $6.66 an hour to $4.25 as well as drastic reductions in healthcare, 1,750 workers from both companies simultaneously walked out on strike on behalf of all canning workers: 'If we accept what Watsonville is offering, then all the canneries will want to pay the same'.[58] Despite consistent opposition from the local Teamster leadership – an unsupportive white-male clique – the Watsonville workers scored better than a draw in what many saw as a hopeless battle, winning a pay rise and health benefits after a protracted struggle supported by TDU activists and the entire Chicano community.

Equal intransigence and solidarity, accompanied by some of the most imaginative and innovative tactics of the whole decade, were shown in the 1989 miners' strike against the giant Pittston corporation. By the time 1,700 Appalachian miners finally walked out over Pittston's demands for work rule changes and cuts in healthcare, the United Mine Workers of America (UMWA) had spent more than a year filing 'unfair labor practice' charges with the National Labor Relations Board to forestall any hiring of permanent replacement workers. The newly effective leadership's 'civil disobedience' stance was enthusiastically backed by thousands of camouflage-clad miners and supporters who blocked roads, held up scab trucks and occupied a coal processing plant. Arrests mounted, court fines rose, but the miners fought on. Supporters from other unions from across America made the pilgrimage to the strike headquarters, 'Camp Solidarity'. In early 1990, the struggle ended with Pittston's withdrawal of most of its required concessions and a return to the contract pattern set in the rest of the industry.

Also in 1989 came a successful strike by Communications Workers of America (CWA) members against telecommunications giant Nynex; after years of sectional competition between the two unions involved, the CWA and the International Brotherhood of Electrical Workers (IBEW), activists on both sides finally achieved unity and mobilised the rank and file to a decisive defeat of the company's drive for healthcare and pay concessions. While a long-drawn-out dispute at Eastern Airlines eventually fizzled out in an abortive attempt at worker ownership, rank-and-file rail workers showed willingness – thwarted by their leaders on legal grounds – to strike in their support; a scattering of successful strikes by hospital workers in New York contributed to the overall atmosphere of militancy.

Strikes like P9, Jay, Watsonville and Pittston continued the development of a new, more class-oriented kind of unionism in the mid to late 1980s. A 1986 photograph shows an all-American P-9 striker, complete with baseball jacket and jeans, raising clasped hands with WatsCan workers at an International Women's Day celebration in March 1986.[59] That picture symbolises all the class unity and awareness produced by the experience of struggle in two cultures worlds apart but united by the same attacks of capital, the same new consciousness of solidarity and the same shared class interests.

In spite of everything, workers in the 1980s continued to wage class struggle not only in its everyday, irreducible sense but also through significant new moves by organised workers in confronting employer aggression and devising more effective strategies. While far from restored to the levels of 'workers' power' attained in the 1970s, rank-and-file trade unionists entered the 1990s with two sharpened weapons: a significant increase in solidarity consciousness, and the understanding of lessons learnt the hard way about the relentlessness and lack of scruple amongst their employers. Accompanying these moves towards stronger, more strategic organisation was the clutch of victories against what had seemed to be, until the late 1980s, an impregnable ruling class.

5
The Workers' TINA: Class Warfare in the 1990s

In the 1990s, the trends of the 1980s grew to their full potential and revealed their true nature. 'Team' became 'lean'; 'cooperation' became 'partnership'; a crude deficit-based Reaganomics emerged as fully fledged neoliberalism; and, most of all, globalisation expanded from leading-edge strategy to total domination of every aspect of employment. The new hardball evinced by the corporate players was based in the ever growing pressures of global competition driving corporations to become ever 'leaner and meaner' in terms of ruthlessness in general and 'lean production' in particular.

GLOBALONEY?

So what was this 'globalisation' cracking the whip over the heads of workers in the 1990s? Despite its suspect glorification in every best-selling book on an eternally 'new' economy, the G-word does denote a distinctive phase in the development of capitalist production. While the 'multinational'-style investment of the 1920s to 1970s saw major corporations opening up plants in other capitalist countries, globalisation meant establishing production 'chains' whereby minimum-cost parts produced in specifically non-capitalist and thus (ultra-)low-wage countries could be reimported into the host country for completion and sale; thanks to trade agreements like 1994's North American Free Trade Agreement (NAFTA), the process was made free from tariff barriers.

The already jaw-dropping size of such global corporate activities suggested to some that multinational corporations had replaced nation states and would now themselves rule the world. Yet such 'globaloney'[1] overlooked the reality that global corporate power in the 1990s remained rooted firmly in the nation state. This was illustrated most publicly by the jockeying for national corporate dominance within world forums like the World Trade Organisation (WTO). But, while less glamorous, an equally crucial function of national governments during the 1990s was to back the 'supply-side' needs of global corporations through the deregulation, privatisation and repression of worker resistance that marked the Reagan and Thatcher years and beyond. Many commentators have pointed out that, despite Thatcher's professed determination to push back the boundaries of the state, her regime probably brokered more state intervention than the most stubbornly corporatist Labour government.

That tradition was continued under the aegis of her successor, the anaemic John Major, whose 'nice guy' image was belied by the torrent of anti-union legislation and privatisation that continued to pour from Downing Street. Nor, finally, was there any escape under the longed-for Labour government, elected in 1997 on an avalanche of popular loathing for Thatcherism. One left-leaning journal summed up the decade with the words, 'If the 1980s were the decade of the Right in the West, the 1990s saw a comparable sweep by the Centre-Left'.[2] Yet that 'centre-left', as exemplified by Blair and Clinton, allowed for no meaningful turning in the neoliberal tide.

'THE WORKPLACE, STUPID'

Government-driven undermining of core national institutions was mirrored in the widespread breakdown and decentralisation of collective bargaining in both the private and public sectors. With the devolution of bargaining to company and even plant level, the 1992 Workplace Industrial Relations Survey (WIRS) could report that 'the traditional, distinctive "system" of British industrial relations no longer characterises the economy as a whole'.[3]

Consonant with the logic of decentralisation, the focus of corporate attention became still more – to rephrase a contemporary election slogan – 'the workplace, stupid'. With the move to enterprise or even plant as profit centre, the 1990s became, even more than most, the decade of 'Labor Crunch Recovery'[4] – a phrase which vividly conjures up the squeeze put on workers through ever longer hours, higher workloads and lower pay. And the key factor in bringing about the recovery in question – for the rate of profit did indeed regain its bloom during the 1990s – was 'lean production'.

Lean production can be understood as the workplace-based counterpart to globalisation. Just as corporations worked towards the standardisation of everything from fast food outlets to shopping malls, so the lean production bundle of work arrangements – 'just-in-time' (JIT), 'constant improvement', contracting-out – became the bulk-standard practice of global corporations in the 1990s. From the US through Britain and increasingly Europe, the combination of labour intensification and 'Human Resources Management' (HRM) rhetoric encapsulated in lean production marched in lockstep with the rise of the global corporation.

The 57-second minute

What most clearly distinguished lean production from the 'team concept' emphasis of the 1980s was the abandonment of the pretence that such systems of work organisation were truly connected with worker 'empowerment'. The ideological 'togetherness' of teamwork became increasingly an optional extra: 'What is becoming clearer is that the teams are no longer regarded as necessary once the dynamics of management-by-stress are at work'.[5]

Such dynamics, largely summed up in the key lean production feature of *kaizen* ('constant improvement'), centred on keeping the work-organisation system in a constant state of stress, exercising continual pressure in order to identify both its weak points and 'those that are too strong ... points that never break down are presumed to have too many resources, and are thus wasteful'.[6] The essential function of the 'team' became to jointly identify such points – including when 'too many resources' included its own members. Despite the glorification of team concept as a vehicle for 'worker empowerment' in direct contradiction to the top-down dictates of Taylorism, within the team framework the basic methods of reducing work time and increasing labour intensification remained those of classic Taylorist work time measurement. As one 1997 GM document blandly stated, 'Workloads are balanced to maximize minutes-per-hour and value-added work content'.[7] The effects of melding the two were impressive: 'Whereas an assembly-line worker at GM's old mass-production plants worked ... 45 seconds of each minute, today's NUMMI [New United Motor Manufacturing, Inc.] workers in California work the standard Toyota 57-second minute'.[8]

Nor was the lean production menu confined to GM or the other two members of the US auto 'Big Three', Ford and Chrysler; its methods and perspectives spread rapidly to other areas of employment. By the mid 1990s, telephone workers, health workers and homecare aides, chocolate producers and postal workers could record their experiences with various forms of 'lean production', including 'reengineering' and TQM (Total Quality Management), in both the US and Britain.[9]

'Charade'

Shorn of the dubious protection afforded by industrywide agreements, even well organised workers found their ability to resist such initiatives impaired. Though many workplace bargaining structures remained in place, the apparent shell of defensive organisation collapsed like a dried-up honeycomb at the first rude push of managerial aggression. A study of British workplace unionism in the 1990s sums up the consequences of corporations' switch from industry to plant level as 'a hollowing out of the union ... and collective representation as a charade'.[10] The absence of formal systems of representation and negotiation was not the problem so much as the emptiness of these structures; once taken-for-granted patterns of accommodation had been eroded.

In the early 1990s, as in the 1980s, a blurring of the oppositional realities of capitalist production weakened most local struggles against the impact of 'lean production'. While resistance often remained strong at the grass roots, the higher echelons of the workplace union organisation succumbed easily to company pressure; 'We inherited a group of senior stewards who ... spent too much time doing what the members wanted ... But over time, they've become more committed to the management's viewpoint', boasted one components plant manager pushing a typical HRM strategy. In this case, the 'commitment' led the senior stewards to recommend a package of new labour-intensifying working practices which the members overwhelmingly rejected, but were unable to resist without leadership support. The workplace union's defection had the effect of 'disarming and demobilising' its own members.[11]

A similar dynamic was reflected at Rover when senior stewards agreed the 1992 'New Deal', a package of flexible working practices, over their members' heads; a grateful chief executive commented, 'The fact that we have been able to enrol the trade union people at Rover in the company's mission and objectives has allowed us to move at a pace that would have been impossible without trade union collaboration'.[12]

In America, cooperation with management objectives went still further; the 1990 GM/UAW 'jointness' agreement increased the number of UAW appointees patrolling the production process and further promoted joint labour–management committees on work organisation. As shopfloor union representatives became increasingly corralled into policing effort and driving speedup, workers' weary disgust at the charade of 'empowerment' was conveyed in the comment, 'Yeah, we have input. We get to decide whether we're hung or shot'.[13]

What Did the Activists Do?

Yet, despite the 'stitching up' of worker resistance inherent in 'lean production', workers continued to fight against its impact, largely because the logic of the system itself confronted them with the twin realities of increased workloads and job losses. At Vauxhall (a General Motors UK subsidiary), 'the rhetoric of participation and "smarter work" was pushed increasingly on to a vanishing direct labour force' at the same time as 'the reality of lean management began to bite'; the result was strike action rumbling throughout 1995–96. In this case, the senior steward leadership had adopted an effective strategy of opposition to 'lean production' which distinguished its technical aspects, like 'just-in-time', 'zero waste' and Statistical Process Control from its ideological trappings. While the technical changes were difficult to resist in their entirety, 'On the crucial matter of the ideological campaign for "hearts and minds", management for the present is trailing the TGWU'.[14]

In the US, such fine distinctions had long been overtaken by the almost universal dissemination of 'lean', but the system's internal contradictions continued to generate a wellspring of rank-and-file resistance. In October 1994, a month-long strike at GM's Buick City assembly plant at Flint, Michigan sparked off a series of local-level disputes centring on 'lean issues' like staffing levels and subcontracting. The strikers' solution to the combination of 'constant improvement' and disappearing jobs was simple: hire more workers.

Although the Buick City strike lasted only four days, it shut down GM plants throughout the company via the impact of 'just-in-time' parts organisation – a lean production 'own goal' which no doubt contributed to the local's success in winning back 779 jobs. As GM plants closed down, their workforces joined the Local 599 picketline, while support for the Flint workers' action spread far beyond the auto industry as workers and activists made the parallel with their own experience of 'the downsizing tidal wave of the early 1990s'.[15]

The wave of GM strikes continued until 1996, culminating in actions at two plants in Dayton, Ohio which lasted 17 days and closed down almost every one of GM's plants in the US, Canada and Mexico. However, the company refused to budge on the workers' demand to stop outsourcing, the lynchpin of GM's strategy. The Dayton workers won their demand for an increase in the workforce, but lost on outsourcing and were forced back to work. Even then, the wave of GM strikes continued and was complemented by actions in the public sector, by immigrant workers in California and by truck drivers under the newly militant leadership of anti-corruption Teamster president Ron Carey, boosted to victory in 1991 largely through the long-term rank-and-file organising of Teamsters for a Democratic Union (TDU).

UTOPIA?

The British trade union movement lacked the caucus-building tradition so significant in the US, but rank-and-file activism brought successful resistance to teamworking in a number of sectors, most notably the postal industry. Postal workers had been in the van-guard of workplace-based resistance from the mid 1980s onwards, their militancy fanned by a 'budget-driven culture' on the part of Royal Mail which made work 'harder, faster and cheaper year in year out'; management's harsh disciplinary treatment of individual workers provoked numerous walkouts which often became the catalyst to a full-scale dispute with fellow workers quick to express their solidarity. It was against this background that the national dispute against teamworking developed in 1996.

The trigger was management's so-called 'employee agenda', which demanded changes to the national delivery system, restructuring of pay and conditions and a wholesale reorganisation of work on the basis of teamworking. The national Communication Workers' Union (CWU) leadership declared the proposal 'a real chance for the membership to share at last in the success of the business'; but the members were less enthusiastic. The proposed team-based changes to the delivery system were seen as the first step towards an almost entirely part-time industry.

Royal Mail's management was determined to pursue teamwork-ing; the local union leadership was equally determined to resist. Activists were clear-eyed about the dangers; workers would be set against one another both within and between the teams, pushed to oust their 'weaker' members in order to reach production targets, while working arrangements previously negotiated with the union would now be 'driven' by the team. As the local leader sardonically noted, 'On one hand you have the employer's pitch that team working will give workers more control over their daily work. But, according to them, to achieve this utopia you have to dismantle all Trade Union negotiated safeguards'.[16]

Local activists representing the rank and file mobilised to fight the agreement. An unofficial meeting called in March 1996 organised the coordination of resistance and called eight one-day strikes, each solidly supported by the membership. The result was a 'failure to agree' (aka management backdown), and the suspension of the joint working parties set up to institute teamworking. The membership's resolute opposition to the lures of 'superficial empowerment', along with an aware and determined local leadership, had overturned a strategy backed by both management and the union leadership.

During the same period, a number of other workplace groups and local union leaderships mounted effective resistance against teamworking, lean production, HRM and 'quality' initiatives. Workers at Cadbury's obtained their company's 1994 'Manufacturing Human Resources Strategy' document, arming them to fight a managerial programme aimed at 'cutting the power of the trade unions ... off at the knees'.[17] The stewards refused to recognise team leaders, and held parallel union meetings to correspond with management-led team briefings. Ambulance workers and other health workers took advantage of the decentralisation of bargaining under National Health Service (NHS) 'trusts' to put more local representatives into office and thus strengthen rank-and-file resistance to the pressures of privatisation. In some accounts, the break up of formerly nationally managed systems such as the NHS resulted, paradoxically, in a 'renewal' of workplace-based unionism.[18]

'TWIN-TRACK'?

On the whole, however, rank-and-file action and resistance was not what interested the union leadership. What they were hotly in pursuit of was 'partnership' with industry and management, which beckoned as an alluring substitute for the much-mourned 'Social Contract' of the 1970s.

In 1994 in the US, the American Federation of Labor-Congress of Industrial Organizations (AFL-CIO) issued 'guidelines to be used in the construction of labor–management partnerships',[19] encouraged by no less an authority than the Clinton administration, which set up the Dunlop Commission on the Future of Worker–Management Relations. As part of its aim of defining 'high-performance workplaces' the Commission advocated, 'where a union is present', a 'full partnership between union leaders and management'.[20] Ultimately, the AFL-CIO gave a lukewarm response to the Dunlop Commission, largely because of its implicit condoning of company unionism. The leadership was optimistic enough to envisage 'partnership' as emanating from *independent* unions in combination with an enlightened management.

During the same period, British union leaders showed equal enthusiasm for partnership with management. In 1994 the TUC published a policy document entitled 'Human Resource Management: A Trade Union Response' in which it called for a 'joint commitment to the success of the enterprise' and argued that 'in a true partnership those conflicts that do occur could be worked out in an atmosphere of mutual respect, trust and goodwill'.[21] Like the AFL-CIO, the TUC maintained that partnership could exist in a context of independent unionism, reasoning that the movement had nothing to fear from HRM-style policies because these had been embraced by unionised companies; the fact that most companies large enough to have HRM policies would be unionised in any case did not enter the argument. The TUC's stance on 'independence' was further undermined by a companion document which allowed for the possibility of 'twin-track' worker representation on European-style works councils by either union or non-union employees.

In fact, very few partnership agreements had actually been concluded in Britain or even the US. The contradictory requirements of independent trade unionism and 'joint commitment to the success of the enterprise' meant that genuine partnership arrangements, as opposed to 'soft', non-union forms of HRM, remained rare in both countries.[22] In the US, GM's Saturn plant was by far the most thoroughgoing example of 'labour–management cooperation'; yet toward the end of the decade, Saturn was to revert to traditional 'adversarial' collective bargaining following a rebellion by rank-and-file activists.[23]

In Britain, the 1992 Rover 'New Deal', though agreed by only a tiny majority of the workforce – 11,961 to 11,793 – was invoked as a genuine partnership agreement, pledging a 'job for life' for its workforce in return for union involvement in flexibility of working arrangements. Unfortunately, the 'job for life' commitment was a charade, as indicated in the wording of the agreement itself: 'The company must continuously improve its ... competitive position through the elimination of waste, increased levels of efficiency and reduced levels of manpower'.[24] While existing workers were kept on, Rover began hiring increasing numbers of workers on temporary short-term contracts, and new absenteeism and lateness procedures were so severe that 'even "permanent" workers face a real risk of the sack'.[25]

New voices?

Across the Atlantic, a notable change at the top of the union leadership nevertheless left the 'partnership' approach intact. In 1995, the twentieth convention of the AFL-CIO saw the first leadership challenge in the federation's 40-year history, led by Service Employees' International Union (SEIU) leader John Sweeney. The incumbent, Lane Kirkland, and his anointed successor, Tom Donahue, were defeated by Sweeney's 'New Voices' faction, demonstrating growing discontent throughout the movement with the dead end of 'business unionism'.

The Sweeney leadership had a newly radical sheen; the AFL-CIO executive board now included an impressive array of women and people of colour, with United Mine Workers of America (UMWA) leader Richard Trumka, who had gained a strong reputation for militancy in the Pittston coal strike, as secretary-treasurer. The new leadership lost no time in declaring its commitment to 'organising' (union recruitment), swiftly revamping the AFL-CIO's dormant Organizing Institute (OI) and launching 'Union Summer', a scheme which trained students for vivid, imaginative organising campaigns. So impressive was the new rhetoric that in 1996 the British TUC brought over the baseball-hatted Andy Stern, a leading representative of Sweeney's SEIU union, to initiate them into the 'organising' mindset.

Some impressive organising activity had already taken place under the aegis of Sweeney's SEIU during this period, notably the 'Justice for Janitors' campaign in Los Angeles, which unionised apparently unorganisable, often undocumented immigrant cleaners in LA's hotels and office blocks. Yet the eventual outcome of this impressive coup pointed to some of the weaknesses in the organising strategy of the 'new' AFL-CIO. In 1995, five years after they had been brought into a huge, bureaucratically managed SEIU local, the Latino janitors teamed up with its African-American members to form the oppositional Multicultural Slate, which staged a rebellion in support of rank-and-file democracy. Despite his imminent ascent to the leadership of a new, more democratically managed union movement, Sweeney denied the dissidents legitimacy and put the local in trusteeship. Eventually, the janitors were transferred to the equally huge Local 1877 – 'a spatial punishment for a local revolt'.[26]

Ultimately, the new, dynamic AFL-CIO retained an essentially top-down perspective on unionisation. A keynote study of organising methods at the time showed conclusively that success in organising depended on 'an aggressive grassroots rank-and-file strategy'; yet the same research suggested that 'unions have made only minor improvements in embracing a more rank-and-file intensive approach to organising'.[27] The institutionally focused and staff-driven approach of the new AFL-CIO leadership was not reassuring in this respect.

But perhaps the most demoralising aspect of the new AFL-CIO leadership was its unquestioning acceptance of 'partnership' ideology. Sweeney's deep-seated belief in partnership was reflected in a number of speeches characterised by phrases like 'It is time for business and labor to see each other as natural allies, not natural enemies' and 'We want to help American business compete in the world and create new wealth for your shareholders and your employees'. Such a mindset was hardly a challenge to the traditional belief of American union leaders 'in the ability of the US economy ... to provide a fair and just distribution of resources'.[28]

'DECATUR IS A WAR ZONE'

But it was precisely this 'fair and just distribution' that was lacking in the experience of the late-twentieth-century worker. Just at the time the AFL-CIO was cooing about partnership with business, the labour-intensifying techniques of 'lean production' were being enhanced by an increasing emphasis on extending and reorganising the working day which ordained new and exhausting working time patterns like ten- or twelve-hour shifts. Euphemistically labelled 'alternative work schedules' (AWS), such initiatives allowed for round-the-clock production, including weekend working, without overtime pay. As the *New York Times* commented, 'The revolution in the 1980s was toward just-in-time inventory. The revolution of the 1990s is toward just-in-time employment'.[29]

Such corporate offensives proved the trigger for three major disputes which turned Decatur, a small town in the heart of the

American Midwest, into a 'war zone' in the summer of 1994. Workers at the corn-processing plant A.E. Staley (recently taken over by the British multinational Tate and Lyle) were the first to rebel when, in the summer of 1992, they were confronted with an 'alternative working schedule' demanding twelve-hour shifts in a three-days-on, three-days-off pattern. The union local, part of the now depleted Allied Industrial Workers, decided to fight, but with a Jerry Tucker-style 'inside strategy' rather than a strike: 'Corporate America has taken the strike and turned it against workers, but by non-cooperation we can still put economic pressure on the company – the only thing they understand'.[30]

The 'inside strategy', implemented from October 1992, 'got to them more than anything else' as production fell by a third, provoking management to ever louder accusations of sabotage and harsh disciplinary actions against individual workers. In mid June, after one worker was fired and ten others disciplined, their fellow-workers walked out. Symbolising the now rampant militancy and unity of the workforce, the next shift reentered the plant singing 'Solidarity Forever'. But less than two weeks later the entire workforce was locked out as the company realised it could run the operation with non-union replacements.

The workers remained defiant; on the day of the lockout, they formed a human chain from Staley to the Caterpillar plant two and a half miles away, each picket carrying a placard declaiming 'Illinois Is A War Zone!' The slogan invoked the solidarity actions which had grown and spread since the first threats to the Staley workforce in early 1992 were matched at the local Caterpillar and Bridgestone-Firestone plants, the other two major players in the 'war zone'.

The fire down below …

In December 1992, Caterpillar unilaterally imposed a 'final offer' which ordained new working conditions remarkably similar to those at Staley; four ten-hour or three twelve-hour days, including weekend and holiday working, without overtime pay. Although the United Auto Workers (UAW) delayed calling strike action, spurts of grass-roots militancy began disrupting the production process; workers staged chanting, whistle-blowing parades through the plant at the end of each shift, festooned themselves with badges and slogan-bearing T-shirts, and called a series of 'hit-and-run' strikes. They won a battle in the ongoing 'T-shirt war' with Caterpillar when the company was forced to reverse its so-called 'personal attire policy';

hundreds of workers had been disciplined – in some cases arrested – for wearing T-shirts, hats and badges with the message 'Permanently Replace Fites' (Caterpillar's $545,000-a-year CEO).

Much as the UAW leadership wanted to avoid another strike, they 'couldn't smother the fire down below'.[31] The Caterpillar workers finally came out officially in June 1994, a year after the Staley lock-out. But although the Caterpillar workers were in the relatively favourable position of being out on strike, rather than locked out, the UAW leadership was timid in pushing this advantage; if anything, as one striker wryly commented, the local union official set out to 'kill 'em with kindness'.[32] The leadership was equally flaccid on the crucial requirement of keeping 'replacement workers' out of the factory. Without UAW support, for all their fervent participation in demonstrations, in 'road warrior' convoys, in all the other subversive but ultimately symbolic features of the Illinois 'war zone', the Caterpillar strikers were unable to halt a steady influx of scabs – many of them union members – into the plant. Sapped by the UAW's contradictory messages of 'partnership' with a contemptuously intransigent corporation while pursuing 'public support' through distancing itself from the 'war zone' mindset of its own members, many workers saw no point in maintaining the fight.

Meanwhile, a third dispute that had been smouldering for about the same length of time joined these two struggles to form an extraordinary display of joint worker resistance in this American-as-apple-pie area. The Bridgestone-Firestone tyre company had been pushing since 1992 for the introduction of rotating twelve-hour shifts and seven-day plant utilisation, as well as a two-tier pay system linked to productivity. Although the leadership of the by now much weakened United Rubber Workers (URW) was no more eager to strike than its counterparts, 'emotions were on high alert ... the union had almost no choice but to strike'. The 4,200-strong Bridgestone-Firestone workforce came out in July 1994, a month after the Caterpillar stoppage.

Bridgestone-Firestone workers proved keen participants in the mobilisations and protests of the Illinois 'war zone' movement. Yet the essentially symbolic action was no match for a sabre-toothed corporate tiger prepared to 'take a long strike'. The company moved to hire replacement workers, and by January 1995 had 2,300 new employees; it was the largest ever replacement of strikers by a private company in the US.

Neither the union nor its membership was in any way prepared for such fast corporate footwork. As so often, workers found it hard to believe that they could be replaced by a whole alternative workforce; 'It was ... as if they had stumbled into a nightmare'.[33] The announcement that their jobs were to be permanently replaced panicked at least 1,000 strikers into going back to work. In March 1996, the embattled URW accepted salvation in the form of a merger with the United Steel Workers of America (USWA), whose president, George Becker, was known for flamboyant international actions like the 1990 campaign to save Ravenswood Steel.[34]

The USWA achieved an impressive number of boycott victories in the tyre workers' dispute, perhaps the reason why the company moved towards a settlement in December 1996. In an ironic 'victory', however, by now the issue of the replacement workers was no longer a problem because most workers were back on the job. Beyond this, the company achieved everything it wanted: continuous plant operation, twelve-hour shifts, a two-tier pay structure, and pay increases tied to productivity. Yet, not surprisingly perhaps, given their draining 27-month struggle, the strikers overwhelmingly accepted the agreement.

'A tortured silence'

While hardly a triumph, the Bridgestone-Firestone settlement represented probably the best outcome of the three Decatur disputes. Almost exactly a year earlier – December 1995 – the other two combatants in the Illinois 'war zone' had been presented with 'offers' so ruinous that Caterpillar workers refused to ratify the contract; a staunch 25 per cent of the Staley workforce voted to reject a 'union-busting' agreement in which the company won the right to unlimited subcontracting, twelve-hour rotating shifts and mandatory overtime. Perhaps the unkindest cut for workers whose cause had become the reinstatement of union fighters was refusal of amnesty for workers fired over union activity. The hard-core activists central to the strike were replaced by a new, far more conformist, local leadership.

Defeat was similarly ground in strikers' faces at Caterpillar, where the UAW had humbly agreed that 150 workers fired for alleged picket-line militancy would be denied arbitration. Along with a number of clauses designed to ban every possible form of resistance, the new contract effectively dismantled representation at the plant. The workplace bargaining committee would be cut in half, with no full-time representatives and no stewards in some areas, and the company assumed the right to unilaterally dismiss grievances it regarded as 'frivolous'. Beyond all this, the contract contained every familiar dimension of new working time arrangements: twelve-hour alternative work schedules, part-time or temporary workers amounting to 15 per cent of the workforce, a two-tier wage and benefit structure for newly hired workers, and much more.

As one supporter described the response of the defeated union activists: 'There's a tortured silence, like someone choking for air after a heavy punch to the stomach'.[35] It would be hard to convey more eloquently the sense of shocked betrayal with which these groups of workers greeted the final defeat of struggles which had changed their lives and to which they had committed their most fundamental hopes and convictions.

'SHUTTING DOWN MOTOWN'

Six months before the two main 'war zone' struggles ended, another major dispute had begun – launched by almost the same set of issues, and doomed to defeat by almost identical factors of company intransigence, union defensiveness and rank-and-file illusions of social 'justice'. The Detroit newspaper strike began in July 1995 over the demand for 1,500 job cuts, along with contracting-out, increased workloads and new work schedules. It was the final straw in a series of ever growing concessionary demands by the owners of the *Detroit Free Press* and *Detroit News*, nationwide multinewspaper corporations Gannett and Knight-Ridder: 'They put demands on the table in 1995 that they knew the unions could not possibly accept – and they forced the strike'.[36]

Jolted out of their customary 'labor–management cooperation' mindset, the six Detroit newspaper locals issued a joint strike call in July 1995. Yet their central strategy for winning the strike, an appeal to readers and advertisers to boycott the papers, failed to impress Knight-Ridder: 'We're going to hire a whole new workforce and go on without unions, or they can surrender unconditionally and salvage what they can'.[37]

From the beginning, the union leaderships at both local and international level were woefully unprepared to confront this level of corporate aggression, unlike the newspaper companies, which 'had spent *years* preparing for their showdown ... They had a scab workforce in place, ready to be sent in without delay'.[38] Much of this 'scab workforce' was drawn from the large African-American population of Detroit, understandably alienated by whites' near-monopoly of the well paid newspaper jobs. Ironically, the experience of the strike itself opened many previously oblivious workers' eyes to racism; but by that time it was too late, at least this time round.

Despite the lack of preparation, the outrage and commitment of the rank and file was not in doubt. The 2,500 strikers acted from the start to supplement the consumer boycott strategy with determined moves to stop production and distribution of the newspapers. In July and August, mass pickets at the *Detroit News* printing plants escalated into all-night actions; local police reacted violently, pepper-gassing a crowd of several hundred pickets who were blocking the plant entrance. After pickets were almost killed when company trucks moved towards the line at high speed, a local judge issued an injunction restricting the number of pickets, providing a welcome excuse for the local union leaderships to tamp down the level of militancy; they changed the next Saturday night picket to a drive around the plant, allegedly to block traffic.

This non-picket marked the last occasion on which any serious attempt was made to use concerted action to block production or distribution of the papers. In July 1996, increasingly frustrated rank-and-file activists formed their own organisation, Action Coalition of Strikers and Supporters (ACOSS), calling on strikers and supporters to 'shut down Motown' as a way of outflanking the increasingly oblivious corporate hierarchy. Meanwhile, the union leadership continued to emphasise boycotting the papers as a central strategy.

In Detroit itself, the boycott appeared highly effective. The number of front-lawn placards announcing 'No Detroit News or Free Press Here' sprouted visibly in the first months of the dispute; the local UAW encouraged workers at the local auto factories to boycott the paper. As a result, circulation dropped by 37 per cent. Advertisers proved surprisingly supportive, withdrawing to the tune of hundreds of millions of dollars. This kind of local solidarity provided an ongoing boost to strikers' morale throughout the long dispute. What it could not do was to win it.

It was hardly surprising that the drop in circulation and advertising failed to bring Gannett and Knight-Ridder to the negotiating table. As nationwide corporations, their Detroit publications were one small part of a multibillion-dollar operation which continued to reap serious profits. At no time during the three-year dispute was the loss of revenue in Detroit more than an irritating thorn in the side of two massive conglomerates owning 118 papers and raking in millions in profits. The strikers' courageous slogan of lasting 'one day longer' than these multibillion-dollar corporations was perhaps 'a pipedream from the beginning'.[39]

Yet strikers' hopes rose when the leadership explored another, legalistic option, making an 'unconditional return to work' offer in February 1997. This apparently ignominious surrender was in fact a precondition under US law for pleading that the employers' handling of the strike constituted an 'unfair labour practice' under the National Labor Relations Act.

At first, the strategy seemed to meet with stunning success; on 19 June 1997 an NLRB judge did indeed rule that the conduct of the strike reflected 'unfair labour practices' and that the employers were legally bound to take the locked-out workers back. In line with its decision, the board issued an injunction forcing the papers to take back the strikers while the case made its slow progress through the courts. It seemed like a turning point in the dispute.

But, to the dismay and astonishment of both strikers and their leaders, the injunction was denied. Though activists had rejected the legalistic route, the decision left them directionless and hurt. As one rank and filer reported, 'Morale is really low. People have called me crying … The leadership plan had us so upbeat about [the injunction] that we never talked about what we would do if we didn't get it'.[40]

But there was one more arrow in the militants' quiver – the long cherished project of a major march and rally in Detroit, attracting nationwide support, which would 'shut down Motown'. This dream was revived by the AFL-CIO's decision to hold its next 'Solidarity Day' march in Detroit. While no march or rally, however vigorous, could have persuaded the newspaper employers to relent, the notion of a protest mobilising national outrage at this assault on workers in a 'union town' reenergised the militants. ACOSS acted quickly to lobby the AFL-CIO, but it took months for the AFL finally to approve a national demonstration for 20–21 June 1997. Even then, organising a nationally based march and rally was left largely to a small number of desperate ACOSS activists working night and day out of a cramped Detroit AFL-CIO office. The one full-time worker 'lent' by the AFL soon found that his main task was to destroy 'the wide perception … that the strike was over',[41] making the task of rallying hundreds of thousands of workers to Detroit to show solidarity an uphill struggle.

Given the obstacles, the numbers were impressive. Over 100,000 workers took part, an estimated 10,000 from outside the state. But, inevitably, the mobilisation fell far short of bringing Detroit to a standstill. As such, the strike lost the only impetus that could have carried it much further forward. While Detroit city buses continued to bear the union-funded legend 'It's not over!', and faithful Detroiters kept the 'No Detroit News or Free Press Here' signs on their lawns, the struggle, waged by a smaller and smaller band of activists, took on an increasingly symbolic character.

As with so many strikes in this era and others, the most positive outcome was a transformed consciousness amongst conservative workers who had rarely taken part in any previous dispute and whose attitude towards their employer had been one of unquestioning acceptance. Many Detroit newspaper employees had worked for the papers for generations and had seen the Detroit News Agency as a 'family' which they had trusted to an extent which made the betrayal still more bitter. One striker vented his fury: 'The CEO said he would fight us till we "all go away or die." ... I am not leaving ... and if I should happen to die first ... I'm teaching the kids to take up where I left off'.[42]

A LONG LIST OF LOST CAUSES ...

Struggles in Decatur and Detroit were matched by struggles across the Atlantic as British workers rebelled against a parallel employer agenda. In early 1993, workers at the Dundee plant of US-based corporation Timex were confronted with a twelve-month pay freeze, layoffs, and a 10 per cent cut in the value of their fringe benefits. The 320 workers, largely women, struck immediately against the proposals; when, 'under protest', they returned to work, the entire workforce was dismissed.

Despite their outrage and fighting spirit, the strikers stood little chance. In true American style, Timex rapidly brought in replacement workers; the plant convenor's conviction that the company would have 'difficulties recruiting enough scab labour with the right skills' was undermined by the relatively unskilled nature of the operation and the fact that in work-starved Dundee there would be no shortage of 'scabs' queuing up for training.

Yet even a limited amount of practical solidarity might have won the dispute. The strikers belonged to the Amalgamated Union of

Engineering Workers (AEEU), a historically strong craft-based organisation, and their dispute was taking place in a heartland of labour struggle. The potential for organising meaningful solidarity was shown when 7,000 workers spontaneously walked out of their workplaces and marched past the factory gates in protest at the lock-out. The Timex dispute 'struck a chord';[43] workers throughout Scotland and beyond turned out for mass pickets at the Timex gates, where Arthur Scargill received 'rapturous applause' for his call for a 24-hour general strike to reinstate the Timex workers.[44] As usual, however, rapture and inspiration were not enough. Despite a resolution in support of the Timex strikers at the annual conference of Manufacturing, Science, Finance (MSF), the supervisory workers' union, MSF and even AEEU supervisors continued working at the plant, 'transporting and training [scabs]', according to the sacked workers.[45]

The Timex dispute became a cause célèbre, inspiring demonstrations outside the American Embassy and even a promise by President Clinton to discard his Timex watch. But consumer boycotts and even the strike committee's new found strategy of 'seeking solidarity abroad' – making links with organised Timex plants in Norway and Denmark – were no match for a powerful and confident multinational determined to break with traditional labour practices.

Similar 'lost cause' struggles, fought with dedication but little hope of real gain without strong union leadership, included the disastrous Burnsall's debacle in 1992–93. Here a group of immigrant workers, again mainly women, challenged an autocratic Midlands small business for the right to membership of the GMB general union. While the dispute could be characterised as a latter-day Grunwick, in this case the problem lay with too little mass picketing rather than too much and 'too violent'. Although the tiny plant lay at the end of a short narrow lane, meaning deliveries could easily have been rendered impassable, the GMB refused to sanction any more than a token picket. Essential supplies passed through with impunity.

The GMB explained its failure to act primarily in terms of the legal limit on picketing, but also invoked the god of 'public opinion'. One critical activist described Burnsall's as 'the supreme example of a strike dominated by pointless "PR"-style perspectives by the local leadership, while real solidarity action ... was put beyond the pale, as usual, by "the law"'.[46] A plethora of similar disputes based in genuine and crucial issues of union derecognition (Arrowsmith's printers), job flexibility (Peugeot), pay cuts and working time changes (Spartan Redheugh, Hillier's engineering plants), plant closures (Lyon's Maid ice cream) or privatisation (Crawley refuse collectors) were greeted overwhelmingly, during these years, by moral rather than practical support. While strikers clearly had a different conception of what was needed – for one Lyon's Maid worker, 'This is class war and solidarity is the only way out'[47] – verbal protestations of solidarity were often accepted as interchangeable with the real thing.

ARTHUR'S BARMY ARMY

Yet only months before, in late October 1992, a seismic shift in the ideological outlook of British society had taken place – a sea change which took the well worn mantra of 'public support' to a new and uniquely transformative level. Two massive demonstrations attracted the kind of 'broad support' lusted after by the TUC as hundreds of thousands of marching workers decked with union banners rocked the centre of London; millionaires leaned out of their Park Lane windows to cheer them on, and supporters crammed the streets as the city ground to a halt. From derided and little-heeded leader of a defeated army, miners' leader Arthur Scargill was rocketed to divine status on the front page of every tabloid in the land, the *Daily Mirror* lauding him, beneath a full-page full-colour photograph, as 'a hero to both rich and poor'.[48] The superintendent of the South Yorkshire police who had arrested Scargill on the Orgreave picket-line in 1984 offered him a public apology.

A revolutionary's drunken fantasy? A socialist's wet dream? No; for a week to ten days this was actually the national mood in Britain, as an Alice in Wonderland-like reversal of the dominant ideology seized the land. And the occasion? The Tory government's announcement of the immediate closure of 31 of the last 50 British Coal pits, meaning 30,000 more miners would lose their jobs.

In response, 'Middle England … rose momentarily as one … The forward march of Thatcherism [was] halted in the coalfields, of all places'.[49] But it was not only the middle class, of course, that was outraged. The foremost constituency under attack was, as always, the working class; and the miners had retained their reputation, it seemed, as that class's spearhead. The attack on the miners sparked the pent-up anger of millions of workers. As an NUM activist put it, 'The pits have proved a catalyst for the massive anger and frustration workers feel about the wrecking policies of this government ... *enough is enough*.[50]

The aftermath of the pit closures announcement saw a storm of demonstrations, solidarity strikes, 'days of action' by trades councils across the country, and pit occupations by miners and Women Against Pit Closures. Public feeling was so strong that the government was forced, almost immediately, to retrench; Tory minister Michael Heseltine, the author of the infamous announcement, apologised to Parliament, the inevitable 'Inquiry' was set up, and the High Court ruled that the closure plans were 'unlawful'. The immediate result was that the government was unable to go forward with its plans for the ten most immediately threatened pits, earmarked for closure by the end of January 1993.

Yet all the outrage in the world, without focused and organised expression, would not ultimately turn the Tories from their course; and that focus and organisation, it soon became clear, would not be forthcoming from the leadership of the labour movement. An early warning was sounded when speakers at the huge October demonstrations included representatives of the Confederation of British Industry (CBI) and the Liberal Democrats, basically a liberal ruling-class party. TUC willingness to embrace a 'broad spectrum' of political and industrial interests was only the beginning of the usual fusty mixture of demonstrations, resolutions and reconvened committees which constituted the TUC's response to working-class anger and despair.

At first, the strength of feeling was such that significant sections of workers acted without waiting for leadership. In the days after the closures were announced, grass-roots activists in rail planned solidarity action and, crucially, power workers at many of the threatened pits went on strike. While demands on the TUC to call a general strike gradually subsided, one sacked miner expressed a general sentiment when he mused, 'Last October, when there was such a wave of public sympathy for the miners, we should have had every union out on strike. People were really on our side; we didn't capitalize on it enough'.[51]

Though Scargill and his 'barmy army' of NUM members struggled valiantly to secure TUC support for wider action, it was not until April 1993 that they received approval for a joint one-day strike with the railway workers; even then, the TUC refused to sanction support from other unions, and the right-wing Union of Democratic Mineworkers (UDM) kept its members at work. And so the opportunity was lost. Though the brouhaha of meetings, rallies, conferences and even the much disputed 'days of action' (which the TUC hastened to explain 'did not include strikes') lasted for weeks and even months, the initial eruption of anger faded into resentment and fatalism. For the second time in ten years, the miners had lost; when British Coal was finally sold off in December 1994, 'only 8,000 miners remained on its book ... in an industry which employed well over a million men at the time of the 1926 General Strike'.[52] And, like that General Strike, the struggle was lost largely through the trade union leadership's fear of what it might have meant to win.

'WORKERS FROM ACROSS THE PLANET'

Unfortunately, the same verdict could be given on what was perhaps the mother and father of all lost causes in the 1990s, the Liverpool dockers' dispute. This was a strike which garnered impressive, in fact dazzling support around the world, while failing to organise even the most elementary solidarity at home. Yet ten years earlier, it could have been won within weeks in the dockers' own back yard.

The Liverpool dispute began in September 1995 after 80 workers were sacked by Torside, a subcontractor of the Merseyside Docks and Harbour Company (MDHC). The Torside dockers mounted a picketline, which 326 MDHC workers refused to cross, only to be sacked themselves. The merged group of sacked dockers refused to take 'severance' and set up their own picket-lines outside the Merseyside ports. A dispute which was to last three years and span at least three continents had begun.

Despite its historical origins in the docks, the Transport and General Workers' Union (TGWU) refused to support the Liverpool dispute on the grounds that it broke the anti-union laws and thus would 'put the union's funds at risk'. It was quite true that the dockers' action broke the anti-union laws; it demonstrated solidarity, almost the first principle the Thatcher government had been at pains to outlaw. The T&G's position, however, was disastrous for the dockers. Within six weeks the company had replaced enough of the sacked dockers to resume operations.

After that it was all smoke and mirrors, though smoke and mirrors more impressive and moving than most. By early 1996 these 460 workers had gained the backing of fellow-dockers as far afield as the USA when longshoremen from Newark, New Jersey, refused to work a ship belonging to one of MDHC's client companies; this international support was replicated by dockers in Canada, Australia, Sweden, Spain, Italy and Japan. Later that year the Liverpool dockers, most of whom had never organised any kind of union event, brought together dockers from across the world in a conference to promote rank-and-file international solidarity.

It worked; 20 January 1997 saw a staggering display of international action as dockers in 27 countries struck for a day to express their backing for the Liverpool dockers. West Coast members of the International Longshoremen's and Warehousemen's Union (ILWU) 'walked off the job from San Diego to Seattle'. Dockers in Denmark, Germany and Japan joined the protest, and 'unions from Hong Kong to Kenya and Spain to Zimbabwe sent messages of solidarity'.[53] On 8 September 1997, the two-year anniversary of the strike, ILWU members shut down all West Coast ports as part of another international day of solidarity.

International action, international conferences; it was impressive, and it was stirring. But none of it got the dockers their jobs back. By contrast, 'If ... Liverpool's tugboat operators had come out on strike, the MDHC's operations would have been frozen virtually overnight'.[54] In fact the tugboat workers, themselves T&G members, had undertaken a number of strike days in support of the dockers at the start of the dispute. Yet TGWU leaders were 'central to stifling such solidarity, arguing that the strikes are unofficial [and] illegal'.[55] Not only the local union leadership but the dockers' own stewards vetoed the tugboat workers' action; likewise, they 'discouraged the several offers of secondary action which came from other workers in ... Merseyside during September and October 1995'.[56] Though rank-and-file dockers – as well as local carworkers, postal and local government workers – chafed for this support, they were unable to move their much respected stewards from the route of solidarity abroad and compliance at home.

In many ways the Liverpool dockers' dispute symbolised a kind of 'globaloney' specific to the labour movement – the notion that international workers' movements can be built with little reference to the strength or otherwise of the movement at home. The dedicated and committed Liverpool dockers could build 'a grassroots organisation that linked together workers from across the planet';[57] yet, on their own home ground, the caution of official and even unofficial union leadership, combined with the lack of an effective rank-and-file network, allowed for their ultimate defeat.

FROM WINTER TO SUMMER ...

And yet, and yet ... articles in British newspapers of the mid 1990s suggested a different, more hopeful picture – one of resurgence and militancy, of the resurfacing of 'old-fashioned' industrial struggle. Responding to the claim of a 'new militancy' among union members by TUC secretary John Monks in the autumn of 1995, activists agreed: 'Monks is right – they are more militant'; 'People are more angry now than they have been for years'. A 'catalogue of work unrest' listed in the *Guardian* listed prospective strikes by telecommunication and engineering workers, civil servants and London Underground workers over pay, safety and the shorter working week. An industrial relations survey, noting that a third of unionised employees had experienced some industrial unrest the previous year, concluded that 'more industrial tension existed under the surface than would appear at first sight'.[58]

Nine months later, the spectre of worker revolt reemerged in the question, 'Is now the summer of our discontent?'.[59] After MPs had awarded themselves a pay rise of 26 per cent, even the non-TUC Royal College of Nursing was moved to fight for more than its own 2 per cent offer, while UNISON members in higher education were disposed to reject a still more miserly 1.5 per cent. Action already being taken by rail workers in ASLEF and the RMT, along with postal workers, was seen as likely to spread, encouraged by an impressive settlement by British Air Line Pilots Association (BALPA) airline pilots with British Airways the previous week.

The constant media surprise at 'industrial tension' was perhaps understandable, given the mystification of what 'exists under the surface' to provoke it. Yet the array of employer offensives cited by workers on the rare occasions they were consulted, from 'rotten wages' and 'more work for less pay' to 'lack of job security', should make such continued conflict less than a surprise. In the 1990s as much as the 1970s – if still more aggressively – employers' agendas were governed by profitability, while workers' less calculated response was encapsulated in the comment of an USDAW activist that 'People don't take strike action for the fun of it, they do it as a last resort'.[60] The key struggles of the early to mid 1990s – Staley, Caterpillar, Detroit Newspapers, Timex and the Liverpool docks – could have been accounted for in the same words.

6
Into the 2000s: Seattle ... and September

The last few years of the twentieth century began with a bang – and ended with anything but a whimper when union activists and environmentalists joined in a triumphant trashing of the supreme symbol of globalisation, the World Trade Organisation. The 'bang' was the successful American UPS dispute in the summer of 1997, which illustrated in action the principles of membership mobilisation and democracy long promoted by Teamsters for a Democratic Union (TDU). While the Teamster president, Ron Carey, was not a member of TDU, his reelection in late 1996 was crucial in affirming an atmosphere in which these principles could flourish within the union – and, from start to finish, govern the conduct of the UPS dispute.

'OH, YEAH?'

A central 'back-story' to the UPS strike was the company's determination to use employee involvement and team concept techniques to coopt and divide the workforce. Two years before the existing five-year pay agreement was due to run out in 1997, UPS had identified team concept as the beachhead which would breach worker unity and create a sufficient degree of divided loyalties to ensure the usual management triumph. Typical company tactics included identifying and coopting 'natural leaders', the quality-circle-style programme KORE ('Keeping Our Reputation For Excellence'), and mantras of 'competitiveness' and 'job security' aimed at undermining workers' unity and morale.

This time, however, the union was ready. In early 1995, when UPS started holding team meetings at a depot in California, Teamster activists were armed with TDU and *Labor Notes* materials which had arrived overnight (by UPS, of course). Some vivid parodies of 'team' ideology ensued, as when 'a union member got up and declared himself team-leader-for-life and all the other members started bowing down before him'.[1] Exasperated, management terminated the programme after six weeks.

This new, TDU-influenced union leadership was also prepared to reject the kind of concessions which former Teamster 'business agents' had meekly accepted for decades. Despite profits of $1.15bn and a more than healthy profit rate of 19.4 per cent, UPS was now demanding expansion of its part-time workforce, increased contracting-out, and a company takeover of union health and pension funds. The 'reward' would be a pay increase for full-timers of 90 cents an hour spread over seven years, while part-timers, whose pay had remained static at $8 an hour since 1982, were offered precisely zero.

Yet worse sets of proposals had seen union leaders rolling over in the past. The difference, in 1997, was not that the company's stance was any worse than in many previous contracts; it was that, at last, the union was prepared to stand up for its members. A central pillar of the Teamster approach was to challenge the spread of part-time work within UPS – not by taking jobs from part-timers, but by making more part-time jobs into full-time ones.

This crucial break from 'business as usual' union collusion – previous Teamster leaders had permitted, if not encouraged, the spread of lower-paid part-time work – was backed by conscious, and extensive, strike preparation. Well before the contract expiration date in July 1997, the union began hiring rank-and-file activists as full-time organisers and developing 'member to member' networks which organised a series of escalating actions aimed specifically at building unity between full-timers and part-timers. In another significant deviation from the norm, Teamster leaders kept members informed on the progress of negotiations throughout; this horrified the UPS negotiator, who argued plaintively that 'In the past, commitments were made to not speak to the members ... the communication of ... negotiations often raises the expectations of those people who ultimately could be voting on the ratification of the agreement'.[2]

'Raising expectations' was, of course, exactly what this union leadership was about. On 2 August, after intensive negotiating had produced no change in the company's 'last and final offer', the 200,000 UPS workers walked out on strike. The goal of 10,000 new full-time jobs not only mobilised an enthusiastic UPS membership but sparked a wave of working-class support across America; national polls showed 55 per cent support for the Teamsters and only 27 per cent for UPS, despite the considerable inconvenience caused by the strike. Capturing the mood, a UPS driver from Atlanta proclaimed: 'We're striking for every worker in America. We can't have only low, service-industry wages in this country'.[3]

As the action took hold, UPS lost $30m a day. Despite its bullish posture, the company began to lose heart: 'If I had known that it was going to go from negotiating for UPS to negotiating for part-time America, we would've approached it differently', a UPS executive later told *Business Week*.[4] In the face of a united, mobilised strike force and a massive wave of working-class support, the once mighty multinational collapsed within 15 days, conceding the bulk of the union's previously 'non-negotiable' demands. The company agreed to create 10,000 new full-time jobs, to raise pensions by up to 50 per cent within the existing Teamster plan, to eliminate subcontracting, and to raise wages by $3.10 an hour over five (not seven) years, with extra increases for part-timers. For the first time in decades, a united, mobilised workforce had decisively defeated one of America's leading corporations.

UPSers were jubilant; but the celebrations extended well beyond them into the wider labour movement. Returning UPS strikers were greeted with cheers and standing ovations as they renewed their deliveries to workplaces around the country.[5] The strike victory was widely seen as a turning point for labour after its long slide into the doldrums: 'For nearly 20 years, unions have endured a string of highly visible defeats ... pundits have concluded that unions are no longer needed or relevant. Now the Teamsters have stood up and said, "Oh, yeah?"'.[6]

FAIRNESS NOT FAVOURS

The decade, then, began its ending on a winning note; and the same might have been said for Britain in the wake of Tony Blair's landslide Labour victory on 7 May 1997. On that triumphant night, even those all too aware of what 'New Labour' held in store for the working class could bask in the illusion, at least, of social transformation. The glorious cascade of revenge as Tory MPs dropped like ninepins from apparently unassailable seats lit up, like a lightning flash, a hidden agenda of class revolt. It was a short honeymoon, however, and a long hangover for those at the sharp end of a government which assured the rich that they would be safe in New Labour's hands, while the trade union movement was held at arm's length with stern admonitions to 'join the real world'.

Blair made his position clear from the beginning: the labour movement was to receive 'fairness, not favours'. This was New Labour code for the firm exclusion of union influence from anything resembling the corridors of power: 'Distancing is scarcely the word to describe the succession of public putdowns [and] denunciations heaped ... on [the] movement ...'. Yet union leaders continued to hope; at one point, Blair was reported to have asked, 'Do these guys really understand that I mean what I say?'. In an almost exact echo of the TUC's disbelief that Thatcher could really be as bad as she had said she was, one senior union leader pleaded after the election, 'I simply can't believe that the attitude adopted in the election period is going to be the normal state of affairs'.[7]

Of course – just as with Thatcher – it was. The Tory cascade of cuts, privatisation, 'labour market flexibility' and low pay (unrelieved by a minimalist minimum wage) continued as Blair stuck unwaveringly to the market forces agenda of his predecessors. Labour's much vaunted Employment Relations Bill boiled down to a US-style system of trade union recognition – the kind which most American organisers now found a burden rather than an asset – a (miserable) minimum wage of £3.60 an hour, and some extensions of unfair dismissal and maternity leave entitlements.

Nevertheless, during what was still the honeymoon period of the late 1990s, the TUC remained anxious to promote itself as a 'social partner' with both business and government. Just after the election, the TUC, along with Barclays Bank, GEC, Unilever, ICI, British Aerospace and other major employers, dutifully signed up to a 'partners for progress' plan sponsored by the government. In his enthusiastic endorsement of 'a more consultative approach' as having 'real benefits' for employers, perhaps the TUC leader had in mind Barclays Bank, which the same week had announced the loss of 6,000 jobs. Indeed, Barclays was cited as 'an example of how the new partnership approach could work'; unions were said to have had a 'constructive role' in implementing the job cuts.[8]

The New Labour regime appeared to begin in suitably non-confrontational mode; one analysis showing strikes at their lowest point since 1891 cheered the TUC, which saw it as evidence of 'trade unions and management working together for the common good ... These figures should nail the myth that trade unions are adversaries and show good employers they have little to fear from a proper partnership relation with trade unions'.[9]

A tree falls in the forest ...

Unfortunately for those with no wish to frighten employers, a plethora of disputes erupted within weeks of Labour's 1997 victory. As early as July of that year, British Airways (BA) cabin staff walked out (or 'sicked-out') over BA's imposition of a pay package which included cuts in overtime, 'back to back' shifts, and extended roster times. Faced with a barrage of management threats against strike action, including sackings, loss of promotion, and lawsuits, 'plane-loads of cabin staff headed straight for their GPs' surgeries with an epidemic of stress symptoms'.[10] While 350 workers took part in offi-cial strike action, over 2000 were 'off sick', costing the hapless British Airways £100m in lost business and still more opprobrium for their managerial incompetence. The outcome was a less dracon-ian form of 'restructuring', though one which retained the basic principle of changed work rules.

While the BA strike was still in progress, one-day strikes by postal workers and London Underground train drivers provoked uneasy comments on the 'growing signs of industrial unrest'. Other such signs included strikes by Birds Eye workers, shop assistants at the elite Harrods store, carworkers at Peugeot, Rolls Royce engineering workers and firefighters in Derby;[11] less publicised were ongoing industrial action by rail workers and college teachers against privati-sation, strikes by bank staff, and unofficial workplace action at Ford's Dagenham plant over the racial harassment of its largely black and Asian workforce.

One way of dealing with the irritating tendency of conflict to recur was to fall back on the comforting assurance that strike action was an irrational response to rational and inevitable developments in technology and work organisation: 'What seems to be fuelling the current discontent is the attempted corporate management of change'.[12] But whatever the explanation offered, the surge of indus-trial unrest seemed to buck the statistics, which were presented in the respected Workplace Industrial Relations Survey (WIRS) as indi-cating 'the virtual disappearance of the strike as a feature of British industrial relations'.[13]

One explanation of the paradox may lie simply in the method whereby strike incidence was reported and defined; one analysis of the WIRS report notes 'a significant discrepancy in the incidence of industrial action between the accounts of worker representatives and managers'.[14] Indeed, WIRS itself reported that 'A quarter ... of union representatives said there had been some form of collective dispute over pay or conditions in the previous year'.[15] Half of these took place without a ballot, suggesting higher levels of unofficial action than recorded by management.

Not only the struggle beneath the statistics, but the actual existence of strikes and conflicts tended to become increasingly obscure; as neoliberalism entrenched its postindustrial 'discourse' in the 1990s, labour reporting itself sank without trace in most news outlets. A two-month-long occupation by engineering workers at Glacier Metals in Scotland, which ended in victory on 1 January 1997, received almost no media coverage in Britain; in America, one eminent labour historian 'stumbled upon' a strike in Morgantown, North Carolina which, he 'soon learnt', was part of 'a decade-long war of position ...'.[16]

Yet obscuring struggles could not stop them from taking place; one paradoxical result of the increased invisibility of strikes in the 1990s was that workers failed to hear of setbacks, as well as remaining largely unaware of strike victories. Less than a year after the UPS victory, rank-and-file action at General Motors (GM) replicated the string of actions in 1996 which had almost shut down the auto giant's entire assembly operation; when workers at a key metal stamping plant in Flint, Michigan walked out in June 1998, 'General Motors plants started going down like dominos'.[17] Twenty-seven of GM's 29 assembly plants, and over 100 parts plants in the US, Canada and Mexico were shut down by the loss of production at two plants in Flint, again demonstrating the vulnerability built into 'just-in-time' delivery systems. The action won the restoration of transferred work, but did not prevent GM from 'spinning off' the whole of its Delphi parts-plant unit, despite promises made to placate the strikers.

'On the line in '95'

Strikes – obscure, victorious, betrayed – were not the only arena of struggle. In early 1999, workers delivered 'a stunning blow' to America's best known example of labour–management cooperation – 'Saturn, the "different kind of car company"'.[18] With a voter turnout of 85 per cent, workers swept aside the United Auto Workers (UAW) 'vision team', which had supported labour–management cooperation, and elected union activists standing for a traditional union-style collective agreement.

The membership revolt was not based on nostalgia for times gone by, but on an unsentimental awareness of the real impact of UAW-supported 'jointness' on workers' everyday lives. The rebels' slogan was 'Rebalance them. On the line in '95'. In a *Labor Notes* translation: '"Rebalance" is Saturn's term for doing the same work with fewer people. "Them" refers to the Vision Team. And "on the line" means: put Vision Team members to work on the factory floor rather than in the quasi-management positions they currently enjoy'.[19] The 'jointness' system meant hundreds of union representatives patrolling the shop floor and maintaining the pressure of work under Saturn's lean production system. These representatives had no share in the onerous conditions, like ten-hour and weekend shifts, imposed on 'ordinary' workers.

The resentment and anger that had been building among the workforce over these injustices exploded once the campaign for a new leadership took root. From silence and isolation blossomed rank and-file involvement, and in turn action blossomed: ' ... people started the tradition of writing letters and putting them out on the shop floor ... It was so different from your usual campaign ... It was your basic grassroots movement'.[20] The Saturn reversal, in its own inconspicuous way, was a classic of materially based shopfloor resistance against the apparently unassailable conjunction of managerial ideology and bureaucratic union consent.

DEFINING THE 1990s

What both the successes and the – undeserved – failures of the late 1990s had done was to show, as always, what was possible. At UPS, the key factor in beating an apparently intractable corporation was rank-and-file membership mobilisation, a precious commodity allowed by most union leaderships to atrophy into 'apathy'; at Flint in 1998, it was the old lesson, given a new twist by high-tech 'lean' and 'just-in-time' production techniques, of how to turn capital's organisation of work against itself. In Britain, signs of 'trade union renewal'[21] in the late 1990s were based, paradoxically, on the impact of privatisation, which sparked new forms of organisation in response to the very structures intended to cheapen labour and weaken worker resistance.

Anti-privatisation actions by London Underground workers continued throughout the late 1990s, culminating in a two-day strike in February 1999 which cost 'business' in London up to

£70m;[22] in May, Felixstowe dockers bucked the trend of defeat and demoralisation in their industry with an 80 per cent vote to strike over attacks on pay and working conditions. A long-running struggle by electricians in construction against flexible working and pay cuts had 'the tabloids scream[ing]: "It's the Winter of Discontent all over again" ...'.[23]

Thus, by the end of the 1990s, the fortunes of the British labour movement were once again left to the 'old-fashioned' resources of the working class. The hoped-for 'employee rights' legislation – that lodestar to which the trade union leadership had hung on so hopefully for so long – conceded very little to workers; while some minimal increase in union recognition did ensue from the passing of the Employment Relations Act in 1999, employers were soon wriggling around even these modest proposals by separating their workforces into different 'bargaining units'. Meanwhile, the Act as a whole retained every iota of the laws which Blair had proudly described as 'the most restrictive on trade unions in the western world'.[24] By now, those laws had been challenged internationally for their contravention of agreements on workers' rights. Yet Blair announced firmly: 'The essential elements of the 1980s legislation will remain'.[25]

It seemed that it was struggle, rather than legislation, which would make the decisive difference to the British labour movement. And it was at this point that, for a transcendent moment, the agenda of capital was brought to a halt with an astounding act of defiance against global capital in which labour – the rank-and-file variety – played an essential part. As the century shifted on its axis, students and workers, anarchists and 'Reagan Democrats', environmentalists and union activists, united in the Battle of Seattle.

THE PROTEST OF THE CENTURY

Seattle was famous worldwide; as the massive street protests flashed across the world on the night of 30 November 1999, anarchist protesters chanted, 'The Whole World Is Watching' – and they were right. But not just anarchists. The major importance of Seattle was that it united a range of anti-globalisation groups – 'tree-huggers', students, anti-capitalist revolutionaries and anti-establishment youth – with a significant constituency of labour activists.

The Seattle demonstrations were not a bolt from the blue, though their impact was. By November 1999, when the now five-year-old

World Trade Organisation was to meet in Seattle's convention centre, a major anti-globalisation movement was already in existence. Fuelled largely by student activists and anarchists, its members had stopped the streets of major cities on a number of occasions to protest against the impact of globalisation. And now, in late 1999, thousands were planning to travel to Seattle for the 'Protest of the Century'.[26]

As early as 7 a.m. on 30 November, the first day of the WTO convention, locked-out steelworkers from the nearby Kaiser steelmill led a march to the convention centre, while in the 'downtown' area, thousands of people were already sitting down, linking arms, and chaining themselves together. The Battle of Seattle had begun.

Organised labour, however, took longer to join in; by the time the AFL-CIO march started, protestors had been occupying the streets of Seattle for over five hours. After penning thousands of union activists inside a huge stadium for interminable speeches, the AFL-CIO finally led a 35,000-strong march to the convention centre; but by then, activists were chafing to join the real action. Although AFL-CIO organisers changed the route of the march to avoid the downtown 'zone of conflict', a significant number of trade unionists broke away and joined the protests. Thousands of workers mingled with environmentalists, fought off riot police, and joined the protestors' heady chant – 'Whose Streets? Our Streets!'.

And the streets of Seattle were, indeed, the people's streets – for a few brief but exhilarating hours in which labour activists played a central part alongside groupings which had, in many cases, regarded labour as part of the enemy. The immortal image of environmental activists clad in giant turtle shells marching, shouting and taking the streets side by side with stereotypically 'macho' truckers sparked the moving epitaph: 'Teamsters and Turtles, Together At Last'.[27] And the action succeeded in the scarcely credible aim of shutting down the WTO conference; only 500 of the 3,000 delegates were able to reach the opening ceremony, which was cancelled. Throughout the day, the business of the WTO was put on hold. In a breathtaking reversal of power and priorities, the masses in the streets had jammed the smoothly running works of the international capitalist class.

It could hardly last. The police began to take their revenge soon afterwards, driving demonstrators back from the city centre to the 'uptown' Capitol Hill district with tear gas and bullets. Even here, however, the union activists who had been central to the 'downtown' protests remained in the thick of the fray, helping to defend the notoriously gay neighbourhood from police attack until the early hours – an action typical of the 'unlikely coalition' of causes, the brief utopia of solidarity which summarised Seattle. As one Teamsters for a Democratic Union (TDU) activist pointed out, 'It was rank-and-file members and reform leaders who were in the streets when the going got tough'. And rank-and-file activism was the force behind the unique configuration of protest which catapulted Seattle 1999 into the headlines and pushed labour, at least temporarily, into the front line of the new millennium.

SEVEN DAYS THAT SHOOK NEW LABOUR

A rather different configuration took brief, but total, control of Britain in that millennium's first year. During one surreal week in September 2000, a 'leaderless revolt'[28] against exorbitant fuel taxes catapulted previously obscure road haulage workers and small farmers into the headlines when they came together to blockade oil depots and refineries: 'These are the actions of desperate people ... We are dying on our feet'.[29]

Within a few days supermarkets were running out of food, ambulance services had imposed speed limits, and funeral directors were reporting that they had enough petrol to pick up bodies, but not to bury them. However, the protest's efficacy was due not only to the blockades but to support for the protests by oil tanker drivers. Compared to the standard 5,000–5,800, only about 100 oil tankers were on the road during the dispute.

The apparently middle-class character of the 'motley alliance of farmers, hauliers and fishermen' conducting the protests, along with the dubious role of the oil tanker companies, who clearly shared an interest in reducing fuel taxes, watered down support from many on the left. Yet this petit bourgeois revolution had a working-class trajectory. The revolt could never have got off the ground if not for unionised oil tanker drivers who supported the protests, respected the blockades, and refused to drive 'scab' oil tankers, effectively paralysing the movement of fuel. While oil tankers normally left the refineries every few minutes, 'during the protest only one an hour got out. And they were carrying fuel for the emergency services alone'.[30]

The self-employed road hauliers were in many cases ex-employees 'contracted out' by cost-cutting transport companies; drivers themselves saw little difference between the two categories. As one tanker driver put it, 'We are all in the same boat. Everyone suffers from high fuel prices'. The 'close-knit community' of the drivers ensured solidarity; 'At the end of the day ... they knew they would have to share the road with us afterwards'.[31]

Such grass-roots connections were invisible to the union leadership, which cited the tacit support of some oil companies as a reason to label the protests a 'bosses' blockade'. For the TUC, the revolt was 'not a legitimate form of industrial action but a challenge to democracy and a crude attempt to hold the country to ransom'.[32] The general secretary of the TGWU ordered his members back to work, saying, 'The campaign has crossed the line from democracy and into anarchy';[33] some union leaders called on the pickets to be hauled in front of the courts like striking miners in the 1980s.

References to the miners' strike were apt; many of the 'middle England' citizens most hostile to the miners in 1984–85 now declared, 'looking back at it', that 'the miners and Arthur Scargill were right to go in for militant action'.[34] Members of the protest coalition made the same connections: 'An Essex farmer admitted this week that only now did he understand and sympathise with the reasons for the miners' strike in the 1980s'.[35]

In many ways, the protest stirred up the latent resentment among the general population at the disappointments of the Blair government; in the words of one taxi driver, 'Blair ... should know that 90 per cent of the public are with them, not him'.[36] Despite its dubious class composition and sometimes xenophobic politics, the movement struck the chord of 'a deep well of frustration and anger'. How, one reporter wondered, could 'terminally uncool people in shell suits ... and tweed jackets get to man the barricades?'.[37] It was exactly such 'terminally uncool people' who had made Blair's 1997 victory possible, but now the '*Sun*-reading, self-employed lorryman' had 'turned rebellious and broken out of New Labour's clutches'.[38]

The political implications of the dispute were brought out by its 'dual power' character; 'pickets are voting on a case-by-case basis whether to let the tankers out of the refinery ... the driver presents his case to the picket-line and awaits their decision'.[39] The parallels with the 'Winter of Discontent' were clear, and were duly made by Labour politicians with 'deep fears ... about the political implications of this crisis'.[40]

Yet, within the ten days allocated for such events, the 'revolution' ended. Union leaders were central to cobbling the final compromise, in which drivers at the Grangemouth refinery were persuaded to take out the tankers on the basis of guaranteeing their 'safety'. The withdrawal of unionised drivers broke the back of the movement; 'By early Thursday morning, the farmers and road hauliers ... knew the game was effectively up'.[41]

The end of the dispute brought little or nothing to those who had thrown their livelihoods on the line in the desperate protest. Despite causing 'mayhem in a way they had never dreamed possible',[42] the farmers' and drivers' basic demands remained unfulfilled. Though the Chancellor threw out vague promises of a budget review, Blair maintained his intransigent stand against lowering the fuel tax. An action which had 'laid low ... the fourth largest economy in the world'[43] had failed for lack of support not from the British working class, but from its historic leaders.

A 'LABOR RENAISSANCE'?

While American workers stopped short of laying low the 'first largest' economy in the world, they too continued to fight. One of the most impressive struggles of the era took place in Charleston, South Carolina, when five dock workers taking part in a mass picket against the use of non-union labour were arrested and charged with 'conspiracy to riot'. The police, massively outnumbering the pickets, injured more than a dozen, while the 'Charleston Five' were seized and put under 7 p.m.–7 a.m. house arrest, with the possibility of five-year prison terms after their trial the following November.

Within a year of the arrests in January 2000, solidarity across America – and the world – had secured the dockers' release. The AFL-CIO threw its weight behind the dockers, working full-time to coordinate a national defence movement, while the West Coast dockers' union, the International Longshore and Warehouse Union (ILWU), pledged to shut down the West Coast ports on the first day of the Charleston Five's trial; pressure was building within the International Longshoremen's Association (ILA), the Charleston Five's own union, to take similar action.

The arrest of the Charleston Five had taken place only days after an anti-Confederate flag march in which their local had played a leading role, making the issue a focal point of opposition to Southern racism; in June, thousands of trade unionists marched in South Carolina to show their support and challenge the bigotry. The state Attorney General described them as 'sympathizers' and 'comrades' (of, clearly, an imaginary Communist Party), adding 'South Carolina is a strong right to work state and these rights will not be trampled upon'.[44] However, by the end of 2001, the state was forced to withdraw from the case by 'the unrelenting pressure of the movement'; the Charleston Five were released after paying only a nominal fine. Not only the dockers but the labour movement could claim victory, and perhaps a turnaround in the notoriously anti-union region: 'The recent battle of the Charleston Five ... gives hope for a labor renaissance in the South'.[45]

Other struggles, by workers as varied as Los Angeles bus drivers and bus riders, New York greengrocery assistants, 'high-tech' Boeing and WashTech workers, Overnite truck drivers, Chicago janitors and nurses in Massachusetts, Washington DC and Michigan, took place in the first two years of the twenty-first century. But on 11 September 2001, labour movement activity in Britain, America and around the world was halted by a stunning event – the flight of two planes into the Twin Towers of the World Trade Center in New York, and the near destruction of the Pentagon in Washington. For a brief moment after 9/11, 'Media coverage ... highlighted blue-collar heroism: the courage displayed by firefighters, police, and the 3,000 union members who cleared the World Trade Center site'. Yet before too long, as always, 'labor got stiffed'.[46] When the jagged wound of the WTC attacks tore an already bewildered nation in half, the wars that followed were mounted against both 'terrorists' and workers.

STANDING ON THEIR GRAVES

Within two months of 11 September 2001, union activists at a conference for local organisers could claim that 'Employers are taking advantage of the situation. They're standing on the graves of 5,000 people to weaken unions'. A New York Hotel Employees Restaurant Employees (HERE) organizer reported being evicted after a manager claimed she had 'called in a bomb threat'. Building trades organisers described how 'tighter security' was an increasing justification for throwing them off unorganised sites; a drive to unionise Delta flight attendants was now stalled under the impact of bomb scares and 'security' issues. A federal workers' representative recounted how management was seizing on the catastrophe as an opportunity to undermine recruitment: 'Security is so tight it's impossible to get organizers in'. At the INS (Immigration and Naturalisation Service), managers had proposed eliminating collective bargaining 'in response to the need for higher security'.[47]

The repression continued into the following year. In November 2002, an American Federation of Government Employees (AFGE) application to represent 800 airport screeners, the first to become federal employees, was rejected by the post-9/11 Transportation Security Administration, part of the new Department of Homeland Security, on the grounds that it would prevent the 'flexibility' needed to fight terrorism. In concert, the Social Security Administration argued that its employees should lose union representation 'because they issue social security numbers, which could be of interest to those infiltrating terrorists into America', while the same all-inclusive 'threat' was also being used to justify widespread harassment of airport screeners.[48]

Yet in a country reverberating from the shock of a catastrophic attack, the links between 'anti-terror' ideology and worker repression were only too easy to make. When teachers in New Jersey were jailed for going on strike in December 2001, images of their children's mentors in handcuffs provoked local wrath against teachers, rather than police: 'After what ... the whole country has gone through, it's a shame that adults have to behave like this'.[49] In December 2001, the AFL-CIO issued a statement dutifully endorsing the 'United We Stand' philosophy, intoning 'This is a time of shared sacrifice ...'.[50]

Open season ...

Yet it was clear that an overall agenda of labour repression was expanded and justified, rather than explained, by the 11 September events. Well before 9/11, the Bush administration was appointing hostile National Labor Relations Board (NLRB) members, 'fast-tracking' the North American Free Trade Agreement (NAFTA) and pushing 'pay-check protection' (preventing unions from deducting dues for political causes). As one activist put it, 'When the Republican Party can announce that [a] top item on their agenda for the year 2000 [was] ... to get rid of labor unions and labor influence in state government, you know it's open season'.[51]

Long before 9/11, Bush had given strong backing to airline management's stance against its workforce. In March 2001, the President issued an executive order preventing a strike by airline mechanics and cleaners; in May, he banned strikes in airlines altogether, an initiative clearly aimed not only at airline workers but 'at sending a message to organized labor'.[52]

The Bush government attacked not only workers' organisation but their living standards. When Bush stole the election in November 2000, the economy was already faltering; as the 'dot.com' bubble burst and 'the foul odor of actually existing capitalism wafted out',[53] no government intervention shielded workers from the brunt of the ensuing recession, or of the ongoing haemorrhaging of manufacturing jobs which escalated with globalisation.

In fact, both employment and pay registered negative growth during the Dubya years. The so-called 'recovery' from the 2000 recession remained obstinately 'jobless'; in his first term, Bush distinguished himself by becoming the first president since the Great Depression to have generated fewer jobs in total than existed when he came into office. By 2000, US workers had added 32 hours to their working year, yet wage growth in 2001 was only 2 per cent.

Unfortunately for those at the sharp end of these statistics, sweeping Republican victories in 2002, enabled by the 'terrorist' zeitgeist, allowed for a still more intensified offensive against labour. Immediately after the elections, a White House adviser suggested expanding the reach of the Taft-Hartley Act and the Railway Labor Act in order to 'strengthen the President's position in labor disputes'; both airline and longshore workers' strikes were included in the remit. As part of a bill which established the much-hyped Homeland Security Department, civil service protections and collective bargaining rights were removed from over 150,000 workers. At the same time, the administration announced plans to privatise the jobs of almost half the entire federal workforce – about 850,000 employees.

A wildcard situation

Yet resistance continued. Defying the new strictures, West Coast longshoremen brought down the wrath of the government upon them in the summer of 2002 with 'the biggest and most high-profile labor battle in the United States since the ... UPS strike'.[54] As the longshoremen's contract approached its expiration date in July, the government began piling on the pressure; Tom Ridge, Director of Homeland Security, contacted the ILWU president to inform him that any disruption of the ports would be seen as a threat to the 'war on terror'. Meanwhile, the port employers' united front with massive corporations like Wal-Mart and Home Depot made it more than usually clear that economic 'insecurity' for major corporations was at issue, as much as any threat to 'national security'.

At the end of September, after weeks of stalling, the dockers were locked out on the grounds of staging a deliberate 'slowdown'; on 9 October the government ordered an 80-day cooling-off period under the Taft-Hartley legislation, then imposed a Temporary Restraining Order which required dockers to 'work at a normal and reasonable rate of speed'. Once again, 'the employers immediately began crying that the union was running a slowdown'.[55] But this time, the employers' association may have overplayed its hand. Not all port employers wanted to continue the stand-off, and nor, necessarily, did the government: 'The Bush administration made a calculation that ILWU militancy and its history of international solidarity was enough to create a wildcard situation'.[56]

On 23 November, a tentative agreement was reached providing some safeguards for current workers against the impact of new technology. As in many such protracted disputes, the settlement could not be called an outright victory, but the 'wildcard' of solidarity won gains that would not otherwise have been possible. Labour was still capable of challenging a viciously anti-union government and a culture dominated by the 'war on terror'.

STRIKES BY SOCIAL DINOSAURS ...

Although Blair had instantly aligned himself with Bush in that war, he had even less luck in imposing a labour truce. Less than six months after 9/11, the media was consecrating 'Britain's revived labour movement' as the 'biggest threat of widespread industrial action ... since Thatcher broke trade union power' was posed by railway workers, civil servants, postal workers, teachers, hospital workers and even police officers.[57]

By July 2002 the 'threat' had become a reality, not least among the one million local government workers who staged a huge national walkout, the largest strike by women in the country's history. The hundreds of thousands of state-employed workers, almost all women, who still received only £4.80 an hour, were 'a group of workers who couldn't be more representative of the modern British workforce', making 'nonsense of the long-fostered image of unions as social dinosaurs'.[58]

As rail workers and, ironically, oil tanker drivers joined the fray, even the discreet Institute of Directors was alarmed at the escalation of struggle: 'We do fear that there's going to be further militancy, there's no doubt about it'. The Institute's 'concern' at the 'general shift to the left'[59] seemed justified when, in November 2002, Britain's 50,000 firefighters walked out on their first national strike since 1977. The workers were demanding a 40 per cent wage rise, which Blair, predictably, dismissed as 'beyond contemplation'. Yet even this massive rise would only bring firefighters' average pay to little over £30,000 a year; many firefighters had to take second jobs in order to feed, house and clothe their families.

Within a week, the dispute had turned into yet another 'crisis'. After an initial 48-hour stoppage, the firefighters returned to the fray on 22 November with an eight-day strike. By the fourth day, local authority employers had made a 16 per cent offer which the FBU accepted, only to see it vetoed by the government as 'costing too much'. The eventual outcome of the dispute, vitiated despite the 'militancy' of its leadership by constant cancellation of the planned strike days, was disappointing – 16 per cent over three years, tied to massive job cuts – but, as always, considerably more than could have been achieved without struggle.

Meanwhile, a rash of disputes in both private and public sectors kept up an uninterrupted challenge to Blair's 'intransigent' stance. In January 2003, the unthinkable happened; workers at Nissan, Britain's 'lean production' poster child and 'Europe's most productive car plant', threatened to strike.[60] While based on a routine pay issue, like simultaneous action by their fellow-carworkers at the traditionally combative Peugeot plant, resistance from the allegedly 'hege-monised' Nissan workers held a particularly strong class meaning.

... and Bolshie militants

An equally 'non-militant' set of workers walked out on July 2003 when British Airways (BA) customer service staff, 'a largely female group ... with no record of militancy' confirmed the verdict that strike action was by no means the preserve of 'social dinosaurs'. The strikers, depicted as 'bolshie militants', had taken action over what was indeed perhaps, in this era, a revolutionary issue: childcare arrangements. BA's imposition of electronic swipe cards to monitor clocking-on and -off times meant the workers, many of them mothers with young children, would lose their existing ability to swap shifts with colleagues in a childcare emergency. Exactly the kind of 'caring' issue for the tabloids to weep crocodile tears over, if not for the fact that its participants had inconveniently bucked the stereotype; women deserted their role as subservient 'service' representatives to organise and represent the 'genuine anger on the terminal floor'.[61]

In the autumn of 2003, postal workers took up the cudgels, ironically just after turning down a call by the new Communication Workers' Union (CWU) leadership for a national pay strike. Almost immediately after the 'no' vote, unofficial action broke out across the country over a series of episodes of management harassment, with walkouts in Oxford, Wolverhampton and London's Mount Pleasant depot – the latter bringing 20,000 workers out in sympathy. The general workplace culture of bullying and intimidation, aggravated by take-home pay of less than £230 a week, had fired an explosion of workplace militancy with scant concern for the secret ballots and official procedures required by the law. It was an extraordinary example, and not the first by postal workers, of how the supposedly invincible anti-union laws could be defied in a moment, simply by – defying them.

AN EARTHQUAKE IN THE MOVEMENT

The postal workers' rebellion from the ranks was all the more significant in that their union leader, Billy Hayes, was a member of the notorious 'Awkward Squad' – a posse of recently elected union leaders who seemed to defy everything Blair stood for. Beginning in the late 1990s with Associated Society of Locomotive Engineers and Firemen (ASLEF) members' surprise election of Mick Rix, a train driver with a 'left labour and Communist Party background', the phenomenon went on to embrace leftist Andy Gilchrist in the Fire Brigades Union (FBU), Communist Party fellow-traveller Bob Crow at Rail, Maritime and Transport (RMT), Kevin Curran, 'a great admirer of the Marxist tradition' at the GMB, and the openly revolutionary Mark Serwotka as leader of the civil service workers' union, Public and Civil Services (PCS). In June 2002, a spectacular defeat for Sir Ken Jackson, 'Tony Blair's pet trade union leader',[62] took place when left-winger Derek Simpson won the leadership of the Amalgamated Engineering and Electrical Union (AEEU) (now merged with MSF and mincingly entitled 'Amicus'). The result caused consternation in government circles; as one report put it, 'the scale of the vote against Jackson is an earthquake in labour movement politics'.[63]

The actions of 'Awkward Squad' leaders did not always match their words. Despite his powerful rhetoric on how the government could find money for the Iraq war but not for the firefighters, Andy Gilchrist undermined his militant reputation in the 2002–03 firefighters' strike by calling off proposed strikes at crucial moments in favour of talks with the employers; one such cancelled action was on 15 February 2003, meaning it could have united striking fire-fighters and anti-war demonstrators on the biggest demonstration in British history.[64] Bob Crow had celebrated his election as RMT leader with a banner announcing 'The Revolution Starts Here', but called off tube workers' strikes prefacing a broader protest against privatisation.[65] Postal workers' leader Billy Hayes, despite his back-ground as a militant activist, had proved less than supportive on behalf of rank-and-file postal workers. Members' reluctance to sup-port the national pay strike was perhaps rooted in the fact that, the year before, 'post workers were marched to the top of the hill, won a massive victory for strike action, and were then marched back down again with a poor deal and no action'.[66]

Thus, although the new 'Awkward Squad' leaders' radical stance might suggest a significant rebalancing of class forces within the British labour movement, the union leadership's bark continued to be considerably fiercer than its bite. According to one UNISON offi-cial, the mass council workers' strike in 2002 saw 'a lot of pissed-off women ...'. For the low-paid women workers who made up the bulk of UNISON's council worker membership, the action itself 'was like they had been given permission ... The lid had been kept on for so long. It just blew off'. Yet the frustrating confinement to one-day strikes brought the strikers from 'euphoria' to 'disappointment'. Much of this was linked, according to the official, to a continued lack of true grass-roots involvement in the internal structure of the union; apart from industrial action, 'there are very few areas in which women can feel free to express their anger and frustration at their pay and conditions'. Despite the new leadership's self-conscious awareness of 'the importance of gender difference', most branches were still 'male-dominated and ... increasingly white-collar domi-nated. There is a class issue within the branches'.[67]

'THE PEOPLE AREN'T AFRAID'

In America, a somewhat better record prevailed in organising non-white, non-male workers – though not always from the official ranks. When 30 Latina workers at a typically dangerous and exploitative IBP meatpacking plant in Washington State were fired for supporting a worker penalised for not keeping up with production, 'the next thing we knew there were hundreds of people' gathered outside in their support. Fed up with deteriorating plant conditions and delays in negotiations, the IBP workers began holding rallies along the plant access road. The action continued for five weeks; though the strikers failed to win their pay demands, 'we gained dignity, we gained a lot of strength', said María Martínez, who became chief union organiser in the area. The post-Carey Teamsters put the local into trusteeship, but the workers contacted TDU and launched a series of effective in-plant actions. The union's biggest victory, said one worker, was changing the climate of fear: 'We were fearful before [Martínez] came. There was fear that ... they would fire us. Now ... the people aren't afraid'.[68]

The revitalised organisation at IBP – finally crushed when management decertified the union in 2005 – symbolised a new wave of immigrant and Latino militancy. In early 2003, Guatemalan workers won a major organising victory at an exploitative laundry company in Georgia; not long afterwards, 8,000 Mexican 'guest workers' joined the Farm Labor Organizing Committee (FLOC) and won a contract with the North Carolina Growers' Association. As FLOC president Baldemar Velásquez proudly pointed out, 'NC was the least unionised state in the country; it won't be now that this agreement is signed'.[69]

Nor was immigrant organisation and resistance confined to the South. Successful efforts by the United Farm Workers to organise strawberry pickers in California led to a contract with Coastal Berry, one of America's largest 'agri-business' corporations, in March 2001.

During the same period, a massive labour-community struggle united low-paid Latino and African-American service and maintenance workers with middle-class, mostly white, graduate students struggling to organise in the 'company town' of New Haven, Connecticut, a poverty-stricken area dominated by the elite and savagely anti-union Yale University.[70]

In Jefferson, Wisconsin, the long-running Tyson strike which began in May 2003 against pay cuts, a wage freeze, and soaring health costs united white and African-American workers in a previously staid, Midwestern community. Only weeks later, a strike by African-American laundry workers at the Cintas corporation in Detroit summed up many of the trends of the early 2000s, including poverty wages versus soaring profits and insane CEO salaries; as one worker yelled, fighting mad, 'I've been here 15 years and I still won't be making ten [dollars an hour] ... They live off us'. Another, asked if he would support strike action, expressed the dynamic of struggle still more succinctly: 'We have no choice. It's the only way we're going to get anything ... they call us partners and they won't even negotiate with us when we come to the table'.[71]

'You want to gain something ...'

However, union leaders' blindness to this logic was demonstrated once more in a key struggle by Californian grocery workers. Rock-bottom labour costs at the giant anti-union behemoth, Wal-Mart, provoked the three main Californian grocery chains, Vons/Pavilions (Safeway), Ralph's and Albertson's, to demand two-tier wages, a wage freeze and, inevitably, increased healthcare contributions. Over 70,000 grocery workers walked out in October 2003.

The strike was given a massive boost at an early point by the support of Teamster drivers in California and beyond. But by its fourth month it had become a 'war of attrition'. The principal union, the United Food and Commercial Workers (UFCW), which had insisted on limiting the strike to the California region, began 'pulling' pickets at some stores after the companies offered talks. As the strike failed to close the main grocery stores, and strike payments dwindled, defeat began to seem inevitable; and in February 2004 the strike ended with only modest gains – healthcare costs would not rise until the third year of the contract – while allowing for the two-tier pay system which had been the strikers' major sticking point. As one activist sighed, 'They got two-tier. Everything we were going against, they got. When you stay out for five months, you want to gain something, not lose what you had'.[72] It was a dismal end to a courageous and committed struggle, undermining still further the apparently impossible goal of organising Wal-Mart.

Other 'atypical' strikers, workers in Atlantic City hotels and casinos, fared better when they struck over 'a share of the wealth' and for contracts which would terminate at the same time as those in Las Vegas, where the entire casino workforce was unionised. From the beginning, the employers refused to accede to this demand, which would have given the union 'tremendous leverage at the bargaining table'. The workers finally declared victory on 3 November, winning limits on subcontracting and pay and health benefit increases. One triumphant striker exulted, 'Thank God, it's done, it's done, it's done ... we got more than we even asked for'.[73] But the employers held fast on the crucial contract expiration issue, insisting on a five-year term.

A CLASS WAR

Successful or not, all these strikes were against the odds, 'against the stream' of an ever more corporate, and, since 9/11, increasingly repressive culture; and, as always, it was concrete issues which galvanised workers into resistance. In Britain, assaults on living standards and working conditions continued to drive the Loch Ness monster of class struggle to the surface; as other groups of workers weighed in to support the firefighters, even the Murdoch-owned *Sun* proclaimed, 'It's A Class War'.[74] Amicus leader Derek Simpson summed up the dynamic: 'The government can't beat underlying trade union principles, because they can't deal with the problems that are there. You can fool some of the people some of the time, but the issues keep coming back ... That's why Blair's popularity is suffering. He has told 'em this and told 'em that but it is not what their own life experiences are telling them'.[75]

Workers' own life experiences, as ever, continued to provoke industrial struggle in both Britain and America in the late 1990s and early 2000s. Perhaps, even in the 'postindustrial' nirvana of twenty-first century Britain and USA, not much had changed. Just as always, even the most 'revolutionary' of union leaders seemed unable to take that most radical of steps – identifying the union in practical and theoretical terms with its rank-and-file membership – and, just as before, that membership continued to fly the red flag of actually existing class struggle. It was rank-and-file action which had constructed the 'Winter of Discontent'; it was the same force which reconstructed it not only in the 2002 'hot British summer' but on countless other occasions when that allegedly spent force resurfaced to startle the commentators. In 2003, it could still be written that 'unions retain the potential to shake governments and make ruling classes shudder'.[76]

Yet, in the twenty-first century just as in the nineteenth and earlier, the roots of that astounding resistance lay not in some idealist impulse to sacrifice but simply in the reproduction of workplace-based contradictions centred on the everyday exploitation of labour. One US writer's concept of the 'two souls of labor's revitalization' in the first years of the new millennium was based on the reality that 'As the employers' assault on workers continues, so do workers' anger and frustration'.[77] In the British Airways strikes of 1997 and 2002, in the Chicano meatpackers' actions against IBP, in the firefighters', London Underground and council workers' struggles, in the Californian grocery workers' and Atlantic City casino workers' strikes of 2004–05, the ruling class remained, at the cusp of the millennium, labour's best organiser.

Part II

What to Make of It All

7
Unions and Unions

'The unions' is the usual term for the organisations written about in this book. What else would we call them?

The problem is that this common usage suggests an image of unions as a homogeneous block; 'the unions' do things, and get blamed for things, whether the leadership or the membership is involved. This can lead to wildly varying descriptions and distortions. In 1970s Britain, 'the unions' were routinely accused of having 'too much power' when their members clearly had too *little* power, if this is judged in terms of wealth and political influence. Fast-forward to twenty-first-century America, and 'A lot of young people see unions as a job protection racket',[1] while at the 2003 Social Forum, a worldwide gathering of radicals, one participant was 'skeptical about the trade unions. The trade unions are conservative ... and tied to the Blair government'.[2] Yet Fiat carworkers on strike against job cuts were leading a mass demonstration at the same event; and, at the precise moment the student was expressing his 'skepticism', British firefighters were on strike in direct defiance of the Blair government.

Which of these groups is 'the unions'? The 'job protection racket'? The marching, striking workers? In writing as if 'unions' were one homogeneous, seamless entity, commentators regularly conflate the two faces of trade unionism: union-as-institution, formal, official, comprising bricks and mortar and financial assets, and union-as-movement, the inner, living content of the organisation, a volatile mix of interests, demands, resistance, membership mobilisation and rank-and-file organisational forms which may differ qualitatively from the 'official' variety. For this reason, one central theme of this chapter is the crucial issue of internal trade union democracy – not as a formalistic, constitutional process but as the direct democracy of workplace resistance and membership involvement, the only soil from which 'unions' can truly grow.

'Too big of a risk ...'

The 'bricks and mortar' side of the union equation is regularly illustrated in union leaders' reluctance to support membership action
posing the threat of legal action, sequestration of funds, etc. The
refusal of the TGWU to lend support to the keynote 1996 Liverpool
dockers' dispute was based on insistence that 'the union' would be
financially broken by defiance of the anti-union laws, leaving it
unable to protect its existing members. When, in March 2000, the
United Steel Workers of America (USWA) suddenly withdrew its
promise to support a joint steelworker-environmentalist rally, one
explanation for the abrupt decision was that 'the possible legal ramifications of what could happen at the rally was too big of a risk'.
The cancellation halted a crucial step forward in the 'Teamsters and
Turtles' alliance between workers and radicals, the most politically
promising aspect of the Seattle anti-globalisation protests.

Yet it was not the steelworkers who felt that action challenging
corporate property relations was 'too big of a risk' – it was the USWA.
The Liverpool dockers who refused to cross a picket-line expressed a
principle considerably more 'valuable' than financial assets –
solidarity. For many rank-and-file activists, the relationship works in
reverse: 'Better to have a union with no building and no bank
account than to have a building and a bank account with no
union'.[3]

WHAT ARE UNIONS FOR?

These opposing arguments represent, again, the two opposing facets
which are simultaneously presented and conflated in the term 'the
unions'. It is this *dual, contradictory* reality that has led to persis-
tently conflicting accounts of the 'limits and possibilities'[4] of trade
unionism, to alternating lurches towards 'optimistic' and 'pessimistic'[5]
assessments of its potential. In fact, the simple truth is that trade
unionism has *both* limits *and* possibilities, can be viewed both opti-
mistically and pessimistically. But what do the 'possibilities' depend
on? What makes 'optimism' (of the will at least, if not of the intel-
lect) anything other than naive?

In one sense, what makes the difference is a 'choice'; whether to
seek to maximise what possibilities there are, or to remain gloomily
preoccupied with the limitations and failures of the movement in a
species of self-fulfilling prophecy. And this in its turn raises the
question: who is doing the 'choosing', and what is it about their

position – in the bureaucracy, at the roots – that persuades them to choose as they do?

One way of approaching this is to look at the attitudes of Marx and Engels, whose overwhelmingly optimistic view of the potential of trade unionism faded to pessimism about its 'bourgeois' character, only to blossom again into delight at the explosion of New Unionism amongst unskilled workers in the late1880s. The 'bureaucratic crust' overlaid upon mid-nineteenth-century British trade unionism did not prevent Engels from 'looking beyond this encrustation, toward the forces that would break through it'.[6]

Not everyone involved in trade unionism, however, is looking in this direction – one explicitly opposed to bureaucratisation, one passionately committed to putting the class dynamic back into the movement. Whereas the lamentable state of organisation in the 1990s pushed the US union leadership towards acknowledging the need for 'the unions' to 'once again ... play a disruptive, insurgent role in society',[7] such 'insurgency' was notably short-lived; any real 'disruption' would threaten the relationships with employers built up so carefully over the decades of 'business unionism'.

The insurmountable problem, for those whose position and strategic outlook belong to union-as-institution rather than as movement, is that significant union growth raises the unacceptable spectre of mobilisation at the grass roots. Living, dynamic unionism, unionism which sees floods of new workers entering the movement, is unionism based on struggle, and unionism which breathes the disruptive air of direct, membership-based democracy. These two elements – grass-roots resistance, membership involvement and democracy – are intrinsically threatening to stable, institutional union existence. But it is these two elements which make unions grow.

The intrinsic status of the institution

In fact, ironically, most examples of explosive growth and organisation take place *outside* the existing union movement, which often does its best to control the associated ferment. Forms of working-class organisation developed through struggle often develop quite independently of formal union structures, and display 'spontaneous' features of committee-based democracy and accountability only too seldom found in the existing movement.

The dynamic of union growth and strength often works in the *reverse* way to that of any institutional pattern; union leaderships have traditionally tended to react to what amounts to self-organising by the grass roots, rather than looking to those roots in order to build, or rebuild, trade unionism. Thus 'In periods of rapid membership growth ... organising amounted to little more than receiving workers into membership';[8] in Britain, 'by the 1970s ... members were pouring into trade unions without any great exertion on the part of the organisation'.[9] Yet such growth often strained institutional resources; the same period saw officials struggling to 'cope with the influx of members wanting to join'.[10]

Workers in struggle become passionate advocates of union organisation, but as a dynamic, class-based union form rather than a dues-building partner with capital. In more than one case of 'organising', union-as-institution stays out of the picture; immigrant construction workers in California, rebuffed by the largely white and by now declining Carpenters' Union, formed their own 'Movement of Drywall Hangers' which conducted a successful strike in 1992 when 'a lot of those people didn't know what a union was yet'.[11]

This indicates two things: that the bureaucracy has seldom been involved in actually *creating* mass trade unionism; and that, without another agency to compel action in the interests of their rank-and-file members, the bureaucracy's interest lies more in safeguarding its own, essentially institutional position than in mobilising the rank and file. By itself, without roots in the rank and file, the trade union bureaucracy is incapable of putting life into trade unionism; left without a 'live' organisational base, the union leadership will scrabble, not to rebuild that base, but to seek the kind of *institutional* solutions which have been most to the fore in the current crisis gripping the movement.

Trade unions – decline and fall?

That crisis expresses itself most irrefutably in the steep decline in union membership. The figures can hardly be questioned; in both Britain and America, trade union membership and density have declined catastrophically since the 1970s, dropping sharply throughout the 1980s and 1990s to reach less than 33 per cent in Britain today, while in the US union density fell to 12.5 per cent overall and a shocking 8 per cent in the private sector by 2005.

Given the vicissitudes of the last 25 years or so – neoliberalism, overwhelming ruling-class hostility, 'deindustrialisation', the haemorrhage of unionised manufacturing jobs – it might be thought surprising that any trade union movement is left at all. The situation can hardly be said to be organised labour's fault. Or can it?

The draconian anti-union tactics of employers like Wal-Mart can hardly be dismissed; but, even after surveying the list of 'macroeconomic' and other structural explanations, even the most conventional analyses politely suggest that the fault may lie with 'the unions' themselves. In both Britain and America, 'Some part of the explanation of union decline ... clearly lies with deficiencies in union organising ... After the 1970s, both movements became especially reliant on their own efforts to recruit new members, and the evidence ... is that they did not spend enough money or put in sufficient effort to resist influences countering membership retention and growth'.[12] A major US study of union organisation indicates that 'union tactics as a group play a greater role in explaining election outcome than any other group of variables, including employer characteristics and tactics'.[13] In other words, how workers vote in union recognition elections is influenced more, overall, by union action – or the lack of it – than by the behaviour of employers, however hostile.

So what are these 'union tactics'? While the amount unions spend on recruitment and organising is important, the overall *approach* to organising – primarily 'top-down' or 'bottom-up' – appears to be the key factor; and all the evidence is that 'bottom-up' works. The research cited above shows conclusively that success in organising is associated with 'an aggressive rank-and-file strategy'. Rank-and-file-based worker-to-worker organising campaigns achieved 'win rates that were 10 to 30 per cent higher than traditional campaigns';[14] some 67 per cent of rank-and-file-based campaigns were successful, versus 38 per cent in which union staffers used more 'professional' tactics like gate-leafleting, glossy mailings or 'house calls' by staffers. Sometimes referred to as 'internal organising', the simple tactic of getting unionised workers to organise the plant, office or store next door has clearly worked.

But, effective or not, worker-to-worker campaigns are not what 'unions' seem to want. Between the mid 1980s and mid 1990s, the average number of 'rank-and-file-intensive tactics' (personal contact by rank-and-file members, small group meetings, rank-and-file organising committees) rose only slightly; only 15 per cent of unions surveyed made significant use of these tactics. The reality of union leaders' reaction to the crisis of union membership, despite rallying calls to 'organise', has been to huddle together in forms of restructuring which, rather than expanding the movement, amount to the kind of 'rearranging the deckchairs on the Titanic' logic represented in the current Service Employees' International Union (SEIU)-inspired debate in America.

'BUREAUCRATIZE TO ORGANIZE'?

The crucial issue in looking at trade union growth and development – one seldom addressed in the movement – is how to combine the necessary degree of institutional stability with the indispensable element of living, direct membership-based democracy. This issue of the leadership–membership relationship is one of the most difficult, but unquestionably the most important, to confront anyone looking at the current condition of trade unionism and the possibilities for its 'renewal'. It is also the one which seems to be most neglected in the current debate over the movement's future.

In America, that debate exploded in 2004 when Andrew Stern of the SEIU, together with the leaderships of the Carpenters union, Union of Needletrades, Industrial and Textile Employees (UNITE), Hotel Employees Restaurant Employees (HERE), Laborers' International Union of North America (LIUNA) and the Teamsters, launched a 'New Unity Partnership', later reconstituted as the 'Change to Win' coalition. Its main recommendation – abandoning the current American Federation of Labor-Congress of Industrial Organizations (AFL-CIO) and restructuring the current 30-odd unions into twelve 'giants' with hugely increased density and thus organising power – has provoked vigorous and ongoing debate, increasingly centred on a split between the 'Stern' and 'Sweeney' factions. At the 2005 AFL-CIO convention, after much preliminary fanfare, the SEIU and Teamsters, along with the United Food and Commercial Workers (UFCW), made the dramatic move of withdrawing from the Federation.

The difference between the two factions is now said to lie with their different approaches to 'growing' the movement – Stern et al. promoting more effective organising of workers through the suggested restructuring and consolidation, while Sweeney's AFL-CIO appears to be turning towards a 'political' perspective involving electing Democrats to office. The disagreement is all the more bizarre in that Sweeney himself was once at the forefront of promoting the 'organising model' of unionism.

Nevertheless, Stern's own proposals scarcely conform to that model. Rather, the 'Change to Win' proposals suggest a sternly top-down structure which would, as one critique puts it, 'bureaucratize to organize'. While the proposed reorganisation along industrial-union-style lines makes some sense given the existing jurisdictional chaos of the movement, it is a reorganisation which utterly excludes the constituency at its heart – the members. The structure of the Carpenters' union, in which 'locals have been reduced to impotent units',[15] gives some idea of the coalition's agenda; merged into huge regional councils, locals have lost all control over bargaining, have no paid officials, and answer to 'business agents' appointed from above, along with other restrictions. As an example of an 'organising' rather than 'service' model, it is not a promising portent.

Yet, as suggested, this 'member-less' orientation prevails throughout most of the union leadership. Rather than looking to 'put the movement into the movement' through the dangerous strategy of mobilising their own members, unions-as-institutions overwhelmingly seek institutional solutions. In the US particularly, the era of union decline has provoked an aggressive pattern of restructuring and 'raiding' which apparently lacks all logic but institutional survival. Mergers themselves are only one aspect of this, although the merger rate has been increasing rapidly, with 46 mergers taking place between 1984 and 1994 and another 16 from 1995 to 2000;[16] alongside this activity, unions have moved to take over organising jurisdictions from other, usually smaller contenders, and, rather than trying to extend membership in their own areas, reaching out to more easily available pools of membership. In recent years, the United Auto Workers (UAW) has organised university clerical staff and part-time lecturers, but not auto parts workers; the United Steel Workers of America (USWA) has organised retail staff, but failed to increase its influence in the growing 'little steel' sector or in low-wage 'enterprise zone' plants. More recently, the Laborers' Union, LIUNA, has taken into membership 50,000 postal workers, and the Teamsters a 20,000-member local of New York City lawyers, housing workers and other public sector employees.[17]

Alongside rearranging the deckchairs, collusion with management is seen as a promising way of securing institutional survival. The UAW's latest variant, 'card-check neutrality', brings partnership into the heart of organising by offering labour–management cooperation in return for employer 'neutrality' in union recognition elections. Asked, 'What can current UAW members do to support organising and growing our union?', the answer comes smartly: 'We must negotiate [employer] neutrality and card check'. (True, another suggestion is 'giving a talk about how your union–management partnership has helped your employer compete more successfully'.)[18]

While the British trade union movement remains less zany than the US in its jurisdictions, mergers have been gaining currency since the 1980s as a 'solution' to union decline, with colossi like UNISON, the Communication Workers' Union (CWU) and Amicus consolidating rather than expanding union memberships. Currently, the prospect of a merger between Amicus and the TGWU, possibly bringing in the GMB to form one huge general union, provoked unexpected approval from 'Awkward Squad' Amicus leader Derek Simpson: 'We don't need to organise – that has failed. The way to grow our union is through mergers'.[19]

True to form, the British union leadership has matched its American counterpart in grasping at the unlikely straw of employer support to keep unions afloat, with the 'sweetheart deals' of the 1980s an early variant. For Britain, the lure of union–employer collusion was enhanced by its state-level representation in the European Union, which gave its blessing in the early 1990s to EU-wide joint works councils. The worker representatives to these councils are not required to be union members, and by 1992, many British trade unions were 'ready to accept that employee representation can no longer be confined to a single channel through trade union membership'.[20] In a bizarre reversal for a movement supposedly dedicated to union organisation, the TUC itself gave support for non-union 'twin track' representation on European works councils.

SHADOW STEWARDS

Yet, in Britain as in the US, research into declining unionism provides convincing evidence that workplace-based organising is key to reviving the movement. Despite the TUC's apparent conception of the membership as 'consumers' and of union officials as 'expert providers of services',[21] recruitment efforts centring on polite offers to potential members of bargain credit cards and mortgage rates have clearly failed to overcome the main obstacle facing union growth – 'perceived union instrumentality'.[22] The principal reason why workers are not joining unions, according to this and other research, is that they are simply not effective enough: 'The central problem faced by unions is the perception that they may be too weak to "make a difference"', a perception sited clearly in the workplace; 'employees are deterred from joining because they believe unions are simply too weak to be able to solve workplace injustices'.[23]

Given this, in Britain as in the US the most effective direction for organising appears to be rooted in the workplace, rather than in external, 'top-down' activity. One study of Scotland's 'Silicon Glen', site of some of the least union-friendly employers in Britain, demonstrates the key role of rank-and-file activists in unionising a set of 'high-tech' electronics companies, including the formidable IBM. Described as 'shadow shop stewards' in that their organising took place outside any formal structure, these activists risked their jobs in order to recruit exactly the 'new economy' workers unions claim to be most anxious to reach. Yet they received scant support from their union, which, after recovering from its surprise, worked to contain, and not facilitate, the activists' request for a concerted recognition campaign. Or, as one 'shadow shop steward' put it somewhat more forcefully, 'I make no bones about it, we need the AEEU to get up off their butts and recognize that there is potential'.[24]

A number of different studies indicate the crucial role of committed rank-and-file activists; in one summary, 'the whole process of collectivisation is heavily dependent on the actions of small numbers of leaders and activists'.[25] Yet the activists who remain involved with informal methods of building grass-roots unionism, who carry out the essential, invisible spadework of organisation, who risk their jobs in the cause of union recognition, battle for visibility in an overwhelmingly institutionalised environment, with little or no support from the official movement. While it can easily be argued that the case is hopeless and that small bands of union activists, overwhelmingly outweighed by hostile employer forces, are not going to rescue the union movement, it is also possible to acknowledge that it is these small bands who are doing the most effective and committed work on rebuilding union organisation, and that they deserve support, resources and recognition from the union movement as a whole – particularly given the convincing evidence in both Britain and in the US that fellow-workers and grass-roots activists provide the best force for recruitment.

Yet the leadership, it seems, has no desire to listen. A recent AFL-CIO summit conference held to discuss the 'crisis in organising' devoted relatively little time, according to one observer, to discussing 'the central task of organizers – helping workers build, from the bottom up, organisations capable of winning better conditions through sustained workplace activity'. Rather, discussion moved on to 'management-style jargon about gaining "market share" ... or more "synergy" between national union and industry strategies'.[26]

WHY BUREAUCRACY?

So why do union leaders shoot themselves in the foot like this? Why, if they want unions to grow, don't they take seriously the rank-and-file methods and perspectives which have been shown over and over to enrich and renew union organisation? Why don't they study, and understand, the lessons of previous periods of union upsurge – marked not by 'partnership' or union mergers but by rank-and-file militancy and direct democracy? Once again we are brought back to the issue of, and the attempt to understand, bureaucracy. What, exactly, *is* the union bureaucracy? How does it develop? And why does it so often, in the time-honoured phrase of the rank and file, 'sell us out'?

There are any number of theories of union bureaucracy, ranging from Michels' classic 'iron law of oligarchy' to stern Trotskyist accusations of leadership betrayal. More recent theories can be grouped into three categories:[27] the 'social position' analysis, emphasising the isolation of officials from members through high salaries and middle-class lifestyles; the critique of union leaders' reformist ideology; and a third 'bureaucracy thesis' stemming from the structural and organisational changes affecting British workplace trade unionism in the 1970s.

While 'social position' explanations of bureaucracy may be self-evident, those which focus on the social democratic or 'Labourist' ideology of union officials and the potential bureaucratisation of workplace organisation deserve a closer look. 'Labourism' – belief in the ability of a corporate state to overcome both the causes of industrial conflict and its unacceptably 'militant' nature – in Britain reached a peak in the mid-1970s 'Social Contract', when union leaders were effectively deployed by the Labour government to cut the living standards of their members. As a consistent critic[28] of such 'statism' points out, the corporatist ideology of the period played a decisive role in the repression of rank-and-file resistance, while failing to provide effective solutions to workers' problems.

The widespread disillusion with incomes policy might seem to automatically discredit 'Labourism', but the response of rank-and-file workers is not usually explicit rejection of such ideology. Despite the turn to Thatcherism by an angry working class, or at least its more highly skilled sections, sustained illusions in the benefits of future Labour governments, along with significant loyalty to 'the union', continue to fog the lens of class consciousness. In this sense, the hold of social democratic ideology not only over the union leadership, but the membership itself, continues to be a significant factor in sustaining trade union bureaucracy.

Yesterday's militant ...

The 'bureaucracy thesis'[29] contrasts with this emphasis on ideology in its focus on the workplace, where the widely noted changes in British managers' approach to shop steward organisation during the 1970s laid the basis for new, workplace-based forms of bureaucracy. The upward progress of individual activists from workplace-based militant to 'outside' union official is familiar; the bureaucracy thesis highlights a 'new direction' for bureaucratisation – *downwards* into the workplace. With invitations onto formal negotiating committees, the extension of office space, secretarial help and other facilities, and time off for union duties, the package was hard to resist.

Any study of the transition from militant workplace trade unionism in the 1960s and early 1970s to the collusion and cooperation of a decade later can hardly ignore such processes. However, the simple existence of new structures and facilities, however significant a shift it may represent, is not enough to explain the docility and indeed enthusiasm of most representatives in, so to speak, venturing in. Nor are the obvious personal temptations; for most stewards in the 1970s, the beginnings of incorporation with management were 'less a matter of "corruption" and more a question of an under-developed class consciousness'.[30]

In other words, as the 'bureaucracy thesis' itself recognises, there are ideological as well as structural elements involved here. Shopfloor representatives, however militant, rarely possess the kind of explicit class perspective which would promote a clear awareness of the direction of management strategy, or the urgent need to maintain union independence.

Yet the role of ideology here is more complex and subtle than that of a straightforward, positive endorsement of 'Labourism' and social democracy. While bureaucracy is usually examined in isolation from the membership, its formation actually arises out of membership and activist practice which combines explicit reformism with a pragmatically 'instrumental' approach. The importance of ideology can lie as much in its *absence* – the lack of conscious alternatives to current praxis, combined with blindness to the dangers of incorporation and institutionalisation – as in positive affirmation of a set of ideas which explicitly allow for reformist 'betrayals'.

These connections are affirmed by the only too common experience of yesterday's activist turning into tomorrow's bureaucrat. However subjectively militant a workplace representative may be, there is usually – for the individual – no explicit ideological barrier between everyday rank-and-file resistance and the kind of pragmatic accommodation with management which too often segues seamlessly into 'selling out'. The tale of defection by workplace representatives, once elected to higher office, is too familiar to be worth retelling – except to say that this is less about individual morality than about the lack, within reformist ideology, of clear or insuperable barriers between militant representation and bureaucratic compromise.

What differs between full-time 'bureaucrats' and union representatives still tied to their members at the workplace is the *objective* structuring of action in one direction (compromise) or another (class struggle). The dynamic hinges on the rooting of conflict in the structural features of capitalism, rather than in preexisting ideology or consciousness. Research into a new generation of 'radical' local officials[31] reveals that, despite their strong views on the conflicting interests of management and workers, most arrived at the same negotiating outcomes as their more conservative colleagues. Struggle which emerges out of the material experience of exploitation tends both to have a more direct impact on consciousness and to provide, given its class base, a more noticeable challenge to the 'default' reformist ideology which otherwise is either taken for granted or unrecognised.

'The working class at its workplace'

From this point of view, it makes sense to relaunch the exploration of bureaucratisation from the base of its opposite – the height of non-incorporated, non-institutionalised trade unionism. During the last major upsurge of union activity in the late 1960s and early 1970s, the strength, tenacity and effectiveness of the movement was based largely on its roots in a form of unionism which directly addressed the daily vicissitudes of the capitalist labour process. Nostalgia aside, it seems that the small workgroups which dominated manufacturing during the 1960s exhibited, if for only too short a time, a 'raw' class-based independence and member-led democracy which allowed for an almost entirely oppositional stance towards managerial interests and objectives. Informal workgroups organised independently to defend and advance basic working-class interests; their representatives operated without notable compromise of or distance from the rank and file.

A considerable factor in this dynamic was the piecework pay system typical of this period in manufacturing. In Britain at least, workgroups were able to stabilise and enhance pay levels by setting group norms of production which circumvented the 'rate-busting' logic of piecework. This clear collective interest, rooted in small and interactive workgroups, bore a direct relationship to the 'effort/reward' logic of exploitation and rooted action in the group rather than the representative. Shop stewards rapidly increased in both numbers and influence during this period, but they emerge almost as instruments of workgroups rather than autonomous actors; the shop steward 'tends to be ... merely recognised by the work group ... the role of the steward can only be explained, at bottom, in terms of the work group'.[32]

While a degree of organisational structure existed in the form of shop steward representation and bargaining, the dynamic of steward–workgroup relations lay firmly with the membership. During this period steward representation emerged almost organically from the concerns of workgroups: 'Shop stewards were closely identified with the work group they represented. They shared [their] working environment ... and were subject to membership control on a continuous and close basis'.[33]

Yet the more developed forms of shop steward organisation could hardly remain marooned in a 'sectional' vacuum. The problem was, as always, the contradiction between direct representation and the collective needs of the membership as a whole. Even in the 1960s, the intransigence of the members had its corollary in the relative caution of their stewards; the need to ensure that weaker workgroups were represented and that some claims were prioritised over others meant that the most militant stewards could find themselves urging moderation on members whose trenchant claims clashed with the interests of other workers. The much quoted axiom of the 1968 Donovan Report that 'Shop stewards are moderates not militants' was backed up by a survey of managers in which a majority saw shop stewards as less militant than their members.[34]

'Get stuffed'? The roots of institutionalism

These contradictions and difficulties emerge clearly from a study of shop steward organisation in a large car factory in the Midlands which offers important insights into the exact nature of the processes leading to internal union ossification and loss of direct democracy. Typically, the strength of this workplace organisation was based in processes of militant piecework-based shopfloor activity, but by the 1970s the Joint Shop Stewards' Committee (JSSC) had become typical of the more formalised shop steward structures described in the 'bureaucracy thesis'. The stewards' overwhelming concern with 'protect[ing] the union organisation' had contributed to a mindset in which the needs of that organisation tended to take priority over those of the membership.[35]

Central to the stewards' impressive successes on issues like pay and labour mobility was the attempt to stabilise, in the interests of the membership, the fundamentally unpredictable course of production demands and management decisions. Yet, for the JSSC, an almost equivalent degree of disruption was posed by the membership: ' ... stewards should not be fooled or pushed around either by their own members or by management'. As one leader advised a steward facing complaints from his section: 'They're a bloody ungrateful lot. You've been doing a good job for them, and the trouble is they don't appreciate it. You tell them to get stuffed'.[36]

Thus, ironically, the need to suppress sectional interests in favour of those of the membership as a whole was central in creating a dynamic of membership suppression. This indicates that the beginnings of bureaucratisation are rooted not in explicit 'social democratic' ideology or organisational structure as such, but in the central contradiction between spontaneous, 'sectional' militancy and the need to organise effectively around workplace issues by uniting the membership and thus, on many occasions, suppressing the specific interest of sectional groups. Members' reluctance to accept the 'logic' of stewards' refusal to act over their specific grievances not unnaturally leads to alienation on both sides; the specific workgroup's resentment at being 'sold out', alongside the ossification of leadership identity and a growing tendency to 'blame the members'.

On this basis, the growth of 'oligarchy', even in a workplace setting, may indeed look like an 'iron law'. But the issue is not the contradiction between the interests of 'sectional' groups and overall effective organisation itself, but the degree to which workplace leaders are able to recognise this contradiction and thus consciously work to combat its tendency towards bureaucratisation; not the clear need to create workplace union organisation and 'protect' it, but the ability of leaders to value the roots and rationale of that organisation as well as its formal structure.

When more fully aware of these dynamics, workplace representatives can maintain a (precarious) balance between effective organisation and direct democracy. The central danger of institutionalisation – of the organisation gaining an existence separate from its original justification – has to be avoided by a process of conscious recognition rather than moral principle. Paradoxically, that awareness has been more fully spelt out within US rank-and-file trade unionism than in the stronger echelons of workplace organisation in Britain.

A UNION GETS BETTER ...

In America, by the 1960s, a combination of union bureaucracy and management suppression had robbed workers of their previous domination of piecework bargaining, a loss which eliminated a crucial source of strength and direct democracy. But, as pointed out at the time by one trenchant workplace activist, Stan Weir, this did not mean that American workers did not organise at the workplace. Rather, their resistance receded into a kind of ghost-structure of collectivism: 'In thousands of industrial establishments across the nation, workers have developed informal underground unions ... composed of several workers each of whose members work in the same plant-area ... Led by natural on-the-job organizers, they conduct daily guerrilla skirmishes with their employers'.[37] These workgroups acted as pressure points forcing an unwilling leadership to at least think about the workplace. One workplace activist succinctly expressed the link between labour market wages and a more fundamental agenda of exploitation: 'We're working under chain gang conditions for cotton-picking wages'.

Such issues, including relentless speedup, fired workers to act against their official union representatives as well as employers. Throughout American industry – in the docks, steel, auto, rubber, mineworking and the oil/gas/atomic sector – rank-and-file union members staged revolts against their leaderships, prompting one bemused journalist to note 'a dramatic shift from the familiar faces [of union leaders] to the facelessness of the rank and file'.[38]

Thus, paradoxically, the greater weight of union repression in the US bred a tradition of effective rank-and-file opposition to union bureaucracy. The various rank-and-file reform caucuses in unions from the UAW to the Teamsters represent, crucially, an issue-based rather than solely electoral approach to challenging union bureaucracy. As a leading Teamsters for a Democratic Union (TDU) organiser put it, 'A union does not get better because the right people get elected. It gets better when members understand their collective power and start exercising it, not just to turn out ineffective or corrupt officials but to fight for their rights at the workplace'.[39] Rather than electoralism per se – often the preoccupation of oppositional groups within British unions (see below), US union dissidents have often gained an impressive measure of success through their simultaneous focus on issues of internal union democracy and concrete workplace needs and concerns – a focus which in its turn builds on and stimulates a much greater degree of membership mobilisation.

The experience of a 1980s dissident group in the New York subway and bus workers' union, based around the serendipitously named *Hell On Wheels* newsletter, provides melancholy testimony to the dangers of electoralism. In contrast to previous initiatives aimed at reforming the notoriously corrupt and bureaucratic Transport Workers Union (TWU) local, Hell on Wheels activists 'expressly rejected the idea that electing new officers was the key to reforming the union and fighting back against the [M]TA [Metropolitan Transport Authority] ... We were convinced that the key ... was organizing the rank and file ... to act on their own behalf'.[40] Their actions in defending rank-and-file workers from the assaults of both management and union were well received by the workforce, who 'enjoyed the muckraking aspects of the newsletter and appreciated that someone was speaking out against management's actions and the union's inaction'. When workers nevertheless proved reluctant to commit their own time and energy to organising, Hell On Wheels activists decided to stand for the union executive as the New Directions (ND) slate. However, their prime aim was still not election per se: 'We ran primarily to give the members an option, a way to register a protest'.[41]

New Directions gained electoral support, winning a significant number of posts on the union executive by the early 1990s. Yet, rather than a new dawn for union democracy and mobilisation, this was the beginning of the end. While, in contrast to the incumbent leadership, the New Directions representatives emphasised that 'it was up to the membership ... to win a good contract', the problem was that neither they nor the members could control bargaining outcomes; the ironclad bureaucracy of the union's inner workings meant that the executive 'didn't even know when or where negotiations were scheduled'.[42]

This impotence caused a split among New Directions supporters. Those who argued that 'ND had failed because we had not been well enough organized ... [it] should keep on doing what it had been doing ...' were overridden by a majority pushing to win top posts in the union in order to get some control over bargaining; 'the need to have good people in high positions overshadowed the need to organize the membership to act on its own behalf'.[43] However, the 'good people in high positions' went on to tread the well worn path to bureaucracy. Many of those elected went on to take permanent staff positions in the union, meaning that they 'very quickly became influenced by the hierarchical methods and outlook of the machine of which they were now part'. By 1997, this group had split from New Directions to form the Rank and File United Slate; in 1999, they finally overthrew the corrupt local leadership.

As a Hell on Wheels veteran points out, 'The fact that the term "rank and file" keeps cropping up, that so many factions have sought an identification with it ... is a recognition that the average union member perceives a difference between the rank and file and the officers'. Yet, like so many other dissident groups, the 'Rank and File' slate began to become its opposite; while infinitely more democratic than its predecessors, it emerged as a force for moderation and battening-down of workplace resistance, confirming most workers' expectation that 'even the most militant reformer will become one of "them"'.[44]

DIRECT DEMOCRACY

Britain's record of internal union dissent failed to reach even these levels of contestation, centred as it was largely on a series of anaemic 'Broad Lefts', which tended to concentrate solely on electoral and 'resolutionary' issues – 'not motivated *as organisations* ... but as electoral and conference machines'.[45] Themselves often undemocratic and exclusionary, these 'electoral slate organisations'[46] focused almost entirely on winning executive and leadership positions, ignoring workplace concerns and issues of internal democracy and membership mobilisation. Not surprisingly, even when they were successful in winning control of union executives and offices, the results for on-the-ground militants were disappointing; formerly trenchant militants in unions like the National Communications Union (NCU), where the left gained control of the executive in 1993, turned, in the main, into cautious guardians of institutional stability.

This often melancholy experience – 'getting the right people elected' – draws attention to the whole issue of participative member-led trade union democracy as a crucial component of union effectiveness. While 'formal' trade union democracy uses representative processes, particularly elections, which typify union-as-institution, the dynamic of participative democracy expresses union-as-movement through direct involvement and open debate based in workers' immediate, shared material concerns.

Rank-and-file union activity rooted in such concerns expresses itself in specific organisational forms, often independent of official unionism, which embody this dynamic via an immediate relationship with grass-roots, production-based workplace structures. At the strongest point of union organisation during the upsurge period, multi-union joint shop steward committees (JSSCs) in the plants, cross-company combine committees and industry committees exhibited a form of direct democracy rooted in members' concrete interests which subverted the institutionally ossified logic of bureaucracy. Their delegate-based committee structure, typical of 'spontaneous' working-class organising, ensured a closeness and accountability to the membership lacking in 'representative' democracy.

The workgroup, shopfloor and mass meetings of 1970s Britain also expressed this dynamic of direct democracy, particularly in activities like strike votes which saw collective decision-making, based on open debate, in an atmosphere of strong, dynamic worker interaction.

The dangers of such democracy were swiftly recognised by management and the state; despite the organisational concessions granted stewards in the 1970s, 'certain facilities did not improve. There is, for example, little evidence of any increase in the use of mass or sectional meetings of workers and stewards …'.[47] Nor did the Donovan 'reforms', despite their wide range, include time off for workplace meetings. In fact the first formal acknowledgement of the existence, and implicitly effectiveness, of mass meetings was their outlawing in the Trade Union Act of 1984, which specifically eliminated show-of-hands workplace strike votes in favour of individual, secret, postal ballots.

As one critic commented, 'The intimate collectivism of the mass meeting is qualitatively different to the loneliness of the secret ballot. The essential logic of the Government's balloting legislation is to both debilitate the collective power of the mass and extinguish the immediacy of workers' anger'. More than any other set of pro-employer decisions on union organisation, this cluster of 'democratic' proposals, removing workers from a collective decision-making experience 'into individualistic insecurity, into the domestic environment of the debt-ridden consumer',[48] revealed the dangers to capital of direct, member-led union democracy.

Blaming the members

The Trade Union Act 1984 was premised on the argument that declining attendance at branch meetings indicated a loss of democracy which could be redressed by formal measures; research at the time proved the opposite. The irrelevance of procedural issues to the complex realities of trade union democracy is affirmed in one in-depth study of workplace organisation, aimed at exploring the assumptions behind the Conservative legislation, which concluded that 'Institutional factors – the structure of the local union organisation and collective bargaining ... were less relevant than the interaction between local leaders and members' commitment to collectivism'. An equally important finding was the link between member-led democracy and union effectiveness: 'effectiveness is most possible on the basis of an involved and participative membership' and 'leadership action ... based on a democratic identification with the collective interests of the membership'.[49]

Unfortunately, in at least two of the five workplace organisations examined in the study, such factors were distinctly lacking. In the National Union of Public Employees (NUPE) branch, based in a hospital, the 'chair' projected an attitude of militant substitutionism: 'You can't have everyone involved. I'm the spokesman. Anything wrong anywhere, they'll tell me'. Tell him they most certainly did; the 'chair' could scarcely walk through the hospital without being besieged by agitated members bringing him their grievances. Yet any notion of these individual concerns being turned into a collective fight was annihilated by contempt for the membership; when one shop steward tried to speak about cuts in her members' working hours, her comments 'were swept aside in a tirade by the chair and full-time official about the stupidity of members who had accepted shorter hours'.[50]

This 'blame the members' syndrome was amply represented by the lay Association of Scientific, Technical and Managerial Staffs (ASTMS) officials in the study, who assumed their right to negotiate on behalf of the membership without even a pretence of consultation, but found it easy to justify their neglect of basic union processes; it was the members' fault. When only 25 members attended a branch meeting on job evaluation, despite their strong feelings about the injustice of the system, it was easy to cite 'membership apathy'. Yet the members' non-involvement was interpreted differently by one disaffected steward: 'I kept repeating, people aren't happy – they're complaining to me. And the answer would come back: if they are not happy they have got to come to a branch. But if you know they're not going to come to a branch you can easily say this'.

The 'unhappiness' of ASTMS members, in fact, was directly related to their representatives' failure to defend their basic interests over job evaluation: 'A lot of people they regraded a while back were very dissatisfied ... The union was too involved with the company on job descriptions'.[51] Another steward pointed out that 'If you actually listened and did things which they asked you to do you certainly would get more people ... You could certainly get a more representative and more involved branch'.[52]

Marched up the hill ...

Ironically, the most democratic among the five organisations also failed to represent its members in a way which retained concern with their basic interests as part of its more consciously 'political' agenda. In the National And Local Government Officers' Association (NALGO) organisation, representing white-collar local government workers, encouraging high levels of membership involvement was a central feature of the local leaders' approach, along with a consistent record of winning solid gains in pay, job security and grading. The members responded with a considerable degree of loyalty, which eventually came into play over an explicitly political issue: the government's 'rate-capping' policy, forbidding local councils to raise their rates despite shrinking central government funding. The NALGO leaders' commitment to a radical anti-rate-capping stance scored impressive success in mobilising white-collar public sector workers whose class position did not always predispose them towards working-class forms of militancy.

Unfortunately, the leadership's opposition was expressed in a 'gesture politics'-style series of one-day strikes which disillusioned the members through what became seen as a pointless cycle of mobilisation and retreat, of being 'marched up the hill and down again'. The leaders' political radicalism blinded them to the dangers of substituting for and lecturing to the members: 'the local leaders were not indifferent to their members' concerns ... but rather were too committed to continuing energetic protest longer than their members'.[53] Perhaps as a result, the NALGO convenor concluded that 'The mass of members [will] always be "economic" in their approach rather than "political"'.[54]

Yet the truth is more complex, as the study showed: '[Some] individuals were pushed into involvement by instrumental factors and then acquired a more intrinsic belief in unionism as a result of that experience ...'.[55] A gap tends to remain, or open up, between 'economics' and 'politics' not as a direct result of members' undoubted political conservatism, but because the desired politicisation remains, or becomes, disconnected from members' direct interests. This gap is, ironically, promoted by the very assumptions implicit in the NALGO convenor's comment: that trade union action can be regarded as economic, or political, but not both.

To counterpose radical policies and worker 'economism' overlooks distinctions between the kinds of priorities and strategies that can actually mobilise rank-and-file members, building class consciousness from below, and perspectives essentially delivered from above. In this respect, both the grimly 'economistic' officials of NUPE and ASTMS and the more idealistic leaders of the NALGO workplace failed to deliver on the essential component of member-led democracy: leadership which connected with, built on and developed the logic of members' own concerns.

TRADE UNION RENEWAL – MAYBE

The same gap between 'economistic' and 'political' perspectives marks much current commentary on trade unionism, even in the context of recent research which cites the possibility of trade union renewal in the wellspring of the workplace. The 'union renewal thesis'[56] suggests that in previously state-owned sectors like telecommunications and local public service provision in Britain, the very pressures of privatisation – decentralisation of bargaining, managerial domination and growing labour intensification – have created a renaissance of direct union representation in workplace-based bargaining units.

This argument emphasises the choice for union leaderships between an orientation in this dynamic, member-led direction and so-called 'responsible' unionism 'with little presence in the workplace'. Yet even a thesis which clearly opts for the workplace as the central site for union renewal is cautious and conditional in its approach to the real nature of workplace unionism, noting critically that 'the issues addressed ... continued to be pay, discipline ... and the organisation of work ... these union groups tended to ignore questions relating to state policies and practices'.[57] Ambivalence between acknowledging the class implications of locating union renewal in the workplace and the need to invoke a broader political agenda continues to dog the 'union renewal thesis' even in the work of its own author.

Ironically, the renewal thesis itself has come under fire for its omission of 'the wider context' and 'absence of political agency'.[58] This critique acknowledges the merits of a 'focus on workers' self-activity and self-organisation at the workplace'; yet analysis of how basic workplace struggles can ignite something beyond themselves is again stalled by the familiar criticism that a workplace-based trade union renewal thesis 'is devoid of a political dynamic, that is a form of agency'.[59] The same reluctance to root the dynamic of political development in actually existing worker activity recurs in a contribution to the same debate which notes that, even at the height of the 1960s–1970s upsurge, 'the political horizon of most militants remained restricted'.[60] In today's situation of an aggressively anti-working class 'New Labour' government, the writer urges the need to 'go beyond the workplace' through promoting a programme of broader political demands which would 'connect with the existing not the desired level of consciousness among activists'.

The same account accurately observes the 'fierce antagonism' of New Labour to 'independence, conflict and militancy', its 'resolute opposition to oppositional, solidaristic trade unionism'. Yet, rather than seeing rank-and-file action which embodies these characteristics as the *foundation* for political development, the insistence on pulling workers over to extraneous political agendas and judging workplace unionism on non-workplace criteria opens up, once again, the familiar gap between where rank-and-file trade unionists are and where radical commentators would like them to be.

THE 'POLITICIST SYNDROME'

The same underlying critique of workplace unionism is implicit in many other theories of trade unionism which seek to revive the movement. Despite routine condemnations of the bureaucracy and its reformist ideology, it is the rank and file who are ultimately blamed for the disabling lack of 'politics' within the trade union movement. In one typical comment on the 1970s upsurge, with its militant wage claims, occupations and head-to-head confrontations with management power: 'It is true that industrial militancy does have a clear political character ... But this militancy retains a non-political veneer by virtue of the fact that it arises from separate segments of the working class at different times, and arises moreover in the absence of a generalised and explicit rejection of the economic and political structures in which these social relations are embedded'.[61]

Any serious attempt to address the political meaning and potential of industrial militancy as it stands is precluded by the implied requirement that workplace-based struggles have to show such 'generalised and explicit' awareness before they can be regarded as in any way political. This precondition itself automatically shifts the focus of the debate to broader objectives such as legislative changes, equal opportunities issues and, in the late 1970s, 'alternative' economic policies – perspectives revolving around a view of politics as a formal process of putting demands and developing policies which, socialist or otherwise, essentially come from above.

'The unions', as *institutions*, are posited as the vehicle of transformative politics, rather than their rank-and-file members – except insofar as those members mobilise around 'union policy' as set by conferences and national executives. In this way, the perception of 'the unions' as homogeneous blocks turns full circle; rank-and-file resistance and political leadership occupy two sealed and separate boxes in which there can be no connection between workers' instinctive rejection of capitalist priorities and the consciously 'political', policy-directed campaigns of left union leaders and their allies.

Yet radical commentators on trade unionism are continually caught within the paradox that 'industrial militancy does have a clear political character'. This paradox recurs in the writings of all these analysts as they swing back and forth from recognition of the class meaning of rank-and-file resistance to despair at its long-term lack of coherent transformative politics. Between these two extremes actually lies a terrain of possibility – the potential for 'instrumental' battles, provoked by the impact of capitalist production relations, to raise consciousness of wider social questions. Recognition of this terrain might allow advocates of trade union renewal to move away from what has been, so far, an unproductive insistence on 'politically correct' policies and towards a praxis rooted in actually existing worker resistance.

Criticism of workplace organisation and rank-and-file militancy for its lack of politics misses the point; consciously 'political' or not, any increase in workers' ability to collectively resist the demands of capital at the point of production poses enormous objective political implications, particularly in a period of union decline and ruling-class domination. If the dynamic, complex, contested process of workplace trade unionism deserves a place in serious discussion of the possibilities of trade union renewal, it seems equally important not to make that place conditional on acceptance of an approved list of politics or policies.

Ironically, the same writer quoted above as criticising industrial militancy for its lack of politics also critically identifies

> a broader 'politicist' syndrome ... which has tended to see trade unions as 'less important' because they are geared to short-term demands which are neither explicitly political nor revolutionary. Particularly in a period which has been increasingly industrial in form ... this 'politicist' syndrome forecloses the possibility of a full analysis of the balance of class forces ... .[62]

And a footnote to this comment pays tribute, almost despite itself, to the inherently political nature of such forces:

> Neither the strength exhibited by the workers' movement during the struggles of the second half of the sixties ... nor the capacity of resistance to the blackmail of unemployment during the seventies ... can be easily ascribed to factors of political consciousness and organisation. One can do so only on the basis of the truism that the class struggle is always a political struggle.[63]

It would be disingenuous to deny that class struggle has not become 'political' in the sense of projecting a revolutionary socialist critique of the capitalist system. But if it is a 'truism' that the class struggle is always political, why brush aside that truth? Perhaps, after all, it isn't *trivially* true, as the term 'truism' suggests. Perhaps it has an enormous, powerful truth set at its centre, a truth that those seeking to promote social transformation would do well to take more seriously. Establishing the connection between the class truth of worker resistance – the spark at the centre of union-as-movement – and the conscious politics of labour movement transformation is the central aim of this book.

8

Punctuation Marks:
A Story of Class Consciousness

As a history of workers' struggles, this book has also, inevitably, been a history of workers' consciousness – a factor which, only too often, blocks workers' concerted pursuit of their own class interests. The simplistic concept of 'false consciousness', often (wrongly) attributed to Marx, can be used as at least a working title for one of the central problems of trade unionism – the lack of awareness of most workers, most of the time, of their collective class interests.

For the cynic, the explanation might seem obvious: there is no class struggle, no clash of class interests between workers and capital – therefore, no 'class consciousness'. Yet the experiences and actions described in this book suggest otherwise. Without a fundamental clash between the interests of capital and those of labour, the impulse and dynamic of these struggles would be hard to explain.

Perhaps, after all, there is something which, equally crudely, might be called 'true consciousness' – a truth which may coexist, unrecognised, with the most misleading aspects of ruling-class ideology. In the words of one arch-theoretician of ideology:

> The active man-in-the-mass has a practical activity, but has no clear theoretical consciousness of his practical activity ... One might almost say that he has two theoretical consciousnesses (or one contradictory consciousness): one which is implicit in his activity and which in reality unites him with all his fellow-workers in the practical transformation of the real world; and one, superficially explicit or verbal, which he has inherited from the past and uncritically absorbed.[1]

How to challenge the uncritical absorption of ruling-class ideology – to unite workers, male and female, with all their fellow-workers, or at least enough of them to make a difference? This remains one of the fundamental questions facing the labour movement and the working class. Yet the answer does not lie in 'our' hands. It can already be found in the history and experience of workers themselves, over and over; and, overwhelmingly, it takes the shape of direct, militant, grass-roots worker resistance.

Yet that resistance itself very rarely springs from any explicit, preconceived rejection by workers themselves of the inherently conflictual system their action exposes and challenges. *Objectively*, working-class resistance challenges the rule of capital, and prevents it imposing its agenda in the unfettered way that it would like. But, *subjectively*, whatever the size of the dispute and its challenge to private capital and the state, most workers, most of the time, have not set out deliberately to make that challenge.

The 'true' side of the consciousness equation is that those involved in major struggles against capital may, and often do, emerge with their outlook on the world fundamentally changed. The question of how and why workers do undergo this transformation, along with the enormous political potential of that process, is considered more closely in the next chapter. The main topic of this one is why, even in the most promising circumstances, they don't – or don't enough to win.

ACTUALLY-EXISTING TRANSFORMATION

Even in the late 1960s and early 1970s, when workers both gained significant concessions from capital and were far more explicitly critical of the system, the level of class consciousness was ultimately limited; the upsurge gave way to the downturn, the downturn to the massive defeats of the 1980s and the doldrums of today.

The failures of the 'upsurge' period have been ascribed to a limited 'economism', a failure to adopt 'broader' political perspectives. Less often considered is why working-class militants failed to recognise the political implications of what they were actually doing. What was lacking here was not militant resistance, but a systematic, explicit awareness of the class value of those fierce, oppositional grass-roots struggles, those significant organisational advances, those sweeping material victories – an awareness which would identify them as advances in a 'war of position' between labour and capital, as vital steps forward which, in order to prevent sliding back, would require conscious consolidation.

Perhaps the first question therefore ought to be: What happened to that heightened level of consciousness? What stopped it from sustaining a level of class awareness strong enough to at least maintain the basics of labour organisation in the face of the assaults to come? What stood in the way of its foremost militants becoming conscious, strategically adept long-term planners in the battle with capital? In attempting to answer these questions, this chapter focuses on a crucial issue which links rank and file with union leadership, activist with bureaucrat, militant with radical: the all-pervading ideology of reformism.

An absence of ideology

The existing nature of class consciousness amongst the majority of workers, whether organised, open to organisation or 'unorganis-able', is reformist. Reformist consciousness, or ideology, reproaches capitalism for its abuses, yet assumes that the existing system can be maintained or improved in a way that can meet most workers' needs and interests satisfactorily and permanently, or at least for the time being; it implicitly accepts the boundaries of the capitalist system, and falls short of offering any meaningful alternative. Most workers, implicitly or explicitly, accept this analysis most of the time, meaning that they subscribe to the 'official' ideology of the mainstream labour movement; while ruling-class ideology is also dominant, this is a more shifting and contradictory allegiance. Those who get exploited for a living are unlikely to seamlessly endorse a set of ideas which justify the economic advantage of those who exploit them.

But though workers more fully accept reformist ideology, this acceptance too is riven with contradictions. The traditional, mater-ial dimensions of reformism, the various improvements and rights which constitute at least the premarket, social-democratic meaning of 'reform', are embedded in labour movement activity and thus shape the consciousness of those embraced by that movement. Yet most worker consciousness falls short of a positive, explicit endorse-ment of reformist ideology – or ideology in general.

Rather, reformism constitutes an *absence* – a lack of any coherent, cohesive analysis of everyday experience, and thus an absence of any alternative to what appear as the inevitable structures of capi-talist existence. Things could be better, which is why reformism is an acceptable approach to reality, but things could not be otherwise. In this sense, reformism is a negative rather than conscious attribute: a 'default' ideology which blurs direct perception of class relations, rather than an optimistic faith in the likelihood of reform; an inability to conceive of the true extent of ruling-class 'immoral-ity', rather than any trust in its benevolence.

Yet despite its lack of affect, reformist ideology is shared from top to bottom of the movement, even amongst the most apparently (and actually) 'militant' activists. As so many examples of struggle in this book show, reformist ideology continues to dominate in even the most furious battles against capital. This ideological strain extends not only upwards to embrace the compromises and 'betrayals' of union leaders but also downwards to influence the most apparently explosive and subversive working-class struggles; struggles which may not set out to overthrow the existing system, but at the same time are triggered by the impact of that system on 'ordinary' lives, and the anger and despair it engenders.

Clearly the 'reformism' of outraged workers engaged in gargantuan struggles against capital, or of combative activists fighting the daily battle on the shop or office floor, is not the same as that of the complacently collaborative union official; yet it remains, at bottom, equally unaware of the depth and sharpness of the fissure between labour and capital. What is missing is not outrage, not militancy, but a more analytical and strategic awareness of the class issues and implications raised in struggle, whether everyday or explosive. Only a tiny minority of the most 'advanced' workers are able to make a qualitative, explicit break with the parameters of capital, to consciously recognise that capital has nothing to offer. In general, the limits of worker consciousness to a partial, sporadic, inconsistent critique of the system still mark the process and outcome of worker resistance. This is why reformist ideology is so important, and why this chapter sets out to more fully understand its inner workings.

Advanced sections and backwards tactics

One way of doing that is to look at the strongest sections of the movement, those layers of workplace organisation most resistant to reformist compromises and most open to a critical overview of the system. The workplace union organisation at the British Leyland (BL) assembly plant at Cowley, near Oxford – 'the most militant in the country', by one account[2] – can be taken as a case in point. Led for many years by a group of stewards with explicitly revolutionary politics, and mobilising a mass of members whose outlook, objectives and experience these stewards shared on an everyday basis, the workplace organisation at Cowley seems to have had the maximum potential for challenging reformist ideology and practice within the labour movement.

The strength of steward organisation at Cowley was exemplified in the dual-power-style 'mutuality agreement' of 1970, which gave workers 'a comprehensive veto over management decisions on work effort and staffing levels. It was unique in the industry. Management loathed it'.[3] This agreement had itself emerged from workers' resistance to the impact of measured day work (MDW), a new payment system introduced to eliminate the powerful workgroup bargaining tool of piecework. Cowley workers fought a six-week strike against MDW in 1970; its defeat and the system's implementation marked a significant management victory. Yet even this failed to stem the tide of workplace intransigence; the 'mutuality agreement' was negotiated almost immediately after MDW in order to stem the tide of stoppages and walkouts.

However, BL management could hardly tolerate an agreement which so clearly encroached on managerial prerogative. In early 1974, it moved decisively against the 'mutuality agreement' with the imposition of a substantial speedup on two assembly lines and in the 'trim shop'; here the workers, all women, instigated an immediate sit-in strike, followed within days by a walkout by the assembly-line workers. These strikes, spontaneous eruptions by the rank-and-file workers affected, were supported by the stewards from the relevant sections. However, when the actions ended in confusion and defeat, management dived in immediately to withdraw recognition from the TGWU deputy convenor, a trenchantly left-wing steward and a key player in the workplace union organisation.

This attack on the powerful shopfloor steward structure at Cowley might be predictable on the part of management; yet management was not the only enemy of rank-and-file struggle and organisation. The local union bureaucracy, including both full-time officials and 'lay' (company-paid) representatives, like convenors on the British Leyland combine committee, 'had been looking for the opportunity to take on the left in the Assembly Plant for some time'.[4] Despite token resistance to the deputy convenor's deposition, it allowed for his replacement by a right-wing maverick who had been selected by the bureaucracy for just this purpose.

This defeat launched an unremitting attack on the left in the plant by the T&G bureaucracy. Many of the bureaucratic shenanigans used to undermine shop stewards would have been laughable if they had not so clearly been aimed at eliminating a shopfloor structure committed to rank-and-file resistance against the wage cuts and labour intensification now assaulting workers. The loyalty of the membership to the activist stewards throughout this internal union offensive was extraordinary, as was their willingness to struggle against the management onslaught; workers' intransigence provided a supportive backcloth to the activity of the left in the plant throughout the 1970s and even into the mid 1980s. But it was not enough to stem the growing collusion of 'senior' union representatives with management, or their hostility to shopfloor resistance. It took the full incorporation of the shop steward body into a series of joint initiatives with management, beginning in the mid 1970s with worker participation, to finally – at least at present – squash all rank-and-file dissent at BL.

The chimera of 'participation'

During the 1970s, the joint attack by management and union officialdom on independent workplace organisation at Cowley went hand-in-hand with an early attempt at 'partnership', the Labour government-backed policy of worker participation. Combine representatives on a BL worker–management body set up in 1976 – the Cars Council – gave union sanction for the closure of four plants which between them employed 2,700 workers, and joined notoriously 'macho' chief executive Michael Edwardes to call on the BL workforce to stop strikes and double productivity.

There is little question that the beginning of the end of effective workplace organisation at BL lay with the full-time convenors' acceptance of worker participation and the logic of 'company profitability'. The question here is why the more grass-roots activist layer was unable to effectively contest that quasi-bureaucratic leadership.

The auguries were promising; if anything, rank-and-file workers at BL were 'more sceptical of participation than most stewards'. The membership strongly supported a boycott of Cars Council elections organised by left-wing shop stewards; 'far from being isolated, we were clearly with the bulk of the workforce ...'.[5] Yet the cadre of workplace activists, despite their own explicit opposition and the strong support of their members, was unable to effectively counter the impact of participation. The stewards' furious opposition to Edwardes' job-cutting 'recovery plan', expressed mostly in leaflets and the branch newsletter, proved impotent in the face of official union collusion and the workers' own desperate desire to 'save' BL.

Steward consciousness – the 'missing link'

The stewards' inability to sustain effective opposition to management chicanery even among a militant membership points to a key issue in the analysis of class consciousness and reformist ideology: that grass-roots worker resistance – the 'kick' from below – expresses an *instinctive* rather than *explicit* rejection of managerial ideologies and strategies. Such 'gut-level' resistance, a crucial force in combating managerial offensives, needs conscious recognition and development. What seemed like an inexhaustible wellspring of membership militancy at Cowley in fact required cultivation and recognition as part of building an effective, class-based counteroffensive.

As usual, management was distinctly better equipped in the ideological battlefield. Edwardes' union-style mass meetings, at which he appealed to workers over the heads of their stewards to support his 'recovery plan', his direct letters to individual workers, were ideological masterstrokes leading straight to the eventual debacle in which workers throughout BL – including Cowley – voted for the elimination of their own jobs.

The shopfloor leadership's commitment to trenchant resistance was not enough to avoid that debacle. Rather than moralistic condemnation and leaflet-based 'campaigns', the situation required direct member-to-member education and involvement, creating a rank-and-file fighting force well prepared for both corporate and official union duplicity. As the 'turkeys for Christmas'-style vote revealed, activists had failed to get across the crucial message of independent trade unionism to enough of their formerly combative, supportive membership to make a difference. While resistance had continued to resurface against enormous odds in the past, and would do so for some time in the future, this enormous force – the most powerful at the stewards' disposal – remained, ultimately, neglected.

This was not a deliberate abandonment. Rank-and-file stewards were themselves shopfloor workers facing the same conditions as those they represented; understandably, they took workers' anger and opposition essentially for granted, tending to complain if members failed to support them, rather than valuing it when they did. Even among the most committed representatives, a 'blame the members' mindset was easy to fall into, an inattention to the crucial task of maintaining links with the members, rather than assuming their permanent, uncontested loyalty. The missing factor was conscious recognition of the value of everyday worker resistance in its direct, instinctive opposition to management, the crystallisation of that opposition into a conscious stance of independent, grass-roots, member-led trade unionism against the siren song of 'common interests' and 'company viability'.

RADICAL REFORMISM?

Many of the stewards at the plant were self-identified revolutionaries or at least socialists, espousing class antagonism at a broader political level as well as instinctively championing workplace resistance. What even this most 'advanced' section of a highly organised industry failed to do was to make a conscious link between socialist politics and the equally political question of everyday workplace organisation. Instead, the more developed workplace activists' class awareness, the more they tended to sideline it into 'political' activity which diverted that awareness from the crucial task of maintaining and building everyday workplace trade unionism.

The confident workplace militancy of the 1970s began to see a damaging disjunction between many similar stewards' political views – often close to socialism and in some cases explicitly revolutionary – and their ability to devise clear-sighted class strategies within the workplace. As the rank-and-file militants of the 1960s and early 1970s developed into seasoned activists, they became increasingly open to socialist politics – an encouraging move in the direction of full class consciousness. But it was a consciousness which led away from the workplace towards the broader political arena espoused by middle-class radicals; and on its way, it lost the potential to strengthen the working class by infusing that greater political awareness into the rank-and-file movement.

From this point of view, a different and perhaps unexpected culprit emerges on the ideological battlefield – the 'radical reformism' of the left. Particularly in Britain, in the later 1970s, middle-class radicals' critique of and lack of interest in workplace-based issues and struggles pushed committed activists away from a recognition of the political meaning of their own activity and, in many cases, towards a diversionary 'prefigurative' programme of workers' plans, workers' cooperatives and 'alternative economic strategies', rather than building on the strength and class potential of their own industrywide rank-and-file organisations.

The same paradoxical 'politicist syndrome' emerges in a study of three more typically combative workplace organisations of the

1970s which had deteriorated into acquiescence, weakness and defeat by the 1990s.[6] At the printing plant examined in the study, the workplace leadership was dominated by Militant, a revolutionary organisation then notorious for its 'entrist' tactic in the Labour Party. While themselves rank-and-file workers with a long history of working and organising at the plant, these activists 'didn't have a real workplace base to their politics. They saw their role as being active in the Labour Party'.[7] At a second plant, the left-wing convenor – 'very much politically minded ... a real socialist'[8] – saw the principal focus for his socialist politics as the local T&G branch, where 'we gradually introduced an element of politics into the branch ... we supported the Right to Work Campaign, the Anti-Nazi League and that'. Yet the left-wing activists involved made 'little attempt ... to try to connect [these] political and socialist arguments ... with the day-to-day interests and concerns of shopfloor union members back inside the factory'.[9]

'So it seeped down'

The problem here was not one of simplistic 'betrayal'; in all cases, the stewards saw themselves as trenchantly committed to resistance against management objectives. What was lacking was a more conscious recognition of the immense dangers now confronting what had at one time been the relatively straightforward task of worker protection and representation; management's panic at the crisis in profitability, its newly focused determination to push back the 'frontier of control', its employment of increasingly sophisticated strategies to achieve this. Because of this missing link with the workplace, the substitution of political idealism for strategic, conscious building of rank-and-file organisation and resistance, key workplace activists failed to develop the long-term strategies and policies of membership education and involvement that might have maintained a more effective workplace barrier against the managerial onslaught of the 1980s.

While sheer 'militancy' was in many ways enough during the peak period of rank-and-file strength, unquestioned reliance on earlier patterns as a response to the shift in managerial strategy of the 1980s was more than inadequate – it was disastrous. 'Spontaneous' worker resistance could no longer be taken for granted in an era of growing unemployment and managerial aggression. Not that grassroots resistance was no longer sufficient – quite the opposite. What was needed was an explicit guardianship of just such struggle as the platform for resistance to the growing lures of union–management 'cooperation' which differentiated 1980s management strategies from the simple 'conflict model' of the previous period.

Here, the lack of connection between leading stewards' embrace of 'politics' and their activities in the workplace meant increasing inability to contest management. The inability of politically conscious workplace leaderships 'to link broad socialist arguments with a practical day-to-day shopfloor strategy within the plant' meant that, ironically, 'the overwhelming majority of shop stewards lacked the socialist politics and self-confidence to reject the argument that only increased efficiency and profitability could save jobs'.[10] At Ford Halewood, where a once staunchly workplace-oriented plant leadership had begun to 'look to the extra-workplace TGWU branch as a short-cut solution to advance workers' interests', senior stewards accepted the company's 'employee involvement' advances in the mid 1980s 'hook, line and sinker'. While some lower-level, work-group-based stewards tried to fight the trend, 'they didn't have the counterarguments ... So it seeped down'.[11]

This 'seeping down' augured a tragedy for workplace organisation and the workforce as a whole. British workers in the 1980s were faced with almost insurmountable obstacles – a trade union bureaucracy which embraced 'new realism', structural changes in industry and the economy, and an intransigent government with a missionary zeal to destroy the movement. The 1980s saw the hugely demoralising defeats of key sectors like steelworkers, printers and miners. But perhaps the greatest defeat was where it mattered most, and where it would have been in many ways easiest to resist – the workplace.

The target for capital's most insidious and most profit-generating tactics, from Taylorism to multiskilling, from 'quality circles' to 'team concept' and 'lean production', the workplace is also where labour is strongest, most nourished by its roots in the concrete issues and contradictions facing the working class. This strength is the foundation for wider struggles, for major strikes, for the possibility of classwide solidarity. In its failure to recognise the central class meaning of its most valuable asset – rank-and-file resistance and membership support – the ideology of left reformism ultimately failed the movement as a whole.

The radical, militant stewards dominant in these once strong and militant plants represented the cutting edge of working-class organisation and struggle. It was not any lack of commitment, any lack of honesty, idealism or class loyalty that was the fatal absence in their response to the disasters of the 1980s. It was the fundamentally reformist ideology of even the extreme 'left' of the movement that undermined the very class basis of their own commitment and development as activists. From this point of view, even the most combative stewards ultimately 'blew it' in their response to the management offensive of the 1980s and beyond.

'WHAT CAN YOU DO?'

Reformism, 'left' or mainstream, is a complex set of ideas, with shifting, patchy attributes of passionate anti-capitalism, belief in the promises of deceitful employers, class loyalty, and pragmatic accommodation to the system – often held within the head of one worker, or one workplace activist. Most of all, workplace activists are themselves workers, and as such reflect most workers' 'default' class consciousness – a consciousness which stems from and reflects the daily experience of exploitation, but rarely 'connects the dots' of that experience within a coherent overview of class relations as a whole.

This is often seen as particularly true in America, where a powerful combination of consumerist and individualist ideology, cutthroat corporate strategies and corrupt, bureaucratic unions seem to pose almost impenetrable barriers to against-the-stream class consciousness. Yet a detailed study of so-called 'middle-class' American workers enjoying, on the basis of long hours of overtime, a suburban lifestyle embellished with the usual array of consumer goods,[12] reveals a different, more complex and in many ways more hopeful picture.

In this comparative survey of workers and middle-class radicals, the workers are revealed as significantly more conscious of class realities than the radicals. While displaying standard patriotism and loyalty to the American way of life, workers were 'scathingly dismissive of the political system'.[13] Radicals' beliefs and goals, while superficially more confrontational, implied a logic of reform which clashed with workers' bleak awareness of the unassailability of an overwhelmingly wealth-dominated, politically corrupt society.

While workers' defence of US society was overwhelmingly based on the iconic concept of *freedom*, one of the central tenets of American ideology, on closer inspection the 'freedom' invoked was a very different creature from American Dream-style 'freedom of opportunity'. Instead, what was valued was freedom from *constraint* – the constraint imposed by those in power. Asked to define 'what's *right* with the political system', a worker replied, 'I think basically the biggest thing is that you've got your freedom, right? ... You do your work, pay your taxes, and the government leaves you alone. That's democracy. That's the good part of the system'. In almost identical words, another worker argued, 'I pay my taxes, don't break the law, and leave me alone'.[14]

This political nihilism centred on a realistic recognition not only of the utter corruption and hypocrisy of the political system, but also of its overriding *power*. It is this power which workers invoked in defining their freedom; a freedom to get out from under the huge oppressive structures which dominated their lives, to build 'autonomous spaces' which could afford them some measure of control over their lives. Such 'spaces' were usually enshrined within the much-prized private sphere of home and family, but were also sought at work, where workers dealt with oppression, boredom and labour intensification by 'quietly struggling for "free spaces"',[15] rather than actively mobilising around their demands and grievances.

The same approach of 'opting out' rather than of resistance, of avoidance rather than confrontation, reflected workers' implicit recognition of their inability to challenge the system through conventional means. To a surprising degree, workers supported the anti-war, pro-environmental goals of radical activists; yet such activity was seen, more than anything else, as *futile*. The mindset of political involvement and entitlement found among the well educated and materially privileged radicals was so absent from workers' lives as to render 'politics' utterly irrelevant. This, rather than lack of support for specific causes, was the main reason why workers rejected radical mobilisation, while any class-based revolutionary alternative remained off the radar screen.

This response reflects the profound sense of *powerlessness* – the apparent impossibility of change, the absence of any meaningful alternative – which emerges as the central aspect of working-class rejection of socialist activity and ideas. A principal expression of this was the almost hypnotic repetition of the question, 'What can you do?'. In a typical comment:

> I think things – some things, anyway – have gotten out of hand. We don't really know what to do about all this stuff. What can you do? It's everywhere. What can you do? You hope, you know. You hope people will come to their senses. But really, what can you do?[16]

Despair transmutes into a mixture of fatalism and pragmatism:

> What are you going to do about it? A lot of times I don't like the weather, but I don't rack my brain trying to think up a way to change it because I know there's nothing I can do about it.[17]

While these stereotypically 'conservative' workers were far from embracing a socialist perspective, the barriers to their mobilisation against capital were negative rather than positive, rooted in the absence of any perceived alternative rather than in any positive, explicit endorsement of ruling-class activity and ideology. The failure either to endorse *or* to reject ruling-class ideology matches workers' general adoption of 'pragmatic' rather than 'normative' acceptance[18] – an ideological abstentionism which, despite strongly resented aspects of class society, substitutes fatalism for active resistance. Marx's famous phrase, 'the dull compulsion of economic relations',[19] sums up this mixture of resignation and economic reality.

Yet this 'absence of ideology', paradoxically, allows for the development of an almost wholly transformative acceptance of class struggle politics if and when they become practically relevant to workers' lives. The potential 'reversibility' of this consciousness is shown in the many fierce anti-corporate struggles taking place among workers very similar to those in the study during the same period. 'The two worlds' – politically abstentionist working-class culture, class-based opposition to the system – met 'when the twelve hundred paperworkers at International Paper's mill in Jay, Maine, went on strike'.[20]

'OCCASIONALLY AND IN FLASHES ...'

Most research on class consciousness[21] provides a depressing picture of contradictory, inconsistent, and 'incoherent' views of society. As one analysis points out, 'the possession of a coherent, well-formed and clearly articulated philosophy is a rarity even in the dominant class, and is probably only found among certain intellectual groups'.[22] It is all the more notable that the strike experiences described in this book suggest that purely industrial struggle can generate a 'philosophy' among workers which approaches (and probably surpasses, in terms of its grounded 'common sense') that of the most coherent intellectuals. While the experience of major struggle may not yet signal 'arriv[al] at political class consciousness, that long-awaited station that figures so prominently in Marxist social theory',[23] the revelations it brings provide a crucial, and indispensable, jumping-off point.

Yet progress towards that destination is not, as often suggested, one of set 'stages' marked by predefined levels of class consciousness, but a dynamic process in which underlying contradictions shake apart everyday acceptance and set in motion the potential for rapid leaps in consciousness. The essentially contradictory, uneven and unpredictable potential of working-class struggle for advances in class consciousness belies static 'models' and 'typologies' of class consciousness; the actual growth of consciousness within struggle is far more volatile, uneven and dynamic. As Rosa Luxemburg put it, working-class consciousness 'does not proceed in a beautiful straight line but in a lightning-like zigzag'.[24]

One major analyst of the kind of 'leaps' or 'breaks' in consciousness experienced in struggle is another classical theorist, Antonio Gramsci. Often seen as the arch-exponent of capital's 'hegemonic' ideological domination, Gramsci also provided invaluable insights into the possible *undermining* of such hegemony through concrete experience. Workgroup resistance, itself a product of the contradictions between ideology and experience, 'signifies that the social group in question may indeed have its own conception of the world, even if only embryonic; a conception which manifests itself in action, but occasionally and in flashes – when, that is, the group is acting as an organic totality'.[25]

Despite the sporadic and often short-lived nature of these 'flashes', their existence and recurrence points to the vulnerability of capital's supposedly impregnable ideological domination. While capital may, so to speak, fool most of the workers most of the time, it is never able to totally defend its fortresses against breaches thrown up by its own internal contradictions. The system which promotes the ideology also creates its continual undermining. And a central element in this volatile, contradictory process is its roots in the dialectical *balancing*, within one consciousness, of two 'conceptions of the world', one subordinate, one transformative.

So, rather than solely the chaotic, 'incoherent' mess of contradictions unearthed by sociologists, working-class 'common sense' can also be described in terms of a *dual* consciousness – a simultaneous holding of conformist and subversive views of the world, both of which can be expressed in one inconsistent statement. As Gramsci suggests, forms of 'class-for-itself' thinking and opposition to the ruling class are 'embryonic' – germinal, so to speak, within the consciousness and experience of the working class at its centre. One account of a typical dispute radicalising once-conservative workers – the US Colt Firearms strike of the late 1980s – describes this embryonic awareness, this 'shadow consciousness' in terms of a 'hidden transcript' of working-class consciousness – an 'oppositional pattern of belief and behavior in which the powerless engage when not confronting power directly'.[26]

C2s AND CATASTROPHES

The very *absence* of ideology noted earlier – a 'pragmatic accommodation' with the system which neither consciously questions nor positively endorses it – is a key factor in the emergence of this 'hidden transcript', in permitting the *undermining* of dominant ideology. The much advertised 'hegemony' of the Thatcherite regime in Britain, for example, saw significant cracks in the early 1990s when thousands of workers who had responded eagerly to its message of 'popular capitalism' received a painful reality check which pushed them from delighted acceptance to disillusionment and class-based anger.

These workers came into the infamous 'C2' category – the electoral equivalent of 'Reagan Democrats' – most associated with the rout of Labour by Thatcher in 1979, and her victory in two subsequent elections. Widely seen as impervious to socialist idealism, this 'white working class' was indeed mostly white, relatively well paid and highly conservative on issues like sexuality, race and gender. Nevertheless, by the late 1980s and early 1990s, it was these very workers who were among the most overwhelmingly disillusioned with Thatcherite ideology – perhaps because, materially, they were closest to its 'glittering prizes'.

The central factor sparking this disillusionment was the inability of many C2s to hold on to one of the major promised benefits of the Thatcher regime – their own homes. Appealing to better-off workers through the wildly popular 'right to buy' policy, which allowed local council tenants to buy their own flats or houses, Thatcher successfully created a pool of lower-income homeowners with all the responsibilities, outgoings and pretensions of suburbia – but with much less than the usual disposable income or job security of this traditionally middle-class sector. Workers previously contained within the relatively austere confines of British working-class lifestyles were now suddenly, it seemed, admitted to a paradise of individual consumerism and property-based affluence.

Yet by the late 1980s and early 1990s, C2 voters' belief in the promise of Thatcherite consumerism had been seriously undermined by the concrete experience of job loss, job insecurity, reduced incomes, and perhaps most painfully, widespread home repossession by creditors. The illusions bestowed by Thatcherite ideology were replaced by cruel reality: 'We are now going backwards', 'struggling to survive', 'It's dire – we've hit the bottom and can't go any further'.[27] The experience produced a political and ideological reversal:

> The shock troops of Thatcherism are in open revolt. The voters of class C2, the skilled manual workers who did so much to propel Mrs Thatcher to power in 1979 ... are swinging back to Labour on an even more drastic scale than the electorate as a whole.[28]

Alongside the loss of 'property-owning' delusions went, of course, a parallel radicalisation associated with the jobs-based struggles of printers, telephone workers and many other members of the much maligned 'white working class' in the 1980s and 1990s. The roots of an 'alternative hegemony' could lie only in the collision of these ideologically colonised workers with material reality.

'KISSY-KISSY SHIT'

Within the workplace, attempts to blur such materially based challenges to ruling-class ideology were consciously accelerated with the spread of 'team concept' to an almost total domination of workplace relations by the end of the twentieth century. The promise of a direct voice in the organisation of work appealed not only to 'progressive' union leaders and commentators but also to many workers. Research into worker involvement in a GM plant in Linden, New Jersey,[29] shows that workers began with very positive views of the system introduced in 1986 as the 'New Linden'.

Nevertheless, the contrast between rhetoric and reality became only too obvious shortly after the introduction of new working practices pitched at giving workers more job control and responsibility, including permission to stop the line if necessary for quality reasons. As one worker recounted, 'I would stop the line ... which took maybe about fifteen, twenty seconds ... but they would go crazy, because, you know ... they're thinking right away they're losing money ...'.[30] Similarly, workers' eagerness to contribute new ideas for the organisation of work encountered unexpected reluctance: 'We used to come up with some good ideas for them, but they didn't want any. You know, "Okay, okay, okay". They didn't want to hear us, you know. They wanted numbers, not ideas'.[31] One worker memorably evoked some of the broader contradictions:

> That parking lot, it used to be salaried; then with the big kissing affair going on, to show we're all equal, they opened it up ... But now, I can't park there ... because I'm not a foreman, I'm not supervision. I said, 'What happened to all this kissy-kissy shit?'.[32]

Given the material disincentives for genuine worker involvement, it is difficult for capital to keep up the illusion of shared interests. The same contradictions surfaced in a recent study of the impact of onerous working conditions in workplace union renewal in Britain.[33] In one West Midlands manufacturing plant, management introduced cell-based production 'teams' at the same time as proposing a restructuring of workplace unionism which 'spoke of "partnership" but [was] in fact ... management led and controlled'.[34] The stewards' initial 'pragmatic accommodation' to the changes was shaken when cell-based bargaining based on flat-rate pay rather than piecework led to a severe drop in pay, while the 'partnership' structure threatened the whole basis of union organisation in the plant. The shopfloor union leaders responded by 're-lay[ing] the foundation for active and participative steward-based structures'.[35] In both the US and Britain, the clash between the ideological promise of 'team'-style initiatives and the underlying realities of exploitation continued to challenge capital's twin objectives of intensifying production and undermining traditional 'adversarial' attitudes.

A MIRROR IMAGE

But what are these 'realities'? Since the late twentieth century, the rise of postmodernist theory has worked to discredit any notion of an objective, external material reality. For postmodernists, there is 'no direct access to "reality". All we know is language ...'.[36] Within this framework, experience and action are constructed by 'discourse'; the world is 'signified' in the shifting images and brand-name fixations evoked by the media, advertising and the internet. Contingency and fragmentation supplant the 'grand theories' of history, capitalism, and class conflict.

In one sense, it is impossible to prove the existence of objective reality. Philosophers have been making this point for centuries; postmodernists have extended it to question still further the already much criticised Marxist concept of a material economic base which can impinge on consciousness. But when postmodernists discuss issues related to the despised economic base, the argument undercuts itself. With claims that consumption is now more economically significant than production, or that 'Bureaucratic hierarchies dissolve as owners and workers work at the same desk or workstation',[37] postmodernist arguments start to bear a remarkable similarity to more down-to-earth promotions of 'lean production' and workplace 'flexibility'. Postmodernists may not acknowledge material reality, but their dismissal of it allows for a very real alignment of postmodernist theory with ruling-class interests and ideology.

For most workers, most of the time, 'discourse' does indeed construct their world; there is no point in denying the overarching role of the media and consumer culture in the commodified world of 'advanced' capitalist societies. But, as shown earlier, 'discourse' can be shredded by the experience of only too blunt material reality. In one description of the experience of workers faced with job loss:

> For Kenosha workers, the Chrysler plant closing catalyzed a sense of having witnessed the true reality of things for the first time. The false picture was peeled away, and in its place they see a world beset by social disorder on a magnitude never before imagined.[38]

The conception of a 'false picture', of a 'true reality' stands in direct contrast to the postmodernist critique.

So what are the connections between arguing for the existence of an objective 'reality', and the understanding of consciousness? Marxist theories on ruling-class ideology, best known for the much maligned distinction between 'base' and 'superstructure', also contain a much broader theory of consciousness in general. The basic Marxist rejection of idealism – the notion that historical progress is brought about by ideas rather than material realities – is often seen as indicating a crude economic determinism. But the resulting emphasis on 'experience [as]the base of all consciousness'[39] allows for the complex insight that consciousness is formed by both ideological symbols *and* objective reality. Both are 'real' elements of the world of workers.

Working-class consciousness is often contradictory because the world itself is contradictory: a mixture of material 'realities' which appear as natural and, so to speak, eternal, and the underlying social relations which are both obscured by those appearances and constantly surface in aspects of working-class experience. The dominance of bourgeois ideology is explained by the fact that so much working-class experience *can* be given an apparently logical 'bourgeois interpretation', while on the other hand 'the radical *inassimilability* of other elements of working class experience to bourgeois views of the world'[40] explains workers' incomplete acceptance of ruling-class ideology – the holes, so to speak, in the ozone layer of 'hegemony'.

The Marxist concept of the 'fetishism of commodities' provides a useful way of explaining these complex interrelationships. Because the things produced within capitalism are, of course, material objects which, like the material objects of nature, can be seen and touched, they are held to be 'natural' in all their properties, including price and labour. As Marx puts it, 'economic categories' present themselves as 'qualities inherent in [their] material incarnations'.[41] The 'economic category' of price appears physically built in to the jacket, the car, the table produced for sale.

Making a living

The same concept comes into play in Marx's analysis of the ideological aspects of the wage contract. The Marxist labour theory of value makes a clear separation between the amount paid in wages, decided on a cost-of-living basis (subsistence), and the value of what is produced. Workers are paid not for their labour but for their 'labour power'; the wage contract requires workers to come to work, to work at work. But the wage they receive for fulfilling that requirement is based not on the price in the market of what they produce – expensive cars, cheap candy – but on how much it costs for them to 'reproduce' their labour – in another words, live to work another day.

Yet the wage *appears* as direct payment for work performed – an appearance maintained by the fact that the worker is paid after the work is done and that 'it is a particular kind of useful labour that he has supplied, and was contracted to supply'. Particularly if wages are paid by the piece or by the hour, they appear 'as a direct correlate of work done'.[42] In this way, working-class *experience* gives powerful support to the essentially reformist view of pay as 'a fair day's wage for a fair day's work'.

So where is the element of contradiction, the source of 'class consciousness'? The relationship is dialectical; if material experience is strong enough to support ideological domination, it is also strong enough to overturn it. If ideological 'hegemony' was based *only* on 'discourse', on non-material, abstract ideas, it would lack the traction of 'common sense', there would be, so to speak, no material evidence to support ideas like that of common interests between employers and workers. Such ideas seem substantiated by, for example, the power and willingness of employers to 'give' workers that urgently required necessity, a job. In this way, relations which are actually class- and capital-specific appear as material 'things'.

Yet this appearance is unable to totally conceal a different material dynamic, that contained in the exploitative relations of capitalist production. The wage may look 'fair', a direct exchange between work performed and reward given – but once the dynamics of profitability come into play, that 'fair' wage may rapidly sink below what might have been an acceptable level of subsistence. The gift of a job is withdrawn peremptorily at the first sign of what for the employer is 'overmanning', for the worker the moral right, and human need, to earn a living.

Though workers in the capitalist labour process produce useful, material 'things', the purpose and logic of this production lies entirely in the creation of surplus value – a logic expressed in Marx's concept of 'abstract labour'. For capital, workers are producing not chairs, hamburgers or health services, but numbers – output, profit, the electronic figures which parade the successes of the stock market. These 'quantitative' priorities continually intrude into workers' 'qualitative' perceptions of the usefulness and value of their labour. As the 'New Linden' worker had said, 'They want numbers, not ideas'.

In one sense the question of consciousness – the interface between 'reality', experience and ideology – is very simple; workers' consciousness is a precise mirror image of the whole capital–labour relation. That relation is structured and limited by the boundaries of capitalist relations of production; so is worker consciousness. The capital–labour relation is riddled with contradictions (employment as provider; employment as exploitation), as is 'default' worker consciousness. Most of all, capital and labour are intertwined through the central relation of exploitation, and this, as expressed in the daily experience of the labour process, is what dominates workers' experience of and response to their class position.

'They know nothing about sewing machines ...'

Nevertheless, it is 'use-value' as much as exploitation-related 'exchange-value' which shapes workers' everyday experience, and produces its own conflicts with an ideology centred on commodification and the market. The cooperation and fraternisation necessary to perform standard work tasks produces a collective consciousness rooted in the essentially practical process of production. Workers as producers, whether of goods or services, are directly engaged in the concrete, hard-headed reality of everyday work routines: the movement of equipment, the operation of machinery, the handling of material and physical 'inputs' like fast food in a restaurant, aging bodies in a nursing home, computer chips on a keyboard. In some accounts, this built-in collectivism and cooperation produces a 'culture of solidarity' which contains an inherent oppositional component; even prosaic, everyday acts of resistance are influenced by preexisting feelings of loyalty and interconnectedness among workers.[43] The 'cultural solidarity' of workers in one typical Midwestern auto plant 'derive[s] from the shared experience of a labor-process that encourages collective effort and an egalitarian ethos'.[44]

The problem for consciousness is that the production-based relationships which generate this solidarity also cluster around workers' intense identification with 'the job', which may in its turn promote an uncritical sense of association with the employer. 'The job' is a two-sided phenomenon; the daily experience of collective effort within the labour process on the one hand, the basis for making a living on the other. The apparent class neutrality associated with workers' essentially *practical* conception of 'the job' extends from its crucial importance as guarantor of the worker's very existence to the equally non-confrontational pride of workers in the quality of their work. A fundamental loyalty to the value of production for use rather than exchange, concrete rather than abstract labour, emerges in the bewildered resentment of many workers over their replacement by 'unskilled' workers in a strike, or the transfer of their jobs abroad, despite what for them is the crucial component of worker knowledge and 'quality' of work.

For workers at the Elizabeth, New Jersey plant of Singer Sewing Machines, closed in 1982, the value of the product and thus Singer's success in the world revolved totally around the skills and worker commitment embodied in the sewing machine itself, rather than abstract goals of productivity and profit:

> I don't believe that the people in the corporate management at Singer know how to run this business. They know absolutely nothing about sewing machines ... I don't think that [the president] knows what a sewing machine is. I really don't.[45]

This focus on production of a useful object, rather than abstract value, evokes a basic conflict with the entire logic of capitalism. Unfortunately, for workers forlornly protesting plant closure or even mobilised into large-scale strike action, this objective politics of use-value often translates into the delusion that a genuine concern with 'quality' will preserve their jobs; workers at the shut-down Kenosha plant, like those at Singer, had 'believed that craftsmanship and quality work would be rewarded with job security'.[46] Similar beliefs and resentments were held by workers at RCA whose jobs were finally, after many moves, shipped to Mexico; one worker's disgusted comment that components from Mexico were 'the lousiest stuff you've ever seen' reflected 'the notion that the superior skills and experience of US workers might somehow insulate [them] from direct competition with Mexicans'.[47]

WHAT IS TO BE DONE?

The collectivism and cooperation embodied in the working-class experience of the labour process, like other aspects of working-class experience, does not automatically create a wider critique of capitalism or act as a conscious spur to worker resistance. Rather, the underlying class loyalty and opposition inherent in that experience becomes central in the mobilisation of resistance triggered by another set of factors: the contradictions of exploitation. Paradoxically, while workers experience their labour as use-value, its function within capitalism as production of abstract exchange-value forces conflict, 'alienation' and job insecurity into that experience. The alternating and conflicting dimensions of consent and resistance within working-class consciousness are captured in Gramsci's 'occasionally and in flashes' evocation of class-for-itself awareness.

The writings of other classic authors, notably Lenin, Luxemburg and Trotsky, enlarge on these connections between preexisting collective culture, resistance and the development of class consciousness. Initially, in the 1902 polemic *What Is to Be Done*, Lenin[48] inveighed against the 'economism' not only of a rival political faction but of workers themselves; the conception of a limited 'trade union consciousness' as the only possible product of industrial struggles, the implicit separation between worker resistance and revolutionary theory, mirrors more recent critiques of 'economistic' militancy. With the claim that trade union struggles per se both prevent any opening for socialist ideas and impose their own 'bourgeois politics' on the working class, revolutionary consciousness is presented as arising 'side by side' with workers' struggle, rather than as rooted in or connected with it: 'Each arises out of different premises' (Kautsky's words, quoted approvingly by Lenin).

Nevertheless, Lenin himself diverged from this perspective both before and after 1902, in both cases when inspired by 'spontaneous' mass struggles. In 1899, after a series of strikes, he wrote,

> Every strike brings thoughts of socialism very forcibly to the workers' mind ... it teaches them not to think of their own employer alone and not of their own immediate workmates alone but of all the employers, the whole class of capitalists and the whole class of workers.[49]

In 1905, when a tidal wave of incipient revolution lent historic weight to his words, he wrote, 'One is struck by the amazingly rapid shift of the movement from the purely economic to the political ground ... and all this, notwithstanding the fact that conscious Social-Democratic influence is lacking or is but slightly evident'.[50] And in 1917, on the eve of the Russian Revolution, he concluded that 'A specifically proletarian weapon of struggle – the strike – was the principal means of bringing the masses into action ... *Only struggle educates the exploited class*'.[51] A very different conception of the dynamics of transformative struggle and consciousness from one rooted primarily in the role of the 'middle-class intelligentsia'.

Again, the dynamic of class struggle and its roots in often the most prosaic material issues emerges in Trotsky's vivid account of the resurgence of the 1905 revolution:

> The typesetters at Sytin's print-works in Moscow struck on September 19. They demanded a shorter working day and a higher piecework rate per 1,000 letters set, not excluding punctuation marks. This small event set off nothing more nor less than the all-Russian political strike – the strike which started over punctuation marks and ended by felling absolutism.[52]

A clearer statement of the potential of 'economistic' struggle could hardly be asked for.

While piecework disputes rarely lead to revolutionary insurrection, the dynamics at work here deserve recognition by those concerned to interrupt the familiar cycle of reformism, betrayal and defeat within the labour movement. The direction of class-for-itself consciousness appears to proceed not from radical or revolutionary intelligentsia to ignorant but grateful working class, but rather in reverse, with even workers who may barely have heard of the concept of 'class' pushed into class struggle and consciousness based, almost entirely, on the material contradictions of exploitation.

While the experience of exploitation clearly fails to generate immediate revolutionary consciousness, it also precludes uninterrupted acceptance of the status quo – simply because the system itself disrupts that very status quo, time and again. The exigencies of profitability preclude any lasting stability, sustained reforms, or uninterrupted advances in working-class standards of living. In this way those at the sharp end of the contradiction, whatever their pre-existing consciousness, are pushed time and again into struggle against, or at the very least disillusionment with, the system – a point recognised by the Lenin of 1905, if not by the Lenin of *What Is to Be Done*. These crucial relationships between experience, consciousness and transformation are the subject matter of the next and final chapter.

9

Transitions and Transformations: Which Side Are You On?

Two possible subtitles were suggested for this book: 'Decline and Resurgence in the Union Movement' or 'Why Workers Lost Their Power, and How To Get It Back'. In fact, both come to the same thing. In order to win 'resurgence' for the union movement, even in the simple sense of significant membership growth, that movement might need something much closer to 'power'.

Power is usually thought of as connected directly to Politics with a big P; politics in a sphere of pomp and circumstance light years away from the central subject matter of this book, rank-and-file organisation and resistance. Yet an equally central theme of this book is the argument that the kind of power workers almost grasped in the 1960s and 1970s is as 'political', if not more so, as the speeches of ministers or the debates at party conferences.

Why this stubborn focus on 'workers' power'? The arguments against spontaneous rank-and-file activity are well known; it is sectional, it is parochial, it is economistic. It also seems to go around in circles. The stewards at Ford's Halewood plant in the early 1970s

> agree[d] with the desirability of political change [but] ... are all too rarely able to stick their heads above the waters of bargaining ... They have no chance to think about 'society', or of where they are going, in anything but a year by year sense.[1]

This accurate description of shopfloor 'firefighting' conveys a powerful image of circular, pointless movement; of wheels of change and progress spinning, uselessly, in the mud. Of one step forward, one step back, rather than Lenin's more hopeful metaphor.

Yet there are a number of countertrends to this apparent futility which need to be taken seriously. Perhaps most eloquently, history itself speaks to the possibility that rank-and-file struggle at times can reach the status of a challenge to capitalist state power. The upsurge of the 1968–74 period at certain points undoubtedly strained the limits of the state and raised the spectre of working-class power in both Britain and America. The 'actually existing' power signalled in these events, a long way from the conventional axes of political decision-making; the enormous but often unrecognised potential of such resistance for a politics with a very different meaning; the need to build this potential from its roots – from the ground up – are at the heart of the concluding theme: transformation.

'A ROUGH PLEBISCITE'

Despite the limitations signalled above, the challenge to the state in the1968–74 period was rooted in highly 'parochial' workplace struggles like those of British carworkers. In the late 1960s, the Labour government's obsession with unofficial strikes produced government Inquiries and Royal Commissions, provoked a frenzy of legislative proposals and brought rank-and-file conflict to the international stage; fulminating against the rash of grass-roots walkouts in the car industry, Prime Minister Harold Wilson 'told a collection of businessmen in New York that strikes were to be the main problem faced by democracy in the 1970s'.[2] Clearly, the Labour government saw 'democracy' as synonymous with the requirement for sustained production; and both appeared to be directly threatened by non-political, 'economistic' production workers.

The dangers of a very different – working-class – form of democracy were spelt out after Ford carworkers supported their workplace representatives rather than union officials in a vote over strike action:

> The verdict of the secret ballot has been over-ruled by the appeal court of the mass meeting. One form of democracy, the kind accepted in this country, has been countermanded by another form, democracy's perverted alternative – the rough plebiscite of the show of hands.[3]

Yet it is this very alternative – this 'rough plebiscite' – which poses the possibility of class and union resurgence. In a world of individual secret ballots and corporate mass media, the opportunities for direct, participative democracy and collective decision-making are few; but when workers struggle they struggle en masse, on a socialised basis built on the socialised character of work itself. The inherent collectivism of such resistance, its built-in challenge to the smooth surface of capitalist ideology – above all, its persistence in the face of all obstacles – have to be taken seriously in considering strategies for revitalising the movement, whether from a perspective of social transformation or the simple quest for a growth in union density.

Yet in current discussions of trade union renewal – the urgent question of how to restore a movement stubbornly drained of its numbers, its social and political impact – the 'rough plebiscite' rarely comes into the picture. Rank-and-file militancy enters the stage, plays a restricted and cautiously monitored role, then is banished in favour of higher-profile, more acceptable historical actors. Resurgent, courageous, posing fundamental challenges to social injustice and union status, resistance from the grass-roots is nevertheless dismissed as somehow less serious than the delibera-tions of academic and full-time union 'experts'. Yet the connection – and the contradiction – between these two strands of the movement persists.

REKINDLING ... ON THE 'HIGH ROAD'?

In the US, following the 1995 victory of John Sweeney's organisation-focused 'New Voices' slate against the AFL-CIO's old-guard leader-ship, even moderate commentators became more inclined to evoke links between trade union growth and a movement-style activism:

> Activists and leaders ... have much more in mind than a simple turnaround in declining union membership. What many of them seek is nothing less than a widespread, full-fledged social movement unionism ... it will take the power of such a movement to transform the institutions, to reestablish the right to organize, and to overcome ... the general powerlessness so widespread in ... society.[4]

Yet a new element is introduced when the authors conclude that such movement-style mobilisation 'will push firms towards the high road, adding important social value ... compatible with strong eco-nomic performance'.[5] A Service Employees' International Union (SEIU) pamphlet, itself entitled *The High Road*, expands on the argu-ment when it stresses 'as a core value – the importance of working together with management to meet mutual goals ... The ultimate goal of unionisation is to foster a cooperative relationship with management'.[6]

Clearly, if we imagine capitalism as capable of taking a 'high road', we can also imagine working with its representatives along the route. It is hardly surprising, then, that 'partnership' appears as one of a list of strategies for union revitalisation, with the SEIU-sponsored partnership agreement at health maintenance organisation Kaiser Permanente cited as an important example of 'expanded workplace participation'.[7]

The problem is that the Kaiser Permanente partnership indicates exactly what not to look for in any strategy aimed at expanding worker power and advancing union effectiveness. The agreement, signed in 1997 by the American Federation of Labor-Congress of Industrial Organizations (AFL-CIO), SEIU and American Federation of State, County, and Municipal Employees (AFCSME), secured union recognition in return for a commitment to 'aggressively market' Kaiser's health plan to other unions. At the time, Kaiser Permanente was closing down so many hospitals and contracting out so much work that it came under federal investigation; the previous year, the company had imposed a wage freeze on thousands of its 'non-professional' employees. Collusion with an employer cutting pay and jobs seems a strange recipe for union revitalisation, however welcome the increased numbers.

Bureaucratic militancy – or militant bureaucracy?

The oddity is that support for 'partnership' with savagely exploitative employers is often coupled, within current US analyses, with 'a new emphasis on rank-and-file participation or mobilisation'.[8] And not only in the US; in Britain, 'the argument has been advanced that a strong organisational base, including active workplace memberships, provides the basis for successful engagement in social partnership policies and practices between trade unions and employers'.[9] The renewed, and frequent, emphasis on the rank and file within this perspective is as puzzling as its link with policies of labour–management partnership. Why the need to constantly reiterate the importance of rank-and-file involvement?

Clearly, union leaders and their supporters at least began to learn some important lessons from the atrophying of the US movement under its 'business-as-usual' leadership. By the mid 1990s, many 'had come to understand that labor's capacity to actually make a social contract required that the unions once again demonstrate their willingness to play a disruptive, insurgent role in society'.[10] The union leaders supporting Sweeney's 'New Voices' slate were relearning the lesson the working class has consistently taught them, that workplace-based organisation and resistance is the force which gives union renewal life and possibility.

Yet the framework within which this objective was set actually reverses the logic of 'disruption' and 'insurgency'. The 'social contract' is a reluctant, institutionalised concession to earlier battles rather than a reciprocal relationship between equal parties; indeed, the weight of employer interest can barely sustain the fabric of the bargain. The social contract may have been created by disruption, but any further disruption can only destroy its 'joint' union–employer balance.

The impressive growth of Sweeney's own union, the SEIU, has been described as 'the fruit of a well-orchestrated militancy'.[11] Yet the internal contradictions between militancy and the 'social contract', like those between 'social movement unionism' and 'partnership', seem to justify the contradictory title of 'bureaucratic militancy' coined for Sweeney-style strategies.[12]

Particularly during the 1990s, when Sweeney's 'New Voices' slate was campaigning for the leadership of the AFL-CIO, the militant side of the coin seemed to gain ascendancy; one SEIU 'justice for janitors' campaign in Washington, DC used civil-rights-style tactics, with workers blocking the Potomac River bridges. When an 'old-guard' AFL-CIO delegate sniffed that the SEIU should 'worry more about building bridges to the rest of society', Sweeney famously responded, 'I believe in building bridges ... But I believe in blocking bridges whenever ... employers ... turn a deaf ear to the working families that we represent'.[13] Yet within two years, the SEIU promised to call off its bridge-blockings and other militant tactics if office-building owners would persuade their cleaning contractors to recognise the union. In direct contrast to its previously confrontational attitude, 'the union was proposing to the owners a partnership, and saying to all those janitors who helped stage protests, "You may now go home"'.[14]

The insurmountable problem for the bureaucratic endorsement of 'insurgency' is that once the rank-and-file cat is let out of the bag it is difficult to restrain its unbridled progress towards a very different set of priorities from those held by unions' corporate 'partners'. The process of rank-and-file mobilisation and struggle works in precisely the opposite direction from the way the 'bureaucratic militants' would have it. The nervous embrace of 'militancy' signals the recognition that it is raw, economistic, rank-and-file struggle, rather than partnership or social contracts, which builds unions. Yet the unacceptable face of such insurgency, for the union leadership, is that it builds them the wrong way – from the bottom up.

WHO ARE 'WE'?

This paradox – that to seek renewal is to tap into rank-and-file energy, which is in its turn to move dangerously close to the independent, unpredictable and explosive dynamic of workplace resistance – has been endlessly rehearsed in the more self-conscious sections of the movement. Even those who ally themselves most closely with 'social movement unionism' are often reluctant to accept the prosaic terrain of workplace-based struggles as a basis for building that movement. Instead, labour-friendly writers eternally seek the mobilising Idea: 'What ideas motivate American workers today, and what seem capable of generating the kind of mobilisations and alliances' once 'synonymous with the economic and civic health of the society as a whole?' demands one writer who wistfully seeks the 'inspiration' evoked in US labour's 1915 anthem, 'Solidarity for Ever'.[15]

Yet, even having found the mobilising Idea, the question arises of who is to promote it, and how it is to find a hearing in a stubbornly 'instrumental' working class. There is no shortage of advocates of demands and programmes among the radical chorus of trade union theorists and organisers committed to rebuilding the movement. The question of how these ideas can actually make a difference, of who somehow will inject them into workers' heads, is answered with an omnivorous 'we' whose task is to develop and promote correct policies and campaigning perspectives, rather than building on the existing terrain of worker struggle.

But who are 'we'? One major SEIU strategist 'clearly means officials and staff when he says "we" should build campaigns "that give our members reason to be involved"'. Rather than being the activists, members are 'to be "activated"' in 'a cannon-fodder version of organising'.[16] Rank-and-file union members seem to occupy a lowly position in the 'we'; their own experience of and attitudes towards organisation and struggle tend to figure, if at all, only in passing. Far more emphasis is placed by such commentators on the demands and policies which 'we' are urged to promote: 'If we – and this "we" must be much more than those now in unions – could create a movement that stopped employers from violating worker rights, suddenly tens of millions of workers would organize and push for better conditions'.[17]

The problem is not that these ideals are misplaced – what labour advocate could oppose the demand for 'social movement unionism', for struggle against the 'violation of workers' rights'? – but that they fail to identify, other than in passing, a central agency with the power of carrying them out. The 'we' *must* be 'much more than those now in unions'; workplace union activists and their members are routinely dismissed as too 'economistic' to be focused on such issues, or perhaps simply too boring: 'This book does not focus on day-to-day activities in ordinary unions ... boring meetings ... routine contracts ... [but] on innovative campaigns in areas of major social change'.[18] And the reluctance to embrace the workplace applies to far more radical voices than these; the revolutionary left, despite its historical and theoretical links with the working class, has often been reluctant to place itself with that class as it is, rather than as the left would like it to be.[19]

Ruling the world

Luckily, workers' own activity has never depended on the approval or recommendations of any of these commentators. The independent dynamic of worker resistance, which constantly undermines political predictions and analyses on both left and right, is above all *resurgent*. The series of mass strikes and workplace struggles documented in this book provide evidence, over and over, of the renaissance of explosive resistance, testifying to the continuation and resurgence of class conflict in an environment constantly presented as an 'end-of-history' scenario for class struggle.

Such resurgence is no respecter of consciousness. The apparent 'dead wood' of working-class conservatism has burst into flame too many times for ideological colonisation to be seen as an impenetrable barrier to revolt; preexisting radicalism is not required for the eagle of class conflict to swoop down and seize astonished and formerly compliant workers in its talons. The leap from a parochial, unreflective 'economism' to passionate expressions of transformed consciousness is almost a routine aspect of the many mass struggles described in this book.

This inspiring potential for transformation is documented in the words of workers involved in such struggles. In Britain, as one engineering worker involved in the 1972 Saltley Gates victory put it,

'For the first time in my life I had a practical demonstration of what workers' solidarity meant. We all felt so powerful. We felt we could rule the world'. A striking print worker, part of the mass movement which freed the dockers at Pentonville, described how 'You could sense the power of the working class, you had seen it in action ... People began to think of how working class power can change things'.[20]

Again in Britain, the same sense of profound transformation was expressed by a member of Women Against Pit Closures in the 1984–85 miners' strike:

> I'd never been involved in anything like it before. It seemed the sort of thing other people did, people who were somehow different from me, people who had a lot of education ... I felt awakened. It was as if I'd woken up in the morning and it had rained and everything was fresh and new ... .[21]

In the US, a member of the support group for the Jay, Maine paper-workers related how 'For the first time in my life, I felt I was actually accomplishing something ... and that I could do something to change the world'. The experience of struggle took workers one step further forward to mapping out perspectives for the movement as a whole: 'As time wore on, people began to sense it was going to take more than a three-mill strike to beat the International Paper Company. It was going to take a new labor movement'. Such revelations led to a clearer class vision of the purpose of worker organisation: 'What I have learned, and am still learning from all this, is that unless all the unions in this country merge into one large union and become serious about helping the workers, there is not much hope for a long, long time'.[22]

In all these cases, and countless more, a group of workers with no prior 'political' or class consciousness waged struggles which challenged the ruling class and brought about a qualitative transformation in their own way of understanding the world. Such struggles are all tiny examples, straws in the wind of the apparently indomitable rightward drive of those in power. Even the massive earlier battles described in this book have the air of faint, silent images long extinguished by the force of global capital. But what they illustrate is that the consciousness of the working class is not for ever colonised or hegemonised. Working-class struggle continues, and with it the possibility of redemption.

ALWAYS THE BRIDESMAID ...

Yet there is another, more pessimistic side to the argument. The roots of transformed consciousness and thus renewed social movement unionism may well lie in rank-and-file struggle; but the trouble is, it hasn't happened yet. It is as if the working class is always the bridesmaid of history, never the bride; always springing from the starting blocks, never finishing the race. While the working class will continue to struggle, even in the least favourable circumstances, it also continues – with increasingly rare exceptions – to lose. What kind of strategy for union renewal can be built out of this never-ending cycle of resistance and defeat? What can be the logical plot of a story that is always starting, never coming to an end?

Once it is established that workers' consciousness tends to be significantly altered by one factor more than any other – materially triggered struggles against corporate power – the next question becomes what *happens* to this transformed consciousness. In fact, new levels of consciousness are rarely sustained much beyond the end of the action. The waters of everyday life begin to close over the heads of even the most committed, impassioned strikers and supporters once the struggle is over; in the case of many long disputes, the post-strike ramifications are serious, with broken marriages, broken lives, families and neighbourhoods permanently scarred and split. Unlike middle-class radicals, workers have little opportunity of turning protest into a lifestyle.

This 'non-sustainability' raises serious questions about the meaning and direction of strike-related consciousness and its role in union renewal. Beyond familiar critiques of economism and sectionalism, other less recognised factors tend to weaken major rank-and-file struggles and undermine their lessons. Among these is the dominance of *morality* in strikers' views of themselves and the enemy.

For all the breakthrough in class and solidarity consciousness that major struggles bring, the experience itself often promotes a moralistic rather than 'scientific' consciousness. Clear-eyed awareness of capital as an unscrupulous class enemy is foreign to workers caught up in a passionate struggle in which they see right, and thus ultimately might, on their side. The notion that 'injustice' per se propels workers into struggle[23] is put into question by most of the strike accounts in this book; but once caught up in their own epoch-making battles, strikers take up the banner of Justice with a tenacity which overlooks the cold realities of capitalist 'morality' and dilutes the crucial need to maintain class independence from capital.

Workers' misplaced assumption of basic moral rectitude on the part of their morally bankrupt employers has allowed for many a false step in what could have been, on an independent class basis, a successful struggle. The last months of the 1987 paper workers' strike in the US, when workers offered a unique opportunity to expose an unscrupulous corporation allowed themselves to be tricked by management promises, are only too typical an example. In the 1984–85 coal strike in Britain, the National Association of Colliery Overmen and Deputies (NACODS) stoppage could have been seized on ferociously as an opportunity for victory, rather than being allowed to drift by while the government manically worked towards a settlement; within the leadership's 'campaigning' mindset, the miners' undoubted occupancy of the moral high ground figured larger than more strategic considerations.

Associated with this understandable tendency of workers to see their struggle as a moral crusade is the conviction that the very justice of their cause will take them to victory. One leaflet put out by Women of the Waterfront (WOW), the organisation of women involved in the 1996 Liverpool dockers' strike, eloquently expresses this dignified stance: 'We firmly believe that we will win this fight because morality and human justice are on our side'.[24] Yet the assumption that the sword of justice will automatically cut to the heart of capitalist chicanery is, unfortunately, part of the lack of class clarity associated with the many 'lost causes' of the 1980s and beyond.

Other factors block the wider lessons of even the most transformative struggles. One study of the 1984–85 miners' strike[25] argues that while miners could not but be aware of the political significance of their struggle, for many Thatcher's malignant enmity seemed reserved specifically for them. This 'special case' consciousness meant that strikers saw the political dynamic of the strike as located primarily in Thatcher's specific vendetta against the miners, rather than in the context of capital's attack on the working class as a whole. As with the Pilkington's Glass Company strikers in Britain in 1970, the company, the police, the press and even the union bureaucracy 'were just aberrations in a world that was still fundamentally reasonable'.[26] To see things otherwise would be to rise to an 'overview' level of analysis of capitalism which, almost by definition, is unavailable to most of the working class, most of the time.

EVERYWHERE IS GOING TO BE TAKEN OVER ...

A third factor, fear of the political implications of pushing the struggle to its limits, plays its own role in undermining that overview. Quoting from E.P. Thompson's classic *Writing By Candlelight* during the British oilworkers' blockade of 2000, one journalist noted that 'it is only when ordinary life grinds to a halt that people "know suddenly the great unspoken fact about our society: their own daily power"'.[27] Yet confronting that 'daily power' was more alarming than empowering for the protestors; some leaders had already decided to end the protest because 'the whole thing had got too big and political groups might take it over'.[28]

Paradoxically, the power of that 'great unspoken fact' is revealed in the fear expressed by both workers and their leaders at the social 'abyss' opened up by struggles which challenge the basic property relations of capital. One factory meeting during the 1986 Caterpillar occupation in Scotland heard the Cassandra-like cry: '... if we win, the whole country is going to be taken over by its workers. Ravenscraig is going to be taken over by its workers, everywhere else is going to be taken over ...'. Yet her prophecy, rather than revolutionary triumph, evoked despair: '... they don't want us to win. We've *no* chance!'.[29]

The prediction came true, of course – state and capital invoked 'the law', the stewards trembled, the occupation was lost. If the Caterpillar stewards had been less cowed by the parameters of the system, if their outlook had been one of class independence rather than quasi-cooperation, the results might have been very different. The sustained worker occupation of a plant holding millions of pounds' worth of capital would have severely shaken the Thatcher government and its anti-union apparatus; the worker's prediction – 'If we win, the whole country is going to be taken over by its workers!' – might have been seen as a glorious prospect, rather than a mortal threat.

For all these reasons and more, while major struggles can be a central driving force for the *opening-up* of workers' consciousness to more transformative perspectives, experience alone is unable to complete the process. While spontaneous struggle is, probably, a *necessary* condition for advancing consciousness, it falls short of being *sufficient*. Once again, the question arises of how to acquire that 'sufficiency'.

As already indicated, there is no shortage of prescriptions for an ideologically ailing working class; unfortunately, as also shown, these tend to be administered without the consent or participation of the patient. Unlike a physical malady, trade union decline is unlikely to respond to any remedy which depends on superior 'expertise' rather than emanating from workers' own experience and commitment. Whatever the merits of the political ideas and programmes posed as vehicles for union renewal, most workers see such abstract ideas as largely irrelevant to their lives.

A perspective which *starts* with the 'necessary condition', and reality, of rank-and-file resistance reverses the argument so often used by theorists of union renewal – that workers must be seized by radical ideas, by a 'vision' of social movement unionism, before they can take meaningful action. To argue for a different direction, a direction rooted in the workplace and the rank-and-file membership, is not to claim that existing worker resistance is consciously 'political' or even immediately capable of 'rekindling the movement'. It is an attempt to offer a different perspective on how these goals might be achieved.

RAMPARTS OF RESISTANCE

In many ways, working-class organisations themselves provide the answers – or the beginnings of answers – to these questions. The solutions they suggest are encapsulated less in 'gut-level' militancy per se than in the organisational forms which, historically, have crystallised such militancy. In its aspect as 'union form' rather than union-as-institution, worker organisation establishes buttresses of class organisation which act within the workplace to block the smooth passage of capitalist requirements. This 'rampart'-like formation is noted by Marx in his assessment of the early stages of union formation: 'Permanent combinations have been formed, trade unions, which serve as ramparts for the workers in their struggles'.[30]

Whatever may have happened subsequently to these 'permanent combinations', the depiction of worker organisation as building 'ramparts' – structures that can survive defeat and build on victory – identifies a crucial agent in any attempt to consolidate and build on the lessons of class struggle: workplace activists. The 'ramparts' of workplace organisation, the 'frontiers of control',[31] are not built out of thin air. The whole structure of workplace organisation and democracy is mediated by workers' *representatives*; the delegate-style emissaries distinguished from almost all other democratic agents by their closeness and accountability to their own constituency and class, the workers they represent.

In some ways, then, the most valuable fruit of the ongoing process of building and maintaining 'ramparts of resistance' in the workplace is its generation of a residue of activists able to recognise and pass on the lessons developed in the organising process. In *The Mass Strike*, Rosa Luxemburg speaks of how 'The most precious, because lasting, thing in this rapid ebb and flow of [struggle] is its mental sediment: the intellectual, cultural growth of the proletariat'.[32] Even in less revolutionary circumstances, this 'mental sediment' is distilled in the more committed and advanced sections of rank-and-file organisation, which act as ongoing vessels of the lessons learnt and the consciousness gained in struggle. At Ford's Halewood plant in Britain in the 1970s,

> The shopfloor leadership was itself produced through the struggles of workers on the shop floor ... These struggles, and the unity that carried groups of workers through them, were crystallised in the shop stewards. The shop stewards' committee is a testament to these struggles. It remained fixed in the world after the fires had died down, it embodied the lessons learned in past struggles and ensures that the embers never become cold.[33]

The *forms* of organisation most likely to encapsulate these lessons are distinct both from the 'broader political forces' advocated by radical labour commentators and from the more conventional institutionalised structures of trade unionism. The structures typically created by workplace-based activists are cross-class or cross-industry networks of various kinds, from joint shop steward committees and combine committees to rank-and-file reform caucuses – committee-based, accountable delegate structures which echo the Russian soviets, Chilean *cordones*, Portuguese *inter-empresas*, Iranian *shoras*[34] of historic struggles. To understand this dynamic, and its central importance, is to acknowledge a crucial element in moving organisation forward and revitalising the labour movement – the activist layer.

'ORGANIC INTELLECTUALS'?

Through all the manifold attacks on independent workplace organisation in both Britain and America, a residue of activists has remained to pose some form of opposition against the unmitigated might of capital. Even in the post-1980s onslaught, workers have continued to be 'mostly organised on the basis of steward forms of representation and involvement. It was this form of organisation that ... provided the bedrock for the continued presence of unions in the factories'.[35]

While the thickness of this bedrock may fluctuate, its dynamic remains the same: a kind of 'combined and uneven development' of workplace representation which means that years of experience are not the sole basis of effective workplace leadership. As British trade union renewal research suggests, changing workplace conditions and subsequent organising continually generate *new* groups of activists whose experience of resistance connects them to the mindset of commitment and radicalism which distinguishes the older layer of militants. Activists are made, not born, and the irony is that it is capitalism which most consistently produces them.

These representatives constitute a crucial section of the working class; a layer *between* the compromised formal leadership and what may be a relatively uninformed, unaware membership. What is unique about them is that they are both directly connected to their members' daily concerns within the workplace and also to much wider networks of cross-class organisation at the roots of the movement. This broader experience both builds class solidarity and inspires interest in and openness to wider political issues; many workplace activists are well-read and informed on both theory and practice.

Such activists tend to be exceptionally committed. Union activity is their way of life, rather than a bureaucratic task to be disposed of as easily as possible. But the roots of such commitment in the rank and file lend it a life and energy in direct contrast with the stifling routinism and constitutionalism of 'official' union activity; an energy both drawn from and generating direct, mobilising forms of worker resistance.

Yet the most important point about this layer of activists is not their own integrity and commitment, impressive though these are in the current 'against the stream' climate. It is that the existence of this layer, standard bearers of militant class unionism within the movement, poses the possibility of building an *in-class* leadership of committed activists able to survive periods of 'downturn' and build connections at the roots of the movement able to influence and lead the next 'upsurge' – from the ground up. It is this leadership from below, a leadership rooted in and part of its membership, which offers the most dynamic – and realistic – answer to the endless cycle of betrayal and defeat.

The basis for such a movement already exists within the current layer of committed workplace activists at the roots of resistance and organisation in both the US and the UK. Such activists continuously construct – out of necessity rather than idealism – cross-class forms of independent worker organisation which, even in current circumstances, can work to maintain solidarity and organisation cumulatively from one struggle to the next. In more promising times, workplace-based activists showed strong interest in explicitly political attempts to build cross-class rank-and-file networks; networks like the Communist Party's Liaison Committee for the Defence of the Trade Unions (LCDTU) mobilised thousands of shop stewards in organising against anti-union government policies, only to be subordinated in the mid 1970s[36] to the CP's courting of left MPs and union leaders. Similarly, the then International Socialism group held a series of movement-wide rank and file conferences involving significant numbers of stewards before succumbing to the ever-present temptation to 'build the party'.[37]

The relative smallness and isolation of activist networks today stems at least partly from the fact that few 'friends' of the union movement devote much time or effort to backing these activists or helping them build and spread the movement from below they so crucially represent. The unique class position of these activists and their role in building social movement unionism must be considered in any serious exploration of today's labour movement and its possibilities for renewal.

Gramsci's conception of rank-and-file activists as 'organic intellectuals' suggests a possible role for 'mainstream' or 'traditional' intellectuals – the kind who write analyses of trade union renewal – in 'channeling the activity of these organic intellectuals and providing a link between the class and certain sections of the traditional intelligentsia'.[38] This 'traditional intelligentsia' is urged not so much to mouth the party line from the sidelines as to operate *within* the working class in concert with its 'organic' counterparts – as facilitators, researchers and educators in the cause of developing actually existing class organisation and resistance.

'A RANK-AND-FILE SEA'

While seldom raised in current discussions of trade union renewal, this approach is concretely illustrated in a number of current initiatives of which the best-known is probably the US rank-and-file reform movement Teamsters for a Democratic Union (TDU). A recent tribute refers to the TDU-based 'transformation' of the Teamsters as 'the most significant victory of any rank-and-file grouping in the twentieth-century history of American unionism'.[39] What produced this 'victory', this 'transformation'? Rather than drowning its supporters' autonomy and experience in abstract programmes and policies, the 'mainstream intellectuals' of the TDU perspective grounded themselves in a dynamic of workplace-based class struggle, an approach which sought to expand rather than to bypass the parameters of workplace union politics. As one founding organiser put it, 'I'd be a fool to use TDU for socialist politics, because it would stay very small. I want it to be very big'.[40]

The parallel project and newsletter *Labor Notes* was launched in1979 to reach out to committed activists across the working class as a whole, supporting their activity with national conventions, rank-and-file network meetings, and 'schools' on a range of workplace-based topics ranging from concessionary pay deals to teamworking. These gatherings provide activists with a dual forum for making cross-movement links and formulating strategy on combating management techniques often seen as acceptable by left union leaders and commentators. By 1999, at its twentieth anniversary conference, *Labor Notes* could pay tribute to 'the rank and file sea on which it floated – the many union activists who kept the project informed, worked on its events, and gave its handbooks, conferences and schools their grounding in day-to-day struggles across the labor movement'.[41]

Attempts at building rank-and-file support organisations have not been confined to the United States; the international activists' network Transnationals Information Exchange (TIE), founded in the late 1970s in Europe, rapidly moved from its original conception as a research network to a more direct role in setting up international meetings and contacts among rank-and-file workers. TIE emphasised a grass roots approach, avoiding the kind of largely symbolic gatherings which tend to simply link together a number of national union bureaucracies. Despite the international emphasis, this essentially workplace-based approach relied on strong national, regional and local initiatives – a recognition of the crucial connections between 'global' and 'local' which put the 'local' first, in contrast to many romantic evocations of global worker networks which overlook the point that the links in the global chain are nationally based organisations. Given this perspective, TIE worked to develop national networks of rank-and-file activists in a range of countries from Germany to Brazil who shared a critical outlook on new working practices and the reorganisation of production.

Part of this development was the growth of a series of national worker-activist newsletters by the mid 1990s. From *Solidaritiet* in the Netherlands, *Express* in Germany, *Labor Notes* in New Zealand, *Rodo Joho* in Japan, *Labor* in Taiwan, *Trade Union Forum* in Sweden, *Collectif* in France and *Trade Union News* in Britain, these initiatives grew during the 1980s and 1990s as part of efforts to pull together a national current of militants in each country. However, the historical and political circumstances which had allowed for the birth and successful growth of *Labor Notes* in 1979 were no longer present for many of these projects. In Britain, by the time *Trade Union News* began publication in 1990, political support for a non-sectarian rank-and-file initiative was largely absent. Despite a promising start, with a rapidly growing circulation of over 4,000 union activists, the paper faltered for lack of day-to-day practical support. Unlike *Labor Notes*, the *TUN* project could take advantage of no 'window of opportunity' on the revolutionary left to provide, as the International Socialism's US group had done in the 1970s, an office and at least 1.5 workers.

As discussed earlier, political suspicion by the left of such initiatives may be rooted in the reversal of perspective they promote. The approach embodied in TDU, *Labor Notes*, TIE, and, briefly, *TUN* bears important distinctions from the usual model of reviving the movement, whether revolutionary, radical or merely pragmatic. The notion that the roots of union renewal may lie in paying attention to what workers are already doing holds little 'sex appeal' for many radicals, while the disproportionate animosity of union leaderships to *Labor Notes* and TDU attests to the enormous threat such rank-and-file networks pose to 'business as usual'. The traditional sectarianism of the revolutionary left, however subtle its forms, acts as a barrier to serious, party-effacing involvement in the kind of non-aligned initiatives essential to consolidating and building on existing forms of rank and file organisation.

Yet these initiatives bring together a representative and diverse section of the working class into a milieu in which socialist, transformative and social movement ideas are 'part of the conversation', rather than being invoked from on high. A *Labor Notes*, TDU or TIE convention typically gathers a working-class and ethnically diverse audience in sharp contrast to that usually mobilised by the radical trade union or revolutionary left. And this poses yet another potential – the chance of overcoming the ethnic, sexual and other divisions plaguing the unity of the working class.

THE STRONGEST LINK

The 'look' of a *Labor Notes* audience signals the potential of rank-and-file workplace organising for confronting one of the most destructive problems plaguing the movement – the fracturing of class by racism, sexism, homophobia. Noting the diversity of such gatherings suggests a logic many community activists may resist – that the workplace is a major site of potential unification across the divisions imposed by capital. For many, an emphasis on workplace union activism ignores crucial issues of gender, race and sexual orientation. Arguments centring on the rapidly increasing diversity of the workforce often suggest that a focus on the organised workplace unjustly excludes those less well organised, particularly women and ethnic minorities – favouring the 'strong' at the expense of the 'weak'.

The pressure on today's labour movement to adopt a more inclusive outlook undoubtedly stems from 'outside' forces like anti-racist, women's and lesbian and gay activism. However, many of these movements have gained their strongest social impact, in turn, from struggles centred in the workplace. To see workplace activism as too insular a movement to embrace diversity is to overlook the practical logic of inclusion which most characterises workplace unionism. Workers who have to act together to organise successfully will be led to prioritise mutual goals over workplace divisions; in fact, those who have already committed themselves to an oppositional outlook in class relations are the most open to understanding the need for racial, gender and sexuality equality. For many the process of arriving at this understanding has involved struggles which unite workers across 'identity' lines and promote an awareness of how divisions over these issues strike at the heart of effective organisation.

Activists themselves make it clear that inclusiveness is not a romantic ideal, but an organisational necessity. In one typical comment:

> Management always tries to turn every union struggle into a racist struggle, so they can put worker against worker. We made a strong effort to bring all races together ... We made sure we had minorities, women, people from

the South ... it's the duty of anybody trying to run an insurrection or a union reform movement to bring in all sections.[42]

Building an effective grass-roots movement has to mean – by definition – including all groups represented in the workforce. And in the real world, this really does mean women, people of colour, people with different sexual identities – as well as the 'white working class'.

To separate different sections of the working class on the basis of 'identity', as in the radical politics of the 1960s – 'for many, the working class came to be identified as only reactionary white men'[43] – is to miss the point that white men, reactionary or otherwise, are part of an ever changing working class which, with globalisation, is increasingly *constituted of* those 'identities', making engagement with race and gender issues within organised workplaces inescapable. And these trends emerge within the organisations of the working class – trade unions. Any reverse stereotype of organised workers as 'male, pale and stale' fails to recognise the composition of a movement which, more than any other social institution, brings together otherwise disparate and conflicting groups: 'The 16.3 million union members include 6.7 million women, 2.5 million African Americans, and 1.6 Latinos. Unions have more women members than NOW [National Organisation of Women], more black members than the NAACP [National Association for the Advancement of Colored People] ...'.[44]

Not only the labour movement, but the workplace. In one typical auto plant, 'The autoworkers' shopfloor culture is shared by all those who get paid by the hour ... It crosses the boundaries of sex, race and ethnicity'.[45] Recent US academic research shows that 'integration of workplaces has proceeded further and with less overt controversy than integration of other social domains'.[46] Similarly, 'the social psychology of workplace relations works for gay–straight relations ... "co-operative interdependence" among gay and straight co-workers tends to reduce prejudice, defy stereotypes, and cultivate affinity and acceptance'.[47]

It would be nice if the fight against racism, sexism and homophobia could be based on idealism, as indeed it often has been; but the undermining of prejudice in the workplace tends to have a more practical foundation. Political correctness sits uneasily within workplace culture, particularly the manual variety; in one typical manufacturing plant, 'Kidding and joking about racial, ethnic and

cultural matters provided a safe outlet for the expression of prejudice and difference'. Yet workplace relations themselves served to
dilute such prejudice: 'Although ... racial and ethnic diversity ...
could have been a source of wide social distance and discord among
workers ... the actual activities and requirements of work, combined
with ... patterns of social interaction, combined to minimize these
divisions'.[48]

In another sense, workplace-based struggles themselves work to
undermine acceptance of oppression and inequality. For American
flight attendants trying to organise and bargain in the 1970s, 'the
sex discrimination barrier loomed so large [they] came to see that
problem as inseparable from the other issues being negotiated'.[49]
British miners came to accept gay sexuality through the support of
lesbian and gay groups for their strike; white, 'all-American'
Professional Air Traffic Controllers' Organisation (PATCO) workers
ruefully compared themselves to Black civil rights activists. TDU
built on the concrete struggles of its original core constituency of
white truckers in a way that made credible and possible today's
multi-ethnic, dual-gender TDU leadership, while Teamsters in
Seattle fought to defend a gay neighbourhood from police attacks.
In an American hospital dispute, husbands took over the domestic
tasks as their wives fought for a union: 'The guys would stay
there with the kids, and we'd stake off and do whatever we were
gonna do'.[50]

These sources of enlightenment are mainly constituted around
issues of exploitation rather than oppression, material concerns
rather than political idealism. At one typical rank-and-file activists'
gathering, 'each of the major food groups in the American ethno-
racial stir-fry ... was sufficiently represented ... Men and women
were present in roughly equal numbers'. Yet the diversity was taken
for granted:

> No one seemed to notice, nor to care enough to be either put off or
> rhapsodic ... The unity extolled at the stewards' conference was concrete
> and strategic. It was celebrated as a tool that had demonstrated its
> effectiveness for making people's lives better.[51]

When concrete circumstances generate a class-based unity and
diversity, the outlook is, paradoxically, more promising than
anything conjured into being by idealist rhetoric. As the same

writer puts it,

> Being active in a union is no magic elixir; it doesn't necessarily cure racism
> and sexism ... Nevertheless, for all the limitations of the labor movement ...
> there's no place else where the left's political concerns gain a hearing and
> have a constituency outside the coffee shops, cultural studies programs,
> and sectarian hutches.[52]

BUILDING BRIDGES – THE CONCEPT OF TRANSITION

Yet 'the left' often fails to appreciate the possibility of access to the
working class via the labour movement. The politics of protest,
of campaigns and programmes so favoured by radical advocates of
union renewal overlooks, in many cases, the issue of *process* – of how
to get from here to there, when 'here' is where working-class resistance and activism exist, and 'there' the broader, inspiring, 'social
movement' vision. In fact, to insist on a vision purified of material
considerations is to avoid the direction of a dynamic, copiously
illustrated in this book, in which broader social movement consciousness stems from concrete struggles, not the other way round.

Ideas which counterpose an idealistic 'there' of social justice to the
existing reality of 'self-interested' workplace struggles miss the point
that such 'self-interest' contains within it the core of struggle against
much broader issues of injustice and inequity; a struggle which can
massively 'empower' both workers and their communities. The
bridge, the transition from one level to the next, lies not in abstract
demands but those which objectively challenge the boundaries of
capitalism.

Simply to ask for, or organise around, basic issues like reasonable
wages, shorter hours, safety at work and (particularly in America)
pensions and health benefits, is to invoke the potentially transformative logic of 'transitional demands'. The contemporary relevance
of this concept, originally theorised in Trotsky's later writings, can
be separated from predictions of 'The Death Agony of Capitalism'[53]
to focus on the insight that 'The demand for more becomes revolutionary when it goes beyond the capabilities of the system to provide the "more". That is the link between the fight for reforms and
social revolution ...'.[54]

The demand for 'more' was at its most challenging in the period
which began this book; the 1968–74 upsurge. Then, workers' growing confidence led them to push against the boundaries of capital to

an extent that provoked the ruling class to nervous prophecies of revolution. Such struggles have been dismissed over and over as insufficiently 'political'. But they had two main merits: they raised the question of social transformation, in concrete terms, to hundreds of thousands of workers; and they also unionised the largest proportion of workers in history.

The upsurge is long over, but the recurrence of struggle points over and over again to the fragility of ruling-class hegemony even in an era of apparently seamless consumerism. Particularly in America, the ideological offensive, relentlessly commodifying almost every area of personal life, has reached unparallelled proportions. Yet even in this environment, workers resist individualism and consumerism to confront the system. Workers in hotels and casinos – the acme of the glitzy culture of privilege – organise and strike for better pay and conditions. The increasingly battered image of 'New Labour' in Britain is further eroded by unexpected and courageous acts of solidarity like airline workers' 2005 walkout in defence of subcontracted Gate Gourmet food workers, while workers continue to surge out in stubborn and frequently illegal action against the structures of an anti-working-class 'Labour' government. It is material conditions, not abstract visions, which raise the possibility of a counterhegemony, which open up a genuine bridge to awareness – by 'ordinary' working-class people – of a different way of running society.

FROM TINA TO THEMBA

The fundamental tension within the union renewal argument between its reformist and revolutionary implications often goes unacknowledged, but is inescapable. Invocations of 'workers' power' sit uncomfortably with more mainstream, but equally sincere, concerns with the future of trade unionism; yet, ultimately, there is no way of squaring the circle. Trade union renewal requires grass-roots involvement and mobilisation, which in its turn raises uncomfortable spectres of militancy and democracy. The dangers of setting free the genie of rank-and-file activity are acknowledged in the limited autonomy provided even to groups of workers triumphantly organised under 'New Voices' leadership and then penned into large, unresponsive locals which undermine the very grass-roots strategies used to bring them into the movement. If unions are to be renewed, workers have to win. When workers win, they raise questions troubling not only to capital but to leaders and supporters of SEIU-style 'bureaucratic militancy'. When workers struggle, they expose too often the fragility of the 'social contract', the fantasy of the 'high road' beloved of union leaders and radicals alike.

If it does not acknowledge the central potential of grass-roots working-class struggles for taking the movement forward, the argument becomes circular. Workplace-based struggle is non-political, therefore 'we' won't support it. 'We' don't support it, most of the time; therefore it never does become, consciously at least, political. How to break the cycle? Socialists, radicals, union full-timers, all those who want to see the movement begin again, need to start where the working class is, rather than where they might like it to be. In this way 'we' can form an organic alliance, mutually reinforcing, between the inspiring visions of social movement unionism and the day-to-day reality of what union members experience at work – the prosaic issues of low pay, long hours, and labour intensification unions were built to fight.

At the time when this book begins, workers in both Britain and America were much closer to the 'there' of successful organisation and resistance than today. They were also closer to 'workers' power' – or at least a lot closer than they are now. They overthrew corporations, they reversed laws, they occupied plants, they organised hundreds of thousands of workers, they brought down governments, they brought the country to a halt. They may not have been 'political enough', but they had the ruling class quaking in its boots.

Within ten years, that power had been lost, and with it the lifeblood of unionism itself. What happened? Few people thought, in the 1970s, that 'the rough plebiscite' represented in workplace-based resistance and member-led democracy was worth preserving. The 'power' that workers held so briefly was not political power, nor even the aspiration towards it; it ignored, mostly, romantic notions of 'workers' control', it largely eschewed 'alternative economic strategies', it failed even to place a general critique of capitalism at the centre of its activity, although by the end of the period a growing number of its key activists were thinking that way. The upsurges of militancy which carried on into the late 1970s did not promote noble ideals which could appeal to the radical, 'prefigurative' left of the time or to today's advocates of a union renewal centred on the 'high road'. Perhaps that was why hardly anyone did anything to recognise, value or consolidate that power; and it slipped out of workers' hands as easily as Thatcher and Reagan, after years of social democratic class betrayal, slipped in.

Throughout capitalism, workers have been continually faced with a historic choice: whether to take the revolutionary fork in the road signalled by class struggle, or to relapse into the reformist ideology which continues to dominate the movement. The untrammelled advance of globalisation seems increasingly to bar the road of class resistance; the loss of the comforting 'social compact' of the postwar decades works to reinforce Thatcher's stern injunction of There Is No Alternative – so common a mantra it was shortened to TINA. Yet, as the South African anti-apartheid movement has instructed us, TINA can be vanquished with THEMBA – There Must Be An Alternative.[55] THEMBA is the Zhosa word for hope.

The perspective advocated in this book is certainly optimistic – but it is not unrealistic. It starts with the continuing, unassailable reality of working-class struggle, in all sections and under all circumstances. Rather than turning aside from that reality and its uncomfortable implications, those who seek a lasting resurgence within the movement are urged to start with the concrete conditions workers face, the organisation and resistance they build in response to those conditions, and the direct democracy and class struggle politics contained within these structures, these 'ramparts', of rank-and-file resistance. In advocating a mutually reinforcing unity to replace the 'unbridgeable gulf' between radical intellectuals and workplace activists, this argument centres on the crucial need to build a class-conscious leadership *within* the working class – ready, perhaps, for the next upsurge. Possibly, in these circumstances, workers will be better equipped to take the independent, united action needed to get their power back.

This book has been written with the aim of convincing working-class activists – 'organic intellectuals' – and the 'mainstream intellectuals' who support them – of that simple message. I hope it works.

Notes

1 THE UPSURGE: 1968–74

1 Paul Ferris, *The New Militants: Crisis in the Trade Unions* Penguin 1972, p.10; Leo Panitch and Colin Leys, *The End of Parliamentary Socialism: From New Left to New Labour* Verso 1997, p.20; Willie Thompson, *The Long Death of British Labourism: Interpreting a Political Culture* Pluto Press, p.89; Alan Thornett, *From Militancy to Marxism: A Personal and Political Account of Organising Car Workers* Left View Books 1987, p.181.
2 Chris Harman, *The Fire Last Time: 1968 and After* Bookmarks 1988, p.226.
3 Aaron Brenner, 'Rank-and-File Teamster Movements' in Glenn Perusek and Kent Worcester (eds) *Trade Union Politics: American Unions and Economic Change 1960s–1990s* Humanities Press 1995, p.112.
4 *Royal Commission on Trade Unions and Employers' Associations* (the Donovan Report) 1968, p.95; Colin Leys, *Politics in Britain* Verso 1989, p.144.
5 J.F.B. Goodman and T.G. Whittingham, *Shop Stewards in British Industry* Pan 1969, 1973.
6 Ken Coates and Tony Topham, *The New Unionism: The Case for Workers' Control* Penguin 1974, p.10.
7 *Labour Monthly* March 1970, p.113.
8 Richard Hyman, 'Changing Trade Union Identities and Strategies' in Richard Hyman and Anthony Ferner (eds) *New Frontiers in European Industrial Relations* Blackwell 1994, p.126.
9 Mike Davis, *Prisoners of the American Dream* Verso 1986, p.127.
10 Stan Weir, 'Rebellion in Labor's Rank and File' in Gerry Hunnious, G. David Garson & John Case (eds) *Workers' Control: A Reader on Labor and Social Change* Vintage 1973, p.56.
11 Robert Taylor, *The Fifth Estate: Britain's Unions in the Seventies* Routledge & Kegan Paul 1978, p.138.
12 M. Shalev, 'Lies, Damn Lies, and Strike Statistics' in C. Crouch and A. Pizzorno (eds) *The Resurgence of Industrial Conflict in Europe since 1968* Macmillan 1978.
13 Jonathan Neale, *Memoirs of a Callous Picket* Pluto 1983, p.67.
14 Jack Trautman, *Postal Workers Fight Back* Sun 1975, p.5.
15 Jeremy Brecher, *Strike!* South End 1997, p.260.
16 *Washington Post* 22 March 1970, quoted in Brecher, *Strike!*, p.259.
17 Trautman, *Postal Workers*, p.6.
18 Ibid., pp.6–7.
19 Dan La Botz, *Rank-and-File Rebellion: Teamsters for a Democratic Union* Verso 1990, p.31.
20 Ibid., p.32.
21 Samuel R. Friedman, *Teamster Rank and File: Power, Bureaucracy, and Rebellion at Work and in a Union* Columbia University Press 1982, p.160.

22 William Serrin, *The Company and the Union: The 'Civilized Relationship' of the General Motors Corporation and the United Automobile Workers* Vintage 1970, pp.186–7.
23 Ibid., p.154.
24 *Wall Street Journal*, 29 October 1970, quoted in Brecher, *Strike!*
25 Peter Hernan, 'In the Heart of the Heart of the Country: The Strike at Lordstown' in *Root and Branch: The Rise of the Workers' Movements* Fawcett Crest 1975, p.49.
26 Stanley Aronowitz, quoting the president of the Lordstown UAW local in *False Promises: The Shaping of American Working Class Consciousness* McGraw-Hill 1973, p.42.
27 Heather Thompson, *Whose Detroit? Politics, Labor and Race in a Modern American City* Cornell University Press 1995, p.193.
28 Ibid., p.199.
29 Coates and Topham, *The New Unionism*, pp.150–1.
30 Michael Crick, *Scargill and the Miners* Penguin 1985, p.45.
31 Taylor, *The Fifth Estate*, p.264.
32 Frank Watters, *Being Frank* Askew Design 1992, p.63.
33 Ibid., p.68.
34 Ibid., p.66.
35 Frank Watters, 'The Battle of Saltley Gates' *Morning Star* 10 February 1982.
36 Ibid.
37 Crick, *Scargill and the Miners*, p.60.
38 John Storey, *The Challenge to Management Control* Hutchinson Business Books 1980, p.17.
39 Margaret Thatcher, *The Path to Power* HarperCollins 1995, p.218.
40 Film Four, 'Who Runs The Country?' in *The People's Flag: A Five-Part Documentary History of the British Labour Movement* Platform Films 1986.
41 Stanley Weir, *U.S.A – The Labor Revolt* New England Free Press 1967.
42 Joseph E. Finley, *The Corrupt Kingdom: The Rise and Fall of the United Mine Workers* Simon and Schuster 1972, p.249.
43 Ibid., p.33.
44 Brecher, *Strike!*, p.265.
45 Quoted in Kim Moody and Jim Woodward, *Battle Line: The Coal Strike of '78* Sun 1978, p.30.
46 Quoted in ibid., p.29.
47 Finley, *The Corrupt Kingdom*, pp.284–7.
48 Brecher, *Strike!*, p.265, quoting *Wall Street Journal* 23–25 June 1970.
49 Moody and Woodward, *Battle Line*, p.33.
50 Kim Moody, *An Injury To All: The Decline of American Unionism* Verso 1988, p.90.
51 Alasdair Buchan, *The Right to Work: The Story of the Upper Clyde Confrontation* Calder and Boyars 1972, p.14.
52 Ken Coates, 'Introductory Review' in Michael Barratt-Brown and Ken Coates (eds) *Trade Union Register 1973*, Spokesman 1973, p.39.
53 Graham Chadwick, 'The Manchester Engineering Sit-Ins' in Michael Barratt-Brown and Ken Coates (eds) *Trade Union Register 1973*, Spokesman 1973, p.121.

54 Peter Jenkins, *Mrs Thatcher's Revolution: The Ending of the Socialist Era* Harvard University Press 1987, p.23.
55 Geoffrey Goodman, *From Bevan to Blair* Pluto 2003, p.169.
56 Ibid., p.145.
57 Alex Callinicos, *Socialists in the Trade Unions* Bookmarks 1995, p.46.
58 Goodman, *From Bevan to Blair*, p.145.
59 Thatcher, *The Path To Power*, p.229.
60 Jonathan Freedland, 'Enough of this cover-up: the Wilson plot was our Watergate,' *Guardian* 15 March 2006.
61 Chris Harman, *The Fire Last time* 2nd edition Bookmarks 1998, p.254.
62 Gerald Dorfman, *Government versus Trade Unionism in British Politics since 1968* Hoover Institution Press 1979, p.94.
63 *Times* 29 January 1974.

2 'HOW LITTLE IT ASKED'
(THE WORKING CLASS): 1974–79

1 Tony Benn, *Conflicts of Interest: Diaries 1977–80* Hutchinson 1990, p.178: 'The astonishing thing about the British working-class movement was how little it asked'.
2 Glen Perusek and Kent Worcester (eds) *Trade Union Politics: American Unions and Economic Change* Humanities 1995, pp.11, 234.
3 Steve Jefferys, 'Striking Into the 1980s' *International Socialism* 5, Summer 1979, p.34.
4 Alan Freeman, *The Benn Heresy* Pluto 1982, p.53.
5 Alan Thornett, *Inside Cowley: Trade Union Struggle and Who Really Opened the Door to the Tory Onslaught* Porcupine 1998, p.77.
6 Gerald A. Dorfman, *Government Versus Trade Unionism in British Politics since 1968* Hoover 1979, p.117.
7 Robert Taylor, *The Fifth Estate: Britain's Unions in the Seventies* Routledge & Kegan Paul 1978, p.176.
8 Henry Friedman and Sander Meredeen, *The Dynamics of Industrial Conflict: Lessons From Ford* Croom Helm 1980, pp.267–8.
9 Thornett, *Inside Cowley*, p.173.
10 Geoffrey Goodman, *From Bevan to Blair* Pluto 2003, pp.216–17.
11 William Serrin, *The Company and The Union* Vintage 1974, p.57.
12 Kim Moody, *An Injury To All: The Decline of American Unionism* Verso 1988, p.119.
13 Ibid., p.94.
14 James R. Green, *The World of the Worker: Labor in Twentieth-Century America* University of Illinois Press 1998, p.235.
15 Aaron Brenner, 'Rank-and-File Teamster Movements' in Perusek and Worcester, *Trade Union Politics*, pp.111–12.
16 Thomas Geoghegan, *Which Side Are You On? Trying to Be for Labor when It's Flat on its Back* Farrar, Straus & Giroux 1991, p.38.
17 Ibid., p.33.
18 Ibid., p.33.
19 Kim Moody and Jim Woodward, *Battle Line: The Coal Strike of '78* Sun 1978, p.12.

20 Ibid., p.35.
21 Georgia Ellis, UAW Local 1663, quoted in Moody and Woodward, *Battle Line*, p.98.
22 Moody and Woodward, *Battle Line*, p.65 (illustration).
23 Dan La Botz, *Rank-and-File Rebellion* Verso 1990, p.53.
24 Ibid., p.69.
25 Moody and Woodward, *Battle Line*, p.32.
26 Philip Nyden, *Steelworkers' Rank and File: The Political Economy of a Reform Movement* Praeger 1984, p.65.
27 Ibid., pp.75–6.
28 Ibid., p.29.
29 Moody, *An Injury To All*, p.244.
30 R. Hyman, 'The Politics of Workplace Trade Unionism: Recent Tendencies and Some Problems for Theory' *Capital and Class* 8, 1979.
31 Joe Rogaly, *Grunwick* Penguin 1977, p.94.
32 Jean Lane, 'Working Class Solidarity: The Battles of Grunwick' *Workers Liberty* October 1998, p.23.
33 Rogaly, *Grunwick*, pp.66–7.
34 Lane, 'Working Class Solidarity', p.24.
35 Leo Panitch, *Working Class Politics in Crisis: Essays on Labour and the State* Verso 1986, p.121.
36 Benn, *Conflicts of Interest*, p.551, entry for 26 October 1979.
37 Hilary Wainwright and Dave Elliott, *The Lucas Plan: A New Unionism in the Making?* Allison & Busby 1982; see also Huw Beynon and Hilary Wainwright, *The Workers' Report on Vickers* Pluto 1979.
38 Wainwright and Elliott, *The Lucas Plan*, pp.101–7.
39 Ibid., p.136.
40 Hilary Wainwright, in Peter Hain (ed.) *The Crisis and Future of the Left: The Debate of the Decade* Pluto 1980, pp.24–5.
41 Richard Prosten, 'The Rise in NLRB Election Delays: Measuring Business' New Resistance' *Monthly Labor Review* 102(2), 1979, pp.38–40.
42 Michael Goldfield, *The Decline of Organized Labor in the United States* University of Chicago Press 1987, pp.190–3.
43 Steve Babson, *The Unfinished Struggle: Turning Points in American Labor, 1877–Present* Rowman & Littlefield 1999, p.166.
44 Moody, *An Injury To All*, p.138.
45 Babson, *The Unfinished Struggle*, p.166, quoting Martin Levitt, *Confessions of a Union Buster* Crown 1993, p.273.
46 Irving Bluestone, 'Human Dignity Is What It's All About' *Viewpoint*, AFL-CIO Industrial Union Department, 8(3), 1978, quoted in Mike Parker, 'Inside the Circle: A Union Guide to QWL' *Labor Notes* 1985, p.6.
47 Mike Parker, 'Inside the Circle: A Union Guide to QWL' *Labor Notes* 1985, p.7.
48 Henry Friedman, in Friedman and Sander Meredeen, *The Dynamics of Industrial Conflict: Lessons from Ford* Croom Helm 1980, p.271.
49 Thornett, *Inside Cowley*, pp.272–4.
50 Benn, *Conflicts of Interest*, pp.413ff.
51 Jefferys, 'Striking Into the 1980s', p.40.
52 Peter Jenkins, *Mrs Thatcher's Revolution: The Ending of the Socialist Era* Harvard University Press 1988, p.22.

53 Benn, *Conflicts of Interest*, p.444.
54 Trevor Blackwell and Jeremy Seabrook, *A World Still to Win: the Reconstruction of the Post-War Working Class* Faber & Faber 1985, pp.146–7.
55 John Storey, *The Challenge to Management Control* Business Books 1980, p.95; emphasis in original.
56 Jenkins, *Mrs Thatcher's Revolution*, p.22.
57 Quoted in Thornett, *Inside Cowley*, p.276.
58 Margaret Thatcher, *The Path to Power* HarperCollins 1995, p.420.
59 Friedman and Meredeen, *Dynamics*, p.279; Peter Taafe, *The Rise of Militant: Militant's 30 Years* Militant 1995, p.142.
60 Thornett, *Inside Cowley*, p.274.
61 Thatcher, *The Path to Power*, pp.444, 455, 458–9.
62 Leo Panitch and Colin Leys, *The End of Parliamentary Socialism: From New Left to New Labour* Verso 1997, p.162.
63 Hugo Young, *One of Us* Macmillan 1989, p.129.
64 Ken Coates (ed.) *What Went Wrong* Spokesman 1979, p.29.

3   GONE WITH THE WIND: THATCHER, REAGAN AND THE EARLY 1980s

1 Alan Thornett, *Inside Cowley: Trade Union Struggle and Who Really Opened the Door to the Tory Onslaught* Porcupine 1998, p.279.
2 Margaret Thatcher, *The Path to Power* HarperCollins 1995, p.405.
3 Ibid., p.403.
4 John McIlroy, *The Permanent Revolution? Conservative Law and the Trade Unions* Spokesman 1991, p.21 (quoting Carrington).
5 McIlroy, 1991, p.21.
6 John MacInnes, *Thatcherism at Work: Industrial Relations and Economic Change* Open University Press 1987, p.46.
7 David Marsh, *The New Politics of British Trade Unionism: Union Power and the Thatcher Legacy* ILR 1992, p.80.
8 Len Murray, interviewed in 'The Thatcher Decade', BBC Radio 4, 11 April 1989.
9 McIlroy, *The Permanent Revolution?*, p.49.
10 Ibid., p.65.
11 Marsh, *The New Politics*, p.71.
12 Trades Union Congress, *Industrial Relations Legislation: The Employment Act 1980 and Employment Act 1982* adopted at the Wembley Conference 5 April 1982, p.17.
13 Mike Freeman, *Taking Control: A Handbook for Trade Unionists* Junius 1984, pp.159, 165, 181.
14 Jonathan Neale, *Memoirs of a Callous Picket* Pluto 1983, pp.100–1.
15 McIlroy, *The Permanent Revolution?*, p.201.
16 John Biffen, cited in Patrick Cosgrove, *Thatcher: The First Term* Bodley Head 1985, p.164.
17 John McIlroy, *Trade Unions in Britain Today* Manchester University Press 1995, p.196.

18   Neale, *Memoirs*, pp.89–90.
19   Jean Hartley, John Kelly and Nigel Nicholson, *Steel Strike: A Case Study in Industrial Relations* Batsford 1983, p.25.
20   Ibid., pp.50–1.
21   Ibid., pp.74–5.
22   Colin Herd, 'The Warrington Brick Brigade' in *Lessons of the Steel Strike* IMG 1980, pp.20–1.
23   Hartley et al., *Steel Strike*, p.112.
24   Ibid., p.40.
25   Thornett, *Inside Cowley*, p.320.
26   Ibid., p.321.
27   Hartley et al., *Steel Strike*, p.148.
28   Bernard Connolly, 'A Strike Against the Tories' in *Lessons of the Steel Strike* IMG 1980, p.11.
29   Ibid., p.11.
30   Hartley et al., *Steel Strike*, p.26.
31   Ibid., p.151.
32   Hugo Young, *One Of Us* Macmillan 1989, p.197.
33   Ibid., p.195.
34   Ibid., p.255.
35   Mike Davis, *Prisoners of the American Dream* Verso 1986, p.157.
36   Ibid., p.208–9.
37   Ibid., p.140.
38   Jane Slaughter, 'Concessions and How to Beat Them' *Labor Notes* 1983, p.10.
39   Ibid., p.11.
40   Ibid., p.12.
41   Davis, *Prisoners*, p.141; emphasis added.
42   Slaughter, 'Concessions', p.37.
43   Ibid., pp.39ff.
44   Chris Toulous, 'Political Economy after Reagan' in Glenn Perusek and Kent Worcester (eds) *Trade Union Politics: American Unions and Economic Change, 1960s–1990s* Humanities 1995, p.36.
45   Perusek and Worcester, *Trade Union Politics*, Introduction, p.20, n.24.
46   Jeremy Brecher, *Strike!* South End 1997, p.312.
47   Jim Woodward, in *Labor Notes* 29 September 1981, p.2.
48   'PATCO Strike Continues' *Labor Notes* 27 October 1981, p.14.
49   Barbara Kingsolver, *Holding The Line: Women in the Great Arizona Mine Strike of 1983* ILR 1989, 1996.
50   Dan La Botz, 'Greyhound Strike – Will it be a PATCO on Wheels?' *Labor Notes* 22 November 1983.
51   Kim Moody, *An Injury To All: The Decline of American Unionism* Verso 1988, p.310.
52   Dan La Botz, 'A Troublemaker's Handbook: How to Fight Back Where You Work – And Win!' *Labor Notes* 1991, pp.117ff.
53   Ibid., p.119.
54   Elly Leary and Marybeth Menaker, *Jointness at GM: Company Unionism in the 21st Century* New Directions 1995, p.32.
55   Michael Terry, 'Shop Steward Development and Managerial Strategies' in George Bain (ed.) *Industrial Relations in Britain* Blackwell 1983, p.70.

56　Ralph Darlington, *The Dynamics of Workplace Unionism: Shop Stewards' Organisation in Three Merseyside Plants* Mansell 1997, p.251.

57　Graham Turner, *Daily Telegraph* 13 February 1981.

58　Mark Dickinson, *To Break a Union: The Messenger, the State and the NGA* Booklist Ltd 1984, p.9.

59　McIlroy, *The Permanent Revolution?*, p.71.

60　Ibid., p.73.

61　McIlroy, *Trade Unions*, p.55.

4　AGAINST THE STREAM: 1984–89

1　Peter Rachleff, *Hard-Pressed in the Heartland: The Hormel Strike and the Future of the Labor Movement* South End 1993, p.110.

2　Michael Crick, *Scargill and the Miners The Great Strike* Penguin 1985, p.87.

3　Alex Callinicos and Mike Simons, *The Great Strike: The Miners' Strike of 1984–5 and its Lessons* Socialist Worker 1985, pp.33–4.

4　Ibid., pp.43–4.

5　Ibid., p.35.

6　Huw Beynon, in Beynon (ed.) *Digging Deeper: Issues in the Miners' Strike* Verso 1985, pp.18–19.

7　Crick, *Scargill*, p.99.

8　*Times*, 7 March 1984, quoted in Crick, *Scargill*, p.101.

9　Callinicos and Simons, *The Great Strike*, pp.75–6.

10　Ibid., p.74.

11　Seamus Milne, *The Enemy Within: the Secret War Against the Miners* Pan 1995, p.21.

12　Ibid., p.25.

13　Beynon, *Digging Deeper*, p.19.

14　Callinicos and Simons, *The Great Strike*, pp.145–6 (quoting from *Economist* 8 September 1984).

15　Milne, *The Enemy Within*, p.22.

16　Ibid., p.369.

17　Ibid., p.370.

18　Quoted in Lynn Beaton, *Shifting Horizons* Canary 1985, pp.227–8.

19　Callinicos and Simons, *The Great Strike*, p.221.

20　Interviews with striking miners, Learning Centre, Sheffield Hallam University 1994.

21　Philip Bassett, *Strike Free* Macmillan 1986, pp.157–8.

22　John McIlroy, *The Permanent Revolution? Conservative Law and the Trade Unions* Spokesman 1991, p.114.

23　The psephological term in Britain for skilled or better-off workers.

24　'Round-table Discussion with Hormel Workers', *Forward* 7(1) January 1987, p.26.

25　Ibid., p.27.

26　Quoted in Rachleff, *Hard-Pressed*, p.19.

27　Julius Getman, *The Betrayal of Local 14: Paperworkers, Politics, and Permanent Replacements* ILR 1998, p.7.

28　Ibid., pp.33–6.

29 Ibid., p.45; emphasis in original.
30 Ibid., p.53.
31 Ibid., p.57.
32 Ibid., p.64.
33 Ibid., p.172.
34 Ibid., p.95; emphasis in original.
35 Marc Lendler, *Crisis and Political Beliefs: The Case of the Colt Firearms Strike* Yale University Press 1997, p.24; see also Rick Fantasia, *Cultures of Solidarity: Consciousness, Action, and Contemporary American Workers* University of California Press, 1988.
36 Richard E. Walton, Joel E. Curcher-Gershenfeld and Robert B. McKersie, *Strategic Negotiations: A Theory of Change in Labor-Management Relations* ILR 1994, pp.77, 105.
37 Mike Parker and Jane Slaughter, 'Choosing Sides: Union and the Team Concept' *Labor Notes* 1988, p.16.
38 Peter Downs, 'Identity Crisis: Unions in the Workplace of the Future' in Bruce Nissan (ed.) *Unions and Workplace Organisation* Wayne University Press 1997, p.103.
39 Parker and Slaughter, 'Choosing Sides', p.4.
40 Kim Moody, *An Injury To All: The Decline of American Unionism* Verso 1988, p.239.
41 Harry Scarbrough and Mike Terry, 'United Kingdom: the Reorganisation of Production' in Thomas A. Kochan, Russell D. Lansbury and John Paul MacDuffie (eds) *After Lean Production: Evolving Employment Practices in the World Auto Industry* ILR 1997, p.142.
42 Andrew Sayer, 'New Developments in Manufacturing' *Capital and Class* 30, Winter 1986, p.63.
43 Dave Ward, 'Postal Workers Unite Against Teamworking' in Sheila Cohen (ed.) *What's Happening? The Truth about Work ... & the Myth of 'Partnership'* Trade Union Forum 1998, p.14.
44 David Marsh, *The New Politics of British Trade Unionism* ILR 1982, p.181.
45 Phil Garrahan and Paul Stewart, *The Nissan Enigma: Flexibility at Work in a Local Economy* Mansell 1992, p.92.
46 Ian Linn, *Single Union Deals: A Case Study of the Norsk Hydro Plant at Immingham* Northern College 1986, p.26.
47 Philip Bassett, *Strike Free: New Industrial Relations in Britain* Macmillan 1986, p.3.
48 Ibid., p.149.
49 McIlroy, *The Permanent Revolution?*, p.124.
50 Charles Woolfson and John Foster, *Track Record: The Story of the Caterpillar Occupation* Verso 1988, p.203; emphasis in original.
51 Ibid., p.76; Ravenscraig was a Scottish steel plant also threatened with closure.
52 Ibid., p.204; emphasis in original.
53 Ibid., p.237.
54 McIlroy, *The Permanent Revolution?*, p.143.
55 Interview with Glenroy Watson, RMT activist, 3 January 2001.
56 McIlroy, *The Permanent Revolution?*, p.198.
57 *Catalyst* 1990, pp.26–7.

58   Moody, *An Injury To All*, p.328.
59   *Forward* January 1987, p.1.

5   THE WORKERS' TINA: CLASS WARFARE
IN THE 1990s

1   Robert Fitch, *The Assassination of New York* Verso 1993, p.171.
2   Advertisement for *New Left Review* 8, March/April 2001 in *Nation* 23 April 2001.
3   Neil Millward et al., *Workplace Industrial Relations in Transition* Dartmouth 1992, p.350.
4   Stephen Roach, *Wall Street Journal* 17 June 1996.
5   Kim Moody, *Workers in a Lean World* Verso 1997, p.90.
6   Mike Parker and Jane Slaughter, 'Working Smart: A Union Guide to Participation Programs and Reengineering' *Labor Notes* 1994, p.25.
7   General Motors, *Competitive Manufacturing Planning Guide*, cited in Steve Babson, 'Ambiguous Mandate ...' in Huberto Juarez Nunez and Steve Babson (eds) *Confronting Change: Auto Labor and Lean Production in North America* Wayne State University Press 1998, p.27.
8   Moody, *Workers in a Lean World*, p.88.
9   Sheila Cohen (ed.) *What's Happening?? The Truth about Work ... & the Myth of* 'Partnership' Trade Union Forum 1998, pp.6–7.
10   Peter Fairbrother, *Trade Unions at the Crossroads* Mansell 2000, p.163.
11   Andy Danford, 'The "New Industrial Relations" and Class Struggle in the 1990s' *Capital and Class* 61, Spring 1997, p.113.
12   Harry Scarbrough and Michael Terry, 'United Kingdom: The Reorganisation of Production' in Thomas Kochan, Russell Lansbury and John Paul MacDuffie (eds) *After Lean Production: Evolving Employment Practices in the World Auto Industry* ILR 1997, p.149.
13   Elly Leary and Marybeth Menaker, *Jointness at GM: Company Unionism in the 21st Century* UAW New Directions 1993, p.50.
14   Paul Stewart, 'Striking Harder and Smarter at Vauxhall: The New Industrial Relations of Lean Production' *Capital and Class* 61, Spring 1997, pp.4–6.
15   Moody, *Workers in a Lean World*, p.30.
16   Dave Ward, 'Postal Workers against Teamworking' in Cohen, *What's Happening??*, pp.13–15.
17   John Tyler, 'Cutting HRM Off at the Knees at Cadbury's' in Cohen, *What's Happening??*, p.42.
18   Cf. Peter Fairbrother, 'Privatisation and Local Trade Unionism' *Work, Employment and Society* 8(3), 1994, pp. 339–56.
19   Committee on the Evolution of Work, *The New American Workplace: A Labor Perspective* AFL-CIO 1994, cited in Bruce Nissen (ed.) *Unions and Workplace Reorganisation* Wayne State University Press 1997, p.19.
20   Mae M. Ngai, 'Workplace Education and Labor-Management Cooperation' in Nissen, *Unions and Workplace Reorganisation*, p.134.
21   Trades Union Congress, *Human Resource Management – A Trade Union Response: Report to the 1994 Congress* TUC 1994.

22 Brian Towers, *The Representation Gap: Change and Reform in the British and American Workplace* Oxford University Press 1997, p.220.

23 Parker and Slaughter, 'Working Smart', p.47.

24 Robert Taylor, *The Future of Trade Unions* Andre Deutsch 1994, p.125.

25 Tony Richardson, 'Onslaught at Rover' in Cohen, *What's Happening??*, p.60.

26 Kim Moody, 'Book review of Andrew Herod (ed.) *Organising the Landscape' Antipode* January 2000, p.208.

27 Kate Bronfenbrenner and Tom Juravich, 'It Takes More Than House Calls ...' in Bronfenbrenner et al. (eds) *Organising to Win* ILR 1998, p.34.

28 Gregory Mantsios, 'What Does Labor Stand For?' in Mantsios (ed.) *A New Labor Movement for the New Century* Monthly Review 1998, pp.52–4.

29 Kim Moody and Simone Sagovac, 'Time Out! The Case for a Shorter Working Week' *Labor Notes* 1995, p.18.

30 Bob Hall, 'US Workers – Fighting from the Inside' *Trade Union News* 15, September–October 1993, p.11.

31 Stephen Franklin, *Three Strikes: Labor's Heartland Losses and What They Mean for Working Americans* Guildford 2001, p.165.

32 *Labor Notes* January 1996, p.14.

33 Franklin, *Three Strikes*, pp.140, 141.

34 Tom Juravich and Kate Bronfenbrenner, *The Steelworkers' Victory and the Revival of American Labor* ILR 1999.

35 Decatur activist, quoted in *Labor Notes* February 1996, p.11.

36 Jack Richards, 'Overview of the Detroit Newspaper Workers' Strike: Some Lessons for the Movement' *Organizer Pamphlet Series* September 1998, p.3.

37 Quoted in Moody, *Workers in a Lean World*, p.29.

38 Richards, 'Overview', pp.3 and 7; emphasis in original.

39 Ibid., p.6.

40 *Labor Notes* September 1997, p.2.

41 Richards, 'Overview', p.40.

42 *Labor Notes* April 1997, p.8.

43 Willie Lesslie [AEEU convenor], *Trade Union News* 13, May–June 1993.

44 Peter Taafe, *The Rise of Militant* Militant 1995, p.510.

45 Bob Duffy, *Trade Union News* 14, July–August 1993, p.4.

46 Gail Squires [UNISON], *Trade Union News* 16, p.3.

47 Speaker at Keele University conference, 1994.

48 Seamus Milne, *The Enemy Within: The Secret War Against the Miners* Pan 1994, p.32.

49 Ibid., p.32.

50 Bob Anderson [NUM Branch Secretary], 'Miners Have Had Enough' *Trade Union News* November–December 1992.

51 Trevor Blackwell and Jeremy Seabrook, *Talking Work: An Oral History* Faber & Faber 1996, p.158.

52 Milne, *The Enemy Within*, pp.32–3.

53 Kim Moody, 'Solidarity in a Just-in-Time World' *Labor Notes* March 1997, p.2.

54 Noel Castree, 'Geographical Scale and Grassroots Internationalism: The Liverpool Dock Dispute, 1995–1998' *Economic Geography* 76(3), 2000, p.288.

55 Michael Lavalette and Jane Kennedy, *Solidarity on the Waterfront: The Liverpool Lockout of 1995–6* Liver Press 1996, p.95.

56 Castree, 'Geographical Scale', p.288.
57 Andrew Herod, *Labor Geographies: Workers and the Landscapes of Capitalism* Guilford 2001, p.199.
58 Lawrence Donegan, 'Spirit of new militancy willing ...' *Guardian* 12 September 1995.
59 Neasa MacErlean, *Observer* 14 July 1996.
60 Donegan, 'Spirit'.

6   INTO THE 2000s: SEATTLE ... AND SEPTEMBER

1   Mike Parker, 'Fighting UPS' "Teamwork" Prepared Union to Win the Big Strike' *Labor Notes* November 1997, p.14.
2   Cf. *Rank and File Power at UPS* Teamster Rank and File Education Foundation (TRF) 2000, p.39.
3   Ibid., p.42.
4   Ibid., p.42.
5   Butch Traylor, 'A Workers' Journal: First Week Back at UPS' *Convoy Dispatch* October 1997, p.4.
6   Jim West, 'Big Win at UPS!' *Labor Notes* September 1997.
7   Seamus Milne, 'Silenced Voices' *Guardian* 12 May 1997.
8   'TUC Seeks Employer "Partnership"' BBC News 21 May 1999.
9   Robert Taylor, 'Labour Disputes at Lowest since 1891' *Financial Times* 10 June 1997.
10 Seamus Milne, 'Doctor, I Feel A Walkout Coming On' *Guardian* 21 July 1997.
11 Taylor, 'Labour Disputes'.
12 Ibid.
13 M. Cully, S. Woodward, A. O'Reilly and G. Dix, *Britain at Work* Routledge 1999.
14 John Stirling, 'Britain at Work ...' *Capital and Class* 73, Spring 2001, pp.173–9.
15 Cully et al., *Britain at Work*, p.208.
16 Leon Fink, *The Maya of Morgantown: Work and Community in the Nuevo New South* University of North Carolina Press 2003, p.1.
17 Kim Moody, 'More Strikes Against Downsizing as GM Flees Flint' *Labor Notes* July 1998.
18 Jane Slaughter, '"Partnership" Takes a Hit at Saturn' *Labor Notes* April 1999.
19 Ibid.
20 Ibid.
21 Peter Fairbrother, *Trade Unions at the Crossroads* Mansell 2000.
22 Reuters, 'Two-Day London Underground Strike to Go Ahead' 10 February 1999.
23 Mark Steel, 'Spark Plug' *Guardian* 25 November 1998.
24 Robert Taylor, 'Election '97: Backtracking Embitters Old Guard' *Financial Times* 7 April 1997.
25 Quoted in *Times*, 31 March 1997.
26 Sarah Luthens, 'Labor to Join "The Protest of the Century" ...' *Labor Notes* October 1999, p.16.

27   Jeff Crosby [President, IUE Local 201], ' "The Kids Are All Right ..." ' *Labor Notes* January 2000, p.8.
28   Patrick Wintour, 'Seven Days that Shook New Labour' *Guardian* 16 September 2000.
29   Reuters, 'British Protests Surge as Fuel Trickles Out' *New York Times* 13 September 2000.
30   Jason Burke, Kamal Ahmed et al., 'A Few Angry Men' *Observer* 17 September 2000.
31   Ibid.
32   Warren Hoge, 'Britain's Disenchanted Kingdom: Strike Takes a Toll' *New York Times* 19 September 2000.
33   Patrick Wintour, 'Down to the Last Drop' *Guardian* 13 September 2000.
34   'The Return of Militancy' *Workers' Liberty* 12 September 2000.
35   Francis Wheen, 'Supporting the Petrol Pickets?' *Guardian* 13 September 2000.
36   Warren Hoge, 'Fuel Standoff in Britain Eases ...' New York Times 13 September 2000.
37   Leanda de Lisle, 'My Friends on the Barricades' *Guardian* 13 September 2000.
38   Warren Hoge, *New York Times* 19 September 2000.
39   *Workers' Liberty* 12 September 2000.
40   Patrick Wintour, *Guardian* 13 September 2000.
41   Patrick Wintour, *Guardian* 16 September 2000.
42   Burke, Ahmed et al., 'A Few Angry Men'.
43   Wintour, *Guardian* 16 September 2000.
44   Dennis Orton, 'Charleston 5 Rally Draws Thousands to South Carolina' *Labor Notes* July 2001, p.1.
45   Peter Olney, 'The Arithmetic of Decline and Some Proposals for Renewal' *New Labor Forum* Spring/Summer 2002, p.15.
46   Priscilla Murolo and A.B. Chitty, *From The Folks Who Brought you the Weekend* New Press 2001, p.330.
47   Chris Garlock, 'After September 11, New Organising Challenges' *Labor Notes* December 2001, p.5.
48   Peter Winch, 'Collective Bargaining Called threat to National Security' *Labor Notes* March 2003.
49   Corey Robin, 'The Politics of Before and After: Labor's War at Home' *New Labor Forum* Spring/Summer 2002, p.68.
50   Hal Leyshon, 'AFL-CIO Stays the Course' *Labor Notes* January 2002, p.1.
51   Ken Riley, 'On The Campaign To Free The Charleston Five' *Social Policy* Winter 2001–02, p.26.
52   Malik Miah and Rich Lesnik, 'Bush: "No Airline Strikes This Year" ' *Labor Notes* May 2001, p.13.
53   Sasha Lilley, 'New Economy R.I.P.', review of Doug Henwood, *After the New Economy* New Press 2003, *Monthly Review* April 2004, p.49.
54   Peter Olney, 'On The Waterfront' *New Labor Forum* Summer 2003.
55   Jack Mulcahy, 'Longshore Union Enforced "No Work" Policy on the Docks – During Lockout' *Labor Notes* November 2002, p.12.
56   Olney, 'On The Waterfront', p.36.

57   Warren Hoge, 'Britain's Revived Labor Movement is Spoiling for a Fight' *New York Times* 15 February 2002.
58   Seamus Milne, 'At Last the Union Tide has Turned' *Guardian* 18 July 2002.
59   Seamus Milne, 'Chaos as Union Rejects Election Result' *Guardian* 18 July 2002.
60   David Gow, 'Nissan's First Strike "Dangerously Close"' *Guardian* 21 January 2003.
61   Kevin Maguire, 'Fear and Anger Drive the Strikers' *Guardian* 29 July 2003.
62   Milne, 'At Last'.
63   Ibid.
64   Martin Smith, *The Awkward Squad: New Labour and the Rank and File* Socialist Worker 2003, p.15.
65   Christine Buckley, 'Union Members Take a Turn to the Left' *Times* 6 June 2001.
66   Smith, 2003, *The Awkward Squad*, pp.16–17.
67   Andrew Murray, *A New Labour Nightmare: The Return of the Awkward Squad* Verso 2003, pp.113–14.
68   Karen Olsson, 'The Shame of Meatpacking' *Nation* 16 September 2002.
69   Teofilo Reyes, '8,000 "Guest Workers" Join Farm Union in North Carolina' *Labor Notes* October 2004.
70   Justin Jackson, 'Yale Unions Unite to Fight Company Town' *Labor Notes* November 2002, p.3.
71   Sheila McClear, 'Detroit Cintas Workers Prepare To Strike ...' *Labor Notes* September 2003, p.7.
72   N. Renuka Uthappa, 'Two-Tiered Grocery Contract Leaves Anger, Questions' *Labor Notes* April 2004.
73   Ivor Peterson, 'Dispute on Contract Length Is Issue in Strike at Casinos' *New York Times* 2 October 2004.
74   *Sun* 26 November 2002.
75   Murray, *A New Labour Nightmare*, p.129.
76   Ibid., p.83.
77   Chris Kutalik, 'Danger and Opportunity: Crisis and the Two Souls of Labor's Revitalisation' *Solidarity News* October 2004, p.4.

7   UNIONS AND UNIONS

1   Naomi Klein, 'AFL-CIO Dropped the Ball on Globalisation Movement' *Labor Notes* March 2001, p.9.
2   Martin Thomas, 'Debating the Future at the European Social Forum' *New Politics* Winter 2003, pp.108–9.
3   Union activist, Transit Workers Union Local 100 (NY), December 2002.
4   Perry Anderson, 'The Limits and Possibilities of Trade Union Action' in R. Blackburn and A. Cockburn (eds) *The Incompatibles: Trade Union Militancy and the Consensus* Penguin 1967.
5   Richard Hyman, *Marxism and the Sociology of Trade Unionism* Pluto 1971.
6   Hal Draper, *Karl Marx's Theory of Revolution: The Politics of Social Classes* Monthly Review 1978, p.110.
7   Nelson Lichtenstein, *State of the Union: A Century of American Labor* Princeton University Press 2002, pp.256–7.

8   Brian Towers, *The Representation Gap: Change and Reform in the British and American Workplace* Oxford University Press 1997, p.81.

9   Andrew Murray, *A New Labour Nightmare: The Return of the Awkward Squad* Verso 2003, p.16.

10 Ibid., p.44.

11 Dan Clawson, *The Next Upsurge: Labor and the New Social Movements* ILR 2003, pp. 102–4.

12 Towers, *The Representation Gap*, p.82.

13 Kate Bronfenbrenner and Tom Juravich, 'It Takes More Than House Calls' in Bronfenbrenner et al. (eds) *Organising to Win: New Research on Union Strategies* ILR 1998, pp.21–4.

14 Bronfenbrenner and Juravich, 'It Takes More', pp.20–4; see pp.22–3 for detailed figures.

15 Herman Benson, 'Must Labor Bureaucratize to Organize?' *Union Democracy Review* July/August 2005.

16 Kim Moody, 'When the Sum Is No Greater Than Its Parts: Union Mergers' *New Labor Forum* 10, Spring/Summer 2002, p.43.

17 Benson, 'Must Labor Bureaucratize', p.5.

18 'Organize, Organize, Organize: Vice President King's route to justice' UAW *Solidarity* May 2003.

19 'Union Mergers Won't Stem Decline' *Workers' Power* 3 February 2005.

20 Robert Taylor, *The Future of the Trade Unions* Andre Deutsch 1994, p.202.

21 John Kelly and Edmund Heery, *Working for The Union: British Trade Union Officers* Cambridge University Press 1994, p.206.

22 Andy Charlwood, 'Willingness to Unionize amongst Non-union Workers' in Howard Gospel and Stephen Wood (eds) *Representing Workers* Routledge 2003, p.70.

23 John Kelly, *Rethinking Industrial Relations: Mobilisation, Collectivism and Long Waves* Routledge 1998, p.48.

24 Patricia Findlay and Alan McKinlay, 'Organising in Electronics: Recruitment, Recognition and Representation – Shadow Shop Stewards in Scotland's "Silicon Glen"' in Gregor Gall (ed.) *Union Organising: Campaigning For Trade Union Recognition* Routledge 2003, p.115.

25 Kelly, *Rethinking Industrial Relations*, p.44.

26 Steve Early, 'AFL-CIO's Organising Summit Looks at "Best Practices" – But Leaves Much Unexamined' *Labor Notes* February 2003, pp.7–10.

27 Edmund Heery and Patricia Fosh, 'Introduction: Whose Union?' in Fosh and Heery (eds) *Trade Unions and their Members: Studies in Union Democracy and Organisation* Macmillan 1990.

28 Leo Panitch, *Working Class Politics in Crisis: Essays on Labour and the State* Verso 1986, Chapter 7.

29 Richard Hyman, 'The Politics of Workplace Trade Unionism: Recent Tendencies and Some Problems for Theory' *Capital and Class* 8, Summer 1979.

30 Tony Lane, *The Union makes Us Strong* Arrow 1974, p.208.

31 Kelly and Heery, *Working for the Union*.

32 A.I. Marsh, *Managers and Shop Stewards* Institute of Personnel Management 1963, pp.15–16.

33 Michael Terry, 'Shop Steward Development and Managerial Strategies' in George Bain (ed.) *Industrial Relations in Britain* Blackwell 1983, p.72.

34 Government Social Survey, *Workplace Industrial Relations* HMSO 1968, p.85.
35 Eric Batstone, Ian Boraston and Stephen Frenkel, *Shop Stewards in Action: The Organisation of Workplace Conflict and Accommodation* Blackwell 1977, pp.31–2, 69.
36 Ibid., p.73.
37 Stanley Weir, 'U.S.A. – The Labor Revolt' in *Single Jack Solidarity* University of Minnesota Press 2004, pp.294ff.
38 Ibid.
39 Quoted in Aaron Brenner, 'Reform Caucuses and Running for Office' in Jane Slaughter (ed.) 'A Troublemaker's Handbook 2' *Labor Notes* 2005, p.281.
40 Steve Downs and Tim Schermerhorn, '*Hell on Wheels*: Organising Among New York City's Subway and Bus Workers' in Ray M. Tillman and Michael S. Cummings (eds) *The Transformation of U.S. Unions: Voices, Visions and Strategies from the Grassroots* Lynne Reinner 1999, p.171.
41 Ibid., p.172.
42 Ibid., p.176.
43 Ibid., pp.178, 183.
44 Ibid., p.185.
45 Jon Johnson [NUPCS], 'Broad Lefts – Are They The Answer?' *Trade Union News* 26, July–August 1995.
46 Martin Spellman, 'Broad Lefts' in *The Coming Crisis in the CWU and How to Overcome It* Nagging Issues 2000, p.20.
47 Terry, 'Shop Steward Development', p.80.
48 Andy Danford, 'The "New Industrial Relations" and Class Struggle in the 1990s' *Capital and Class* 61, Spring 1997, p.127.
49 Patricia Fosh, 'Local Trade Unionists in Action' in Fosh and Heery, *Trade Unions and their Members*, pp.138–141.
50 Sheila Cohen, 'You Are The Union' *Studies for Trade Unionists* Workers' Educational Association, 14(53), April 1988, p.18.
51 Ibid., pp.16, 13.
52 Ibid., p.29.
53 Fosh 1990, pp.111–2.
54 Cohen 1988, p.30.
55 Fosh, 'Local Trade Unionists', p.138.
56 Peter Fairbrother, 'British Trade Unions Facing the Future' *Capital and Class* 71, Summer 2000.
57 Ibid., p.58.
58 Gregor Gall, 'The Prospects for Workplace Trade Unionism: Evaluating Fairbrother's Union Renewal Thesis' *Capital and Class* 66, Autumn 1998, p.150.
59 Ibid., p.154.
60 John McIlroy, 'New Labour, New Unions, New Left' *Capital and Class* 71, Summer 2000, p.16.
61 Leo Panitch, *Social Democracy and Industrial Militancy* Cambridge University Press 1976, p.253.
62 Leo Panitch, *Working Class Politics in Crisis: Essays on Labour and the State* Verso 1986, p.189; emphasis in original.

63 Giovanni Arrighi, 'Towards a Theory of Capitalist Crisis' *New Left Review* 111, September–October 1978, p.23. Cited in Panitch, *Working Class Politics*, p.211.

8 PUNCTUATION MARKS: A STORY OF CLASS CONSCIOUSNESS

1 Antonio Gramsci, *Prison Notebooks* (ed. Quintin Hoare and Geoffrey Nowell Smith) International 1971, p.333.
2 Alan Thornett, *Inside Cowley: Trade Union Struggle in the 1970s* Porcupine 1998, p. xiii.
3 Ibid., p.15.
4 Ibid., p.16.
5 Ibid., pp.115, 125.
6 Ralph Darlington, *The Dynamics of Workplace Unionism: Shop Stewards' Organisation in Three Merseyside Plants* Mansell 1994.
7 Ibid., p.171.
8 Ibid., p.61.
9 Ibid., p.100.
10 Ibid., pp.102, 108.
11 Ibid., p.217.
12 David Croteau, *Politics and the Class Divide: Working People and the Middle-Class Left* Temple University Press 1995.
13 Ibid., p.55.
14 Ibid., p.109.
15 Ibid., p.181.
16 Ibid., p.72.
17 Ibid., p.73.
18 Michael Mann, 'The Social Cohesion of Liberal Democracy' *American Sociological Review* 35, 1970, pp. 423–39.
19 Karl Marx, *Capital, Volume 1* Lawrence & Wishart 1970, p.737.
20 Croteau, *Politics and the Class Divide*, p. xxviii.
21 Mann, 'Social Cohesion'; Mann, *Consciousness and Action among the Western Working Class* Macmillan 1973; J.H. Westergaard, 'The Rediscovery of the Cash Nexus' *Socialist Register 1970*; Westergaard, 'Radical Class Consciousness' in M. Bulmer (ed.) *Working-Class Images of Society* Routledge and Kegan Paul 1975.
22 Nicholas Abercrombie, Stephen Hill and Bryan S. Turner, *The Dominant Ideology Thesis* George Allen & Unwin 1984, p.141.
23 Rick Fantasia, *Cultures of Solidarity: Consciousness, Action and Contemporary American Workers* University of California Press 1988, p.178.
24 Rosa Luxemburg, *The Mass Strike* Merlin 1925, p.73.
25 Gramsci, *Prison Notebooks*, p.327.
26 Marc Lendler, *Crisis and Political Beliefs: The Case of the Colt Firearms Strike* Yale University Press 1997, p.4.
27 Giles Radice and Stephen Pollard, *Southern Comfort, More Southern Comfort* and *Any Southern Comfort?* Fabian Pamphlets 555 (1992), 560 (1993) and 568 (1994).

28 *Guardian* 1990 (nd).
29 Ruth Milkman, *Farewell to the Factory: Auto Workers in the Late Twentieth Century* University of California Press 1997.
30 Ibid., pp.7–8.
31 Ibid., p.9.
32 Ibid., p.172.
33 Peter Fairbrother, *Trade Unions at the Crossroads* Mansell 2000.
34 Ibid., p.151
35 Ibid., p.154.
36 John Kelly, *Rethinking Industrial Relations: Mobilisation, Collectivism and Long Waves* Routledge 1998, p.109.
37 S. Crook, J. Pakulski and M. Waters, *Postmodernisation: Change in Advanced Society* Sage 1992, p.38.
38 Kathryn Marie Dudley, *The End Of the Line: Lost Jobs, New Lives in Postindustrial America* University of Chicago Press 1994, p.151.
39 Philip Corrigan, Harvie Ramsay and Derek Sawyer, *Social Construction and Marxist Theory* Monthly Review 1978, p.20; emphasis in original.
40 Corrigan et al., *Social Construction*, p.21.
41 Karl Marx, *Resultate, Capital Volume 1*, NLR/Pelican 1976, p.1046.
42 Corrigan et al., *Social Construction*, pp.21–2.
43 Fantasia, *Cultures of Solidarity, passim*.
44 Dudley, *End Of the Line*, p.108.
45 Katherine S. Newman, *Falling from Grace: The Experience of Downward Mobility in the American Middle Class* Vintage 1988, p.189.
46 Ibid., p.124.
47 Jefferson Cowie, *Capital Moves: RCA's 70-year Quest for Cheap Labor* Cornell University Press 1999, p.131.
48 Hal Draper points out that many of the ideas associated with classic 'Leninism' in fact owe more to Kautsky: 'The Myth of Lenin's "Concept of the Party": Or What They Did to *What Is to Be Done?*' (first drafted 1963), *Historical Materialism* 4, Summer 1999.
49 V.I. Lenin, 'On Strikes' in *Collected Works, Volume IV* Progress Publishers 1960, pp.315–17.
50 V.I. Lenin, 'The St. Petersburg Strike' in *Collected Works, Volume VIII* Progress Publishers 1960, pp.92–3.
51 V.I Lenin, 'Lecture on the 1905 Revolution' (1917) in *Collected Works, Volume XXIII* Progress Publishers 1960, pp.239–42; emphasis added.
52 Leon Trotsky, *1905* Vintage 1971, p.85.

9   TRANSITIONS AND TRANSFORMATIONS: WHICH SIDE ARE YOU ON?

1 Huw Beynon, *Working For Ford* Penguin 1984, p.318.
2 Ibid., pp.281–2.
3 Peter Jenkins, 'Ford and the Squalid Silence' *Guardian* 6 April 1971, quoted in Beynon, *Working For Ford*, p.305.
4 Lowell Turner, Harry C. Katz and Richard W. Hurd, *Rekindling the Movement: Labor's Quest for Relevance in the 21st Century* Cornell University Press/ILR 2001, p.21.

5   Ibid., p.21.
6   Service Employees' International Union, *The High Road: A Winning Strategy for Managing Conflict and Communicating Effectively* SEIU 1999.
7   Turner et al., *Rekindling the Movement*, p.10.
8   Ibid., p.10.
9   Peter Fairbrother, *Trade Unions at the Crossroads* Mansell 2000, p.312.
10 Nelson Lichtenstein, *State of the Union: A Century of American Labor* Princeton University Press 2002, p.256.
11 Ibid., p.256.
12 Ibid., p.260.
13 Dan Clawson, *The Next Upsurge: Labor and the New Social Movements* ILR 2003, p.28.
14 Mike Parker and Martha Gruelle, 'Democracy is Power' *Labor Notes* 1999, p.29.
15 Lichtenstein, *State of the Union*, p.270.
16 Parker and Gruelle, 'Democracy is Power', p.14.
17 Clawson, *The Next Upsurge*, p.193.
18 Ibid., p.25.
19 See Hal Draper, *Socialism From Below* (ed. E. Haberkern) Humanities 1992 for a penetrating analysis of this tendency.
20 Ralph Darlington and Dave Lyddon, *Glorious Summer: Class Struggle in Britain 1972* Bookmarks 2001, pp.60, 174.
21 Lynn Beaton, *Shifting Horizons* Canary 1985, p.86.
22 Jay-Livermore Falls Working Class History Project, *Pain on Their Faces: Testimonies on the Paper Mill Strike, Jay, Maine, 1987–1988* Apex 1998, pp.xvii, 12, 21, 31, 77.
23 John Kelly, *Rethinking Industrial Relations: Mobilisation, Collectivism and Long Waves* Routledge 1998, pp.27–9.
24 Michael Lavalette and Jane Kennedy, *Solidarity on the Waterfront: The Liverpool Lock Out of 1995/96* Liver 1996, p.65.
25 Penny Green, *The Enemy Without: Policing and Class Consciousness in the Miners'* Strike Open University Press 1990.
26 Tony Lane and Kenneth Roberts, *Strike at Pilkington's* Fontana 1971, p.202.
27 Francis Wheen, 'Supporting the Petrol Pickets?' *Guardian* 13 September 2000.
28 Jason Burke, Kamal Ahmed et al., 'A Few Angry Men' *Observer* 25 September 2000.
29 Charles Woolfson and John Foster, *Track Record: The Story of the Caterpillar Occupation* Verso 1986, p.76. Ravenscraig was a Scottish steel plant slated for closure.
30 Karl Marx, *The Poverty of Philosophy* Progress Publishers 1973, p.150.
31 Carter Goodrich, *Frontier of Control* Pluto 1970.
32 Rosa Luxemburg, *The Mass Strike* Merlin 1925 (1906), p.35.
33 Beynon, *Working For Ford*, p.229.
34 Cf. Sheila Cohen and Kim Moody, 'Unions, Strikes and Class-Consciousness Today' *Socialist Register* 1998, p.120.
35 Fairbrother, *Trade Unions at the Crossroads*, p.315.
36 Willie Thompson, *The Good Old Cause: British Communism 1920–1991* Pluto Press 1991, p.160

37 Jim Higgins, *More Years for the Locust: The Origins of the SWP* IS Group 1997, pp.94ff.
38 Antonio Gramsci, *Prison Notebooks* (ed. Quintin Hoare and Geoffrey Nowell Smith) International 1971, p.4.
39 Lichtenstein, *State of the Union*, p.259.
40 Kenneth C. Crowe, *Collision: How the Rank and File Took Back the Teamsters* Scribner 1993, p.61.
41 *Labor Notes* conference brochure 1999, p.18.
42 Interview with Tom Hopp, UAW activist at Saturn, February 2004.
43 Michael Zweig, *The Working Class Majority: America's Best-Kept Secret* ILR 2000, p.53.
44 Clawson, *The Next Upsurge*, p.15.
45 Kathryn Marie Dudley, *The End of the Line: Lost Jobs, New Lives in Postindustrial America* University of Chicago Press 1994, p.107.
46 Cynthia Estlund, *Working Together: How Workplace Bonds Strengthen a Diverse Democracy* Oxford University Press 2004, p.68.
47 Ibid., p.100.
48 Rick Fantasia, *Cultures of Solidarity: Consciousness, Action, and Contemporary American Workers* University of California Press 1998, pp.77, 79.
49 Georgia Panter Nielsen, *From Sky Girl to Flight Attendant* ILR 1982, p.119.
50 Fantasia, *Cultures of Solidarity*, p.165.
51 Adolph Reed, Jr, *Class Notes, Posing As Politics and Other Thoughts of the American Scene* New Press 2000, p.203.
52 Ibid., pp.203–4.
53 Leon Trotsky, *The Death Agony of Capitalism and the Task of the Fourth international: The Transitional Program* Pioneer 1964 (1938).
54 Draper, *Socialism From Below*, p.210.
55 Cf. Bill Fletcher and Richard Hurd, 'Beyond the Organising Model' in Kate Bronfenbrenner et al. (eds) *Organising to Win: New Research on Union Strategies* ILR 1998, p.37.

Index